S0-BEA-893

Tourism Analysis: A Handbook

STEPHEN L. J. SMITH

Tourism Analysis

A Handbook

Copublished in the United States with
John Wiley & Sons, Inc., New York

Longman Scientific & Technical,
Longman Group UK Limited,
Longman House, Burnt Mill, Harlow,
Essex CM20 2JE, England
and Associated Companies throughout the world.

Copublished in the United States with
John Wiley & Sons, Inc., 605 Third Avenue, New York, NY 10158

First published 1989
Reprinted 1990

British Library Cataloguing in Publication Data

Smith, Stephen L. J.
Tourism analysis : a handbook.
1. Tourism. Demand. Forecasting.
Mathematical models
I. Title
339.4′891

ISBN 0-582-30150-5

Library of Congress Cataloguing in Publication Data

Smith, Stephen L. J., 1946-
Tourism analysis.

Bibliography: p.
Includes index.
1. Tourist trade. I. Title.
G155.A1S57 1988 380.1′459104 88-4730
ISBN 0-470-21093-1 (Wiley USA only)

Set in Linotron 202 10/12 pt Times

Produced by Longman Singapore Publishers (Pte) Ltd
Printed in Singapore

Contents

*(1) *refers to relative difficulty of method.* (1) = *low;* (2) = *moderate;* (3) = *high.*

Preface

The purpose of this book is to introduce the reader to a variety of quantitative methods useful for tourism analysis. Such an apparently prosaic purpose makes this book distinctive in the tourism field. Anyone interested in learning more about practical methods for studying and analysing tourism has traditionally had three places to turn. This implies choice, but the quality of the choices has not been good. First, he could turn to traditional statistical texts or methods books from other fields. These books give excellent advice on the methods they cover, but the relevance of the methods to tourism is left to the reader's imagination. Alternatively, a student or scholar could consult tourism texts. There he would find an abundance of tourism concepts and problems. Only rarely, though, would these texts provide step-by-step details on how to use the concepts to solve real problems. Finally, one could turn to tourism research journals. Here he would likely find a rich harvest of substantive findings and some methodological contributions. The problem, though, is that most of the quantitative methods used in tourism journals tend to be limited in their variety and relatively simplistic in design. Further, the exact steps involved in applying the procedures are frequently left undescribed. If they are described, the methodological discussion is too often wooden, wordy, and ungrammatical.

I have found such a situation wasteful of time and effort; my students found it maddening and depressing. This book grew out of my desire to provide my own students with relatively clear and detailed explanations of the use and limitations of some of the more important and useful quantitative procedures used by tourism analysts.

The approach I adopted was to gather tourism-relevant methods from a wide range of sources over several years and then systematically, candidly, and practically to discuss their use. The methods I have included in this book are not an exhaustive listing of all methods used by tourism analysts, but they are among the most useful. I have not bothered to cover the basic statistical procedures common to social science research – these are handled well in hundreds of statistical texts available in any university library or bookshop.

The book is divided into ten chapters. The first introduces the challenges facing anyone who does tourism research: the lack of credible data, the diversity of the industry, its geographical complexity, the uncertainty of the future, and the lack of overall industry organization. The chapter goes on to identify some of the strategies employed to cope with these challenges. These strategies, which are also related to basic planning and policy analysis questions, form the structure of the book.

The second chapter introduces the basic units of analysis of tourism research: the traveller and the trip. The problems of defining tourism, tourists, and trips are reviewed. Some suggestions about the types of definitions to be used and about what types of variables are especially useful for describing travellers and trips are identified.

Chapters 3 to 10 represent the heart of the book. These contain the profiles of the various methods used in tourism analysis. Each profile is a detailed discussion of a particular procedure related to the theme of the chapter. To ensure ease of reading and comprehension, the format of the profiles is as similar as possible. Each begins with a description of the method: what it is, how it relates to other methods, and who developed it (if the method is associated with one or more specific authors). The description also explains the types of problems that can be solved with the method and identifies the limitations and assumptions pertinent to the use of the method. The next section in each profile is a detailed explanation of the actual procedures. The format of this explanation is step by step: a 'cookbook' approach.

It should be noted that the level of difficulty of the various methods differs substantially. Some require only basic arithmetic skills and easily collected data. Others require large, expensive, machine-readable data sets and competence in sophisticated multivariate techniques. Still others fall in between. A 'difficulty level' for each method has been noted in the table of contents to guide the reader in selecting those methods on which he may wish to concentrate. A level of (1) indicates procedures that require minimal quantitative skills and research designs; level (2) procedures that are more demanding; level (3) procedures that are the most complex. Level (3) methods typically require access to machine-readable data sets (or the resources to develop them) and computer-based statistical routines.

Finally, each method's profile concludes with an illustration of how the method can be applied to a typical problem. Some of these examples are based on hypothetical data sets. Most, however, are drawn from tourism literature or industry problems.

Although the book is unashamedly a methodological book, and although I enjoy working and playing with quantitative methods in tourism, I would count the book a failure if it inadvertently convinced students that the pursuit of methodological expertise without recognition of larger and more substantive issues was a worthy use of time for a tourism student or professional. Some analytical skills should be a part of every tourism professional's credentials, but they are no substitute for a broadly based, liberal education about the nature of the physical world, the social world, and the human experience. This book should not, therefore, be the only book on tourism in a student's or professional's library, but it should definitely be there.

The writing of this book gave me much pleasure, but it exacted a cost from me, my family, and my friends. I pay the price for my obsessions willingly – and I am fortunate in having kith and kin who have been willing to support me with patience and good humour. I gratefully acknowledge the contributions of the following individuals to this book:

My wife, Carol, and daughters, Kristin and Stephanie, who would prefer me to spend more time practising tourism with them and less time writing about it in my office. Leslie June and Bryan Smale who allowed me to use our friendships to obtain free editorial and consultation services. They also helped me retain my belief that this book was possible and worth while. Every author should have such friends and critics!

The publisher who had the faith and optimism to stick with me through a project that took much longer than anyone had expected. Several anonymous reviewers who gave valuable advice on how to improve the usefulness (and sales, it is to be hoped) of *Tourism Analysis*. I do not know your names, ladies and gentlemen, but I thank you.

Elfi, Carol, and Cindy who typed and retyped the manuscript. Carol also spent additional hours helping me with the format of the manuscript, tables, and figures.

And finally, a woman whose life and love enriched me and all who knew her. It is to her memory that I dedicate this work: Dorothy Tanner Sidell.

Acknowledgements

We are grateful to the following for permission to reproduce copyright material:

The author, C. W. Churchman for an extract from pp. 142–143 of *Introduction to Operations Research* by Churchman, Ackoff and Arnoff (John Wiley & Sons Inc. 1957); Crane, Russak and Co. for table 7.1 from table 15 p. 274, figs. 7.4 & 7.5 from figs. 18 p. 276 & 24 p. 292 (Gunn 1979); Department of Park and Recreation Resources (Michigan State University) for an extract by S. L. J. Smith from pp. 55–60 of *Michigan Tourism: How Can Research Help?*; Department of Tourism and Small Business, Saskatchewan for fig. 7.10 from Map 1 p. 5 and an extract from App. D p. 2 (Balmer, Crapo & Associates); the Literary Executor of the late Sir Ronald A. Fisher, F. R. S., Dr. Frank Yates, F. R. S. and Longman Group Ltd. London for table A.1 from table II i of *Statistical Tables for Biological, Agricultural and Medical Research*, 6th Edition, 1974 (Fisher & Yates); Dr. J. W. Frazier for fig. 7.7 from fig. 1 (Fridgen, Udd & Deale 1983); The Geographical Association for fig. A.2 from fig. 3 (Pinder & Witherick 1975); the Editor, *Journal of Travel Research* for figs. 7.8 & 7.9 from figs. 1 & 2 (Smith 1983a); the Editor, *Land Economics* for table 9.6 from table p. 96 (Pearse 1968); Michigan State University Agricultural Experiment Station for tables 3.2, 3.3, 3.4, 3.5, 3.6 & 3.8 from tables 5–9 and an extract from p. 12 (Stynes & Mahoney 1980) National Recreation and Park Association for an extract (App. A) (Cocheba & Langford 1981); Regional Science Association (University of Illinois) for fig. 9.1 from table V by Dunn on p. 111 of *Papers and Proceedings of the Regional Science Association* Vol. 6, 1960; Texas Agricultural Experiment Station (Texas A&M University) for fig. 7.6 from fig. 1 p. 8 (Gunn & Worms 1973); the Society of American Archaeology and the author, D. A. Pinder for fig. A.1 from *American Antiquity* Vol. 44, No. 3, 1979; Venture Publications for tables 6.4, 6.5 & 6.6 from table 1, 2 & 4 (Smith & Thomas 1983); the Editor, *Visions in Leisure and Business* for table 3.7 from table 4 (Smith & Smale 1982).

Whilst every effort has been made to trace the owners of copyright material, in a few cases this has proved impossible and we take this opportunity to offer our apologies to any copyright holders whose rights we may have unwittingly infringed.

CHAPTER 1

The content, challenge, and strategy of tourism research

Introduction

Tourism is a major industry. For years, industry planners and consultants had been predicting that tourism would grow to become the twenty-first century's largest industry (e.g. Papson 1979; Leisure Industry Digest 1985). The magnitude of the industrial growth that prompted such predictions can be appreciated from the fact that per annum increases in world tourism receipts for the period 1972 through 1983 averaged 13.2 per cent (Tourism Canada 1984). By 1983, the absolute value of world receipts was estimated as nearly $1 trillion (US). And in 1986 they were estimated at over $1.8 trillion (US), fulfilling those predictions 14 years ahead of schedule.

Although the dramatic growth of tourism has been under way since the end of the Second World War, many individuals, businesses, and government agencies concerned with tourism have only recently begun to pay serious attention to its implications. Professional standards for industry operations, the responsiveness of governmental policy initiatives, the level of industry planning, and the opportunities for university-level education in tourism fall far short of that appropriate for such a large industry. There are many reasons for this situation, but ultimately much of the responsibility is due to: (1) a lack of credible information about the importance of tourism; and (2) a tradition in tourism that places little emphasis on the high-quality research that would produce the necessary credible information.

The need for better information extends from the classroom to the boardroom. Students, planners, policy analysts, entrepreneurs, and decision-makers need better data if they are to understand the forces affecting tourism and how tourism, in turn, affects society. Improvements in data collection and information dissemination await improvements in research and research education. Although most countries have some form of tourism data-collection procedures, there is significant variation in the quality of the data collected as well as in the sophistication of analyses applied to the data once they have been collected.

Until recently there were few university-level tourism courses in North America and other countries. Most post-secondary educational institutions providing tourism education offered only vocational training programmes in such activities as bartending, cooking, or front desk operations (Tourism Canada 1983). The rise of university courses and programmes has been slow, and was limited initially to business schools. Only in the last decade or so have departments of recreation and leisure studies, geography, planning, and other fields begun to recognize tourism as a formal specialization. Independent tourism diploma programmes are still rare, although growing in number.

Tourism is, in the minds of many professionals, largely a matter of marketing and administration. While these activities are important, the field is much more. Planning, development, and policy issues transcend the practical and limited aspects of marketing techniques. Future education of tourism professionals will need to have a greater emphasis on product development and industry evaluation. Tourism, as a popular form of leisure behaviour, also offers social scientists a valuable opportunity for better understanding of some forms of human interaction and how these affect other people and the landscape on which they occur.

These opportunities for study can be exploited best if one explicitly recognizes that tourism is a multifaceted field. It requires research from many social science perspectives as well as those of various professions. The range of research problems in tourism can be appreciated by examining, in turn, the nature of tourism in several guises: as a human experience, as a social behaviour, as a geographic phenomenon, as a resource, as a business, and as an industry. We shall do this in the next section.

Content of tourism research

Tourism as a human experience. Tourism is an activity that individuals do and usually enjoy. To understand much of the tourism phenomenon, we must understand individual behaviour – the psychology of tourists and potential tourists. The development and testing of models that help explain the antecedents and consequences of human behaviour are an important research priority in tourism. Such information can be of particular value in designing both new tourism products and marketing campaigns to promote these products. Knowledge of how individuals make decisions about alternative products, what sources of information they use, how they evaluate that information, and how they structure their experiences can offer important benefits to business practice as well as to our general understanding of the tourism experience.

When human beings travel, they frequently use objects as part of their travel experience. Artefacts such as cameras, tour books, and casual clothing have become part of the tourist sterotype in many countries. The role of these artefacts as mediators or filters between the tourist and the landscape or society being visited is a poorly understood phenomenon.

Another aspect of the interaction between the tourists and the destination that is quite important in certain contexts is the desire for 'authenticity'. Authenticity in this sense refers to the subjective feeling that one is experiencing the essential quality of another culture. The conditions that create a sense of authenticity are of interest not just to local tourism operators who can benefit from the artful creation of this feeling but also to those scholars who seek a better theoretical understanding of human motivations and perceptions. More generally, the perspectives of psychology and social psychology have much to offer to the development of tourism research. Tourism, in turn, offers these social sciences an opportunity to examine a special and important form of human experience that often exists outside the more conventional forms of human behaviour.

Tourism as a social behaviour. While tourism is an individual human experience, it is usually shared with other people. Even when travelling alone, a tourist will come into contact with other people and social institutions. Many of the decisions related to a tourism experience are influenced by both the individual's psychology as well as his socialization experiences and self-perceived social role. The tourist comes into a new area and meets both local residents and other tourists. These meetings range from the briefest and most casual anonymous encounters to intense interpersonal interactions. Friendships may be formed or conflicts may be created. Tourists can unintentionally contribute to the deterioration of the social fabric if they come in large numbers, inject unprecedented levels of new income, and display radically different forms of public behaviour than the residents are accustomed to.

Tourists may become the victims of crime or may commit socially unacceptable acts themselves. Knowledge of the social interaction of tourists with each other and with residents and local institutions can contribute to ameliorating potential conflicts and can enhance our understanding of social behaviour and of the structure and functioning of different societies.

Tourism also raises many economic questions. Individuals and families assess their desire for a vacation against their financial resources. A community weighs the merits of greater funding of a local attraction that will draw more tourists against other uses for the same public funds. A tourism operator considers the potential risks and profits of expanding his business. The study of economics is the study of allocation of resources among competing uses. The way these decisions are made involves personal psychological issues or industrial and policy decisions – but in all cases those decisions have social implications. The allocation of personal resources for a vacation tells the analyst something about the social values of a family. The community's decision about greater support of tourism development indicates the social value the community places on economic growth. The entrepreneur's choice reflects his perceptions of social trends that influence the demand for his product.

Tourism as a geographic phenomenon. Travel from an origin to a destination is an inherent and distinctive characteristic of tourism. Local and regional industries are often organized along geographic boundaries. These organizations may be as specific as a local travel and convention bureau or they may encompass several states, such as the Travel Industry Association of America regions. Tourism destinations often rely on a strong image of place in their advertising. Images of beaches, the attractions of local cultures, the dynamism of a city skyline, or the solitude of a mountain range are familiar geographic concepts used to promote destinations.

Geographic research contributes to tourism knowledge in several ways. It helps to identify and analyse the existence of functional tourism regions that can then be used as a basis for developing or evaluating the geographic coverage of a tourism association's structure. Forecasting travel volumes between origins and destinations is another important area of geographic research. Analysis of the morphology of tourism regions, resort communities, and tourism corridors is also important for tourism planning. More generally, the geographic perspective provides an important context for the work of other social scientists who also study tourism.

Tourism as a resource. Many communities are interested in adding tourism to their inventory of businesses because it has the potential to bring in money from other regions with minimal environmental impact. Tourism can also be a positive force for the preservation of significant local sites, festivals, and cultural activities. The tourism receipts from visitors to Historic Williamsburg, in Virginia, are responsible in large part for supporting the ongoing restoration of this colonial capital of Virginia. When tourists are attracted to local communities by virtue of their unique qualities, whether environmental, historic, or cultural, then tourism can be harnessed to help protect and enhance those qualities.

The success in attracting tourists to enjoy and support significant local features, unfortunately, carries the seeds of its own destruction. The daily arrival of tens of thousands of visitors in communities whose permanent population may only be a few thousand can very quickly overwhelm the very qualities that originally attracted tourists. The perspective of tourism as a community resource is one that requires a realistic assessment of both the benefits that tourism may produce and the costs it may impose. A management and planning strategy that combines business interests, environmental concerns, and social awareness can often optimize the returns from tourism to communities.

Such a response, as reasonable as it sounds, is rare in practice and difficult to implement. As Mings (1978) has noted, there are three traditional responses by government when faced with the conflicts of tourism costs and benefits. They can take a 'hands-off' approach by ignoring the problems and hoping that they will 'just go away'. The second course of action is to withdraw their support for tourism and attempt, perhaps, to discourage private, profit-oriented activity in tourism. This is an over-reaction similar to the over-enthusiasm for promoting tourism naïvely exhibited by some public officials and planners in the early 1970s. The third possibility is to re-examine the role of tourism in the community to rationalize its development, control its costs and negative impacts, and promote the benefits. In the short run, of course, the first two courses of action are simpler to follow and may be politically popular. In the long run, the wisest course of action is to balance environmental, business, management, and social concerns so that tourism is recognized as a potentially dangerous but also potentially valuable resource.

Tourism as a business. Tourism, to most people who work in the field, is their source of employment and income. These individuals, or their employers, can benefit from research that: (1) improves the efficiency of business structures and administrative arrangements; (2) improves strategies for coping with the risk and uncertainty inherent in the industry; (3) offers a firmer basis for marketing efforts; and (4) offers improved guidelines for managing employees, training new workers, and for professional development of older employees.

The tourism industry is especially vulnerable to exogenous forces. Political instability or terrorism in a foreign country will both harm the tourist travel to that country and offer unanticipated benefits to alternative destinations. Outbreaks of disease, natural disasters, meteorological problems, changes in currency exchange rates, new taxation legislation, or alterations in border-crossing formalities can quickly and dramatically alter the relative appeal of competing destinations. Very often tourism operators rely on personal experience and personal contacts with other operators to help them understand, anticipate, and cope with these problems. Their coping mechanisms, however, can be improved only if they have access to professional literature, workshops, or consultants (either private or governmental). The effectiveness of these sources of information depends on the degree to which they are based on empirically tested knowledge. There is a need for both practical tourism research and for the extension of basic scholarly research to the problems of tourism operators.

Tourism as an industry. Tourism is not just several thousand businesses, it is an industry with important policy implications. More accurately, perhaps, it is a group of several related industries: transportation, accommodation, food services, attractions and events, and retail activities. An important characteristic of the tourism industry is that it is labour-intensive. A given level of revenue supports many more jobs in tourism than the same level of revenue would support in automobile manufacturing or oil refining, for example.

Tourism is also an important source of interregional and international cash flows. Governments at all levels encourage tourism development because it can bring in new wealth which can create new jobs. They should also be concerned about the social and environmental effects of tourism. Policies designed to maximize benefits and to minimize problems work best if they are based on empirical research.

In many countries tourism is strongly linked to advertising. State and provincial budgets allocated to tourism advertising in North America run into millions of dollars (see the US Travel Data Center's publication, *Survey of State Travel Offices*, for annual budgets). Expenditures of this magnitude from general tax revenues can be sensitive political decisions. Competition for tourism advertising budgets is intense; policies and practices governing the awarding of those contracts can be subjected to equally intense scrutiny. Tourism research can play an important role in state and provincial advertising in several ways. Although advertising is still fundamentally an 'art', promotional campaigns will be more successful if they are based on market research. Research results can also be used to help guide the choice of advertising media, messages, and audiences as well as providing some rationale for the allocation of public budgets for promotion.

Many facilities used by tourists are owned and operated by public agencies: state and provincial parks, historic sites, ferries, museums, public stadia, environmentally significant preserves, and more. The management guidelines of these facilities may sometimes place tourism far down on the list of priorities. The Canadian national park system, for example, was originally established through close cooperation between the federal government and the Canadian Pacific Railroad to promote railroad-based tourism. The current policies of Environment Canada Parks, however, places much higher emphasis on environmental preservation. The tension between those who favour preservation and those who favour controlled development has not been resolved, even after a century of debate. Similar conflicts may be found easily in other countries and between a variety of public agencies.

Research is needed in tourism to develop and apply methods for estimating tourism impacts on communities and to guide the efficient allocation of resources among competing claims. Tourism certainly has the potential for promoting economic growth in many regions, but the potential is not always as great as some local boosters might like to believe. Assessment of the potential for new or expanded tourism development can help ensure that a government obtains the greatest job creation and income generation possible with the available budget.

A basic principle in economics is that resources should be allocated in accordance with their value in alternative uses. Most market-driven economies operate on the assumption that prices, as they develop under the condition of pure competition, are the best indicator of the value of resources in alternative uses. Pure competition, of course, does not always exist. In particular, governments must make decisions about the use of publicly owned resources without reference to market prices. Policy analysts and planners need research tools to help them estimate appropriate economic values of public resources in the absence of market-place pricing mechanisms.

Challenges of tourism research

The tourism industry is in a time of change. Those who study the industry as well as those who operate tourism enterprises will need new skills and new ideas if they are to meet the coming challenges and to take advantage of the opportunities that are emerging. As an example of how government can respond to the need for better information, the Canadian Ministry of Tourism, in cooperation with Statistics Canada, established a National Task Force on Tourism Data in 1985. The mandate of the Task Force was to identify information and data needs in the tourism industry and to make recommendations about how that information could be collected and disseminated to those who need it. The Task Force identified five major challenges facing improvements in data collection: (1) the lack of credible measures for describing the size and impacts of tourism in the economy; (2) great diversity in the industry, with some policy analysts questioning whether tourism is a single industry or a group of related industries; (3) major variations in tourism phenomena from place to place and at different geographic scales of analysis; (4) fragmentation and a lack of organization; and (5) an uncertain and dynamic future, with prospects for further growth and the threat of new and unexpected problems (National Task Force on Tourism Data 1985a and b).

Tourism operators, planners, analysts, and decision-makers need to recognize these issues and prepare to confront them. The implications of these five challenges especially affect research in tourism. The priorities and methods associated with the definition of research problems, the collection and analysis of data, and the dissemination of information based on research findings must recognize the problems and challenges the field faces.

Although these five challenges were identified separately, they are closely related. The lack of credible measures about the size of the industry is due in large part to its diversity. Its diversity and geographic characteristics contribute to the lack of organization. The potential for future growth depends upon resolution of problems about organization and credibility. Much of the appeal of tourism destinations is found in their geographic qualities and the unique regional or cultural characteristics of tourism businesses. Overcoming the fragmentation and lack of organization in the field, therefore, must not be confused with forcing a boring homogeneity on tourism businesses and attractions. Before proceeding with an examination of the strategies of tourism research, it may be helpful to examine each of these challenges in greater detail – remembering, of course, the connections between them.

Lack of credible measures

Tourism often lacks credibility in the eyes of policy analysts and decision-makers because the field is poorly defined and because the data used to substantiate many of the claims concerning the size and importance of the industry are inadequate. When one attempts to measure the magnitude of tourism in a state's economy, for example, an analyst might suggest including some percentage of motorists' expenditures on fuel as part of tourism-related revenues. What percentage can be claimed legitimately? Should automobile travel connected with overnight business trips and conventions be counted as part of tourism? If not, does this imply that business-related airline travel and hotel expenditures should also be excluded? There are no universally accepted answers to these questions.

The potential for double-counting is another aspect of the lack of credible measures. A hotel with a restaurant and bar may report restaurant and bar receipts together in one document and may separate them in a different document. If a researcher is not careful about the purpose, coverage, and conventions used in different documents or secondary data sources, he could inadvertently count restaurant or bar receipts twice.

A data-collection problem even more frustrating than double-counting is the omission of data. This problem stems from the use of Standard Industrial Classification codes (SICs) to label industries. Many national governments use SIC codes to define industries; a discussion of these codes and their application to tourism is described in Chapter 2. It is sufficient for now to note that one difficulty with the use of SICs is that any business can be classified in only one category. The decision about which category is based on the business's primary source of revenues. If the establishment described in the last paragraph derived most of its revenues from the letting of rooms on a nightly basis, it would be classified in the SIC category 7011, 'Hotels, motels, and tourist courts' (this is the US code; other countries have other codes). This classification would apply whether the hotel offered only rooms or a restaurant and gift shop along with the rooms.

The problem of omission of data occurs when an establishment conducts a significant volume of tourism-related business but earns most of its revenues from other sources. The West Edmonton Mall in Edmonton, Alberta, for example, was the world's largest mall in the mid-1980s. It is classified as a retail establishment because of its large volume of retail sales. With over 3 million visitors a year who come from origins well over 160 km (100 miles) away – many of whom stay at the attached hotel complex and use the mall's indoor beach and theme park – it is also a major tourist attraction in Alberta. Estimation of the size of the tourism industry in Alberta, if based on receipts associated with those firms who have tourism-related SIC codes only, would miss a significant portion of the total tourism receipts in the province.

Even counting the numbers of tourists an area receives is not as simple as you might initially think. Different governmental jurisdictions have different definitions of 'tourist'. Some are more restrictive than others. Totals obtained by adding reported figures together from different sources that use different definitions will produce misleading results. This problem is discussed further in Chapter 2.

Tourism analysts occasionally use the concept of a multiplier as part of their estimation of the economic impact of tourism. Multipliers are difficult to calculate precisely under the best circumstances. They require substantial amounts of very detailed data. The econometric methods used are also difficult and require a high level of statistical expertise. Some of the dangers inherent in using multipliers in tourism are described in Brian Archer's aptly named book chapter, 'The uses and abuses of multipliers' (Archer 1976).

Diverse industry

Consider your last vacation. You may have purchased a travel book from a local bookseller and read about a new resort that appealed to you. You booked a reservation at the resort through a travel agent and reserved an airline seat at the same time. While waiting for your departure date, you bought some new luggage and perhaps some resort clothing. When the departure day arrived, you called a local taxi company to get a ride to the airport and then rented a car at the other end. While on the trip you ate at local restaurants, danced in local clubs, bought local crafts, and visited some attractions. You purchased gasoline for your rental car and picked up a few sundries at a drugstore. You may have even had to visit a clinic for treatment of your sunburn. Part way through your trip you called home to tell everyone how wonderful the vacation was and to make sure someone was keeping an eye on your home.

Between the time you began planning your vacation and the time you arrived back home to share your photographs and travel tales, you made tourism-related purchases from a bookstore, a travel agent, three different commercial transportation firms, an accommodation establishment, several food-service operations, different retail shops, a medical clinic, and a telecommunications business. On your next holiday you may use an entirely different set of tourism commodities.

In addition to these direct providers of tourism commodities, one can identify other types of organizations and firms that help support the tourism industry. Gee, Choy, and Makens (1984) suggest classifying tourism organizations into three levels: (1) direct providers; (2) support services; and (3) tourism development agencies. Direct providers refer to the most obvious type of tourism businesses: hotels, airlines, rental car agencies. Support services are less obvious but still essential for the tourism industry: tour organizers, travel publishers, contract laundry services, contract food services. Tourism development organizations include planning offices, government ministries, and universities offering advanced education in tourism.

One can note still other firms that contribute to tourism activity. These include business services such as accounting, investment, legal, and insurance firms. Manufacturers, normally not included in any definition of tourism, also play an important role. These are the providers of the physical resources the direct providers and tourists depend on: luggage, cameras and film, aircraft, buses, automobiles, crafts, and other souvenirs. The close connection between these firms and tourism may be more obvious if you consider what would happen to the volume of business of such firms if tourism ceased to exist.

The point here is not to argue for the most inclusive definition of tourism, but to make clear the diversity of firms and organizations associated with tourism and the difficulty of trying precisely to delimit the scope of the industry.

Geographical phenomenon

Tourism implies travel from one place to another. The movement of people in space means that tourism is fundamentally a geographic phenomenon. Beyond this is the reality that tourism varies dramatically in form and function from place to place. The tourism attractions in Lancaster County, Pennsylvania are quite different from those in Rio de Janeiro or Anaheim, California. Yet all three places are well-known tourism destinations. An understanding of the role and impacts of tourism in each locale requires an appreciation of the differences in the geographic situation of each. These differences include local customs, climate, level of economic development and the tourism infrastructure, types of attractions, and the area's previous experience with tourism.

Tourism also means different things at different geographic scales. The questions asked when planning, developing, and evaluating tourism in a local community are different from those asked for an entire state or province. They are different again when the focus of attention is on an entire country and then at an international level. Analytic and planning questions, data precision, definitions, and even the purposes of doing research and planning vary according to the scale of the problem being addressed.

Unorganized industry

The diversity of tourism businesses as well as their widespread geographical distribution and the many scales at which tourism operates discourages coordinate planning, marketing, and research efforts. With some exceptions, most tourism industry sectors (accommodation, food services, transportation, retail goods, and events and attractions) do not attempt to coordinate either marketing or product development. Cooperative data-collection efforts and data-sharing agreements are especially rare in the private sector. All this is not due to the lack of any compelling reason for cooperation. On the contrary, significant benefits can often be derived when different firms and organizations work together. The major reasons for the lack of organization may include the fact that the majority of tourism businesses are small to medium-sized firms. Canada, for example, with a population of about 24 million (one-tenth that of the USA) supports approximately 100 000 separate tourism businesses (House of Commons Debates 1984). Most of these employ fewer than 25 people. The large number of firms, combined with limited experience in sophisticated cooperative business ventures and an often intensely competitive environment militate against greater industry organization. Some tourism industry organizations have emerged, to be sure. These include regional tourism associations, national industry groups such as the Alliance of Canadian Travel Associations, and even international trade organizations such as the Cruise Lines International Association. Generally, however, the industry is still fragmented.

The lack of organization is also apparent in the great heterogeneity of college and university curricula and courses and in the lack of industry-accepted standards for product definition and classification. With respect to education, tourism courses were once concentrated in business schools, but are no longer limited to them. Tourism is taught in departments of geography, planning, economics, and leisure studies. The phrase 'tourism education' may refer to vocational training in food services as well as to graduate education of social scientists interested in tourism. Standard curricula for some types of job training programmes have been developed and implemented, such as that by George Brown College for the hospitality and food-services sector in Ontario, Canada. Most tourism curricula, however, are based on the individual efforts and insights of faculties working in small, independent groups with occasional advice from industry representatives. There are no nationally accepted guidelines for university-level tourism education.

In the case of product definition and evaluation: again there are no accepted standards. The variety of definitions of the word, 'tourist', alone is indicative of the inability of the industry to define itself. Without agreement on basic conceptual definitions it is of no surprise to observe that standards of industry performance or product quality are also highly disparate. Some private firms, such as the publishers of Michelin guidebooks or the American Automobile Association as well as some public agencies such as Tourism Ontario have developed classifications and evaluation criteria for accommodation and food services. Although these are widely recognized and respected by the travelling public, the systems still reflect the particular values of the classifying agency rather than industry-wide standards. Participation in classification procedures remains largely voluntary for most tourism operations.

Yet another factor contributing to the lack of organization of the industry is the complex interplay of private firms and governmental agencies in the provision of services and facilities. A single community may have facilities offered by independent local businesses, franchises, multinational firms, local municipal government, state or provincial agencies, a federal agency, and private non-profit foundations. The mandates and policies governing each type of organization are frequently different from each other and may even be in direct conflict.

Industry of the future

The best of times and the worst of times for tourism are in the future. Whether or not tourism will remain the world's largest industry in the next century, the needs for information, research, and planning will continue. For example, tourism is generally seen as a 'clean' industry, with relatively low levels of pollution in comparison to manufacturing industries. Pollution, however, is not the only type of problem or disruption an industry can create in a community. Tourism can stimulate inflation, contribute to the growth of crime, alter the social fabric of a community, and lead to the deterioration of traditional folkways and local sites. Tourism professionals in all sectors of the industry need to be able to anticipate future costs and benefits more accurately if they are to be managed successfully.

There are, in brief, many complex forces affecting the evolution of the tourism industry. Those forces also complicate the work of researchers and planners involved in tourism. At the same time, they increase the urgency for objective, scientific study of the industry's problems and prospects.

Strategies of tourism research

The potential strategies of tourism research are as diverse as its content and challenges. If you review the introductory material on the challenges facing tourism researchers, you will be able to identify some of the major research strategies necessary for effective planning and policy analysis. Six major themes are addressed by planners and analysts; (1) marketing and tourist-demand questions; (2) identification of opportunities for development, especially in the context of site selection and regional development priorities; (3) definition of the geographic structure of the industry; (4) description and evaluation of tourism destination regions; (5) determination of the value of public resources used in tourism; and (6) estimation of the economic magnitude of the industry.

These six themes of tourism planning and policy analysis form the framework for the methods discussed in this text. Each chapter addresses one theme or an aspect of a theme. To begin, marketing and demand questions are discussed in Chapters 2 to 5. Chapter 2 describes the problems associated with defining and describing tourism. Two perspectives are noted: using the tourist as the unit of analysis and using the trip as the unit of analysis. Both are necessary; each has distinctive variable and measurement issues associated with it; and each addresses important questions in tourism analysis. An innovative approach to defining tourism as an industry is also presented in Chapter 2.

Tourism, as noted previously, is not just an individual experience. It is also a group or social phenomenon. One important task in tourism marketing is the definition of groups of tourists with similar motivations – market segmentation. The logic of market segmentation as well as some of the procedures used by market planners are described in Chapter 3. Chapter 4 continues the emphasis on marketing by focusing on how tourists make decisions. The use of attitudinal and motivational questions in tourism research is also addressed The final marketing task considered is forecasting. Five procedures for forecasting trends are reviewed in Chapter 5.

In Chapter 6 we turn to the supply side of tourism and examine three site-selection procedures useful for tourism planning. These procedures include site selection for individual firms as well as a method for evaluating the potential for regional expansion of tourism. Chapter 7 introduces the concept of tourism regions. A review of the definitions, uses, and types of tourism regions and some basic principles of regionalization provide the background for our review of four regionalization procedures. Chapter 8 presents a range of useful indicators and analytic techniques for describing and evaluating tourism regions. Methods of measuring internal transportation linkages, spatial patterns of facility distributions, the overall attractiveness of a tourism region, and more is provided.

Chapters 9 and 10 bring us to problems associated with policy analysis and resource allocation. A basic task, noted previously, for government researchers and planners is to be able to measure the value of resources used in competing applications. Five different methods used to establish the economic value of non-market goods are reviewed and criticized in Chapter 9. Chapter 10 raises the issue of how to estimate the economic magnitude of tourism in local areas.

This book makes an important and original contribution to tourism research through its breadth of coverage. A wide range of issues summarized by the phrase 'planning and policy analysis' is recognized and addressed. Specific tools to solve specific problems in planning and policy analysis are presented and related to the challenges the industry is facing. These tools will be welcomed and used by all who wish to understand tourism better and want to improve the effectiveness of their own analysis.

Summary

Many challenges confront the tourism industry. Among the most basic of these are: (1) the lack of credible measures and objective analysis; (2) the diversity of the industry; (3) the complexities created by the geographical characteristics of the industry; (4) the lack of industry organization; and (5) the need to anticipate future developments. Much of the research that has been done in tourism has emphasized the marketing perspective. Although marketing is an important subject in the industry, it is inadequate as the primary research emphasis. Fortunately a growing number of social scientists are beginning to look at tourism; their perspectives and skills will make important contributions to our more complete understanding of the field. Attention is needed, in particular, in the general area of planning and policy analysis. Six themes can be identified in this area; these serve as the focus of this book: (1) marketing issues; (2) identification of opportunities for development; (3) definition and measurement of the geographic structure of the industry; (4) description and evaluation of tourism destination regions; (5) determination of the value of public resources to assist in resource allocation decisions; and (6) estimation of the economic magnitude of tourism.

CHAPTER 2

Defining and describing tourism

Introduction

Samuel Pegge reported the use of 'tour-ist' as a new word for traveller *c.* 1800; England's *Sporting Magazine* introduced the word 'tourism' in 1811. Despite the fact that both words have thus been part of our language for almost two centuries, there is still no single accepted operational definition for either. The lack of consistent and accepted definitions is a continuing source of frustration for tourism planners and analysts. Inconsistency in definitions among various governmental and industrial groups also has the potential to reduce the credibility of the field in the eyes of its critics. This failing is, in part, behind the reluctance of some macro-economists to even accept the notion that tourism is a real industry. From a practical perspective, definitional inconsistency makes comparisons of tourist flows and other related phenomena between jurisdictions difficult, if not impossible. The development of cumulative data sources and of interregional and international data banks to support tourism analysis depends upon the development of a consensus about working definitions of tourism, tourist, and similar terms. Progress has been made over the last decade towards agreement on definitions for international tourism. Agreement on domestic definitions, especially in the context of comparisons between nations, is still far in the future.

Tourism research and policy analysis utilize two major units of study: the person and the trip. Each unit of study or analysis has special definitional issues and a variety of specific variables associated with it. We will examine these issues and some of the major variables for each unit of study in this chapter. To conclude the chapter, we will consider a definition of the field of tourism that has potential to overcome the problems of a lack of credibility and inconsistency found in other definitions of tourism.

Defining the person

International travel

For the purpose of defining and classifying international travellers, the World Tourism Organization (WTO) guidelines (WTO 1981) are perhaps the best known. These guidelines evolved out of the first recommendations made in 1937 by the Committee of Statistical Experts of the short-lived League of Nations (OECD Tourism Committee 1973). Their definition described an *international tourist* as anyone visiting a country, other than that which is his usual place of residence, for more than 24 hours. The Committee of Statistical Experts excluded by direct reference individuals arriving to take up work or residence, students attending schools, commuters who cross borders on their way to work, and travellers who do not stop *en route* through a country regardless of the length of time physically present in that country.

The International Union of Official Travel Organizations (IUOTO) resurrected and modified the Committee's definition in 1950 by including students on study tours as tourists and by specifying a new type of traveller called an *international excursionist*. An excursionist is an individual travelling for pleasure who visits another country for less than 24 hours. Also, IUOTO defined *transit travellers* as those individuals who pass through a country without stopping, regardless of the time they spend in the country or as those individuals who travel through a country in less than 24 hours and make only brief, non-tourism stops.

The United Nations formulated a 'Convention Concerning Customs Facilities for Tourism' that expanded the earlier definition of a tourist by specifying a maximum length of stay of six months. They retained the other components of the earlier definition.

About a decade later, another United Nations conference, the 1963 Conference on International Travel and Tourism, drew a distinction between *tourists*, who stayed for more than 24 hours, and *visitors*, who stayed for less than 24 hours. This distinction is identical to that made by IUOTO in 1950 between tourists and excursionists. Terminology referring to this distinction was examined in 1967 by an 'Expert Statistical Group' working under the United Nations Statistical Commission. They suggested that the distinction be made between *tourists*, who stayed overnight, and *day visitors* or *excursionists*, who did not. This latter category, according to the Group, also included those individuals previously classified as transit travellers.

Again after a lapse of approximately a decade, the United Nations Statistical Commission convened in 1976 an international conference involving representatives of the WTO, the United Nations Conference on Trade and Development, the Conference of European Statisticians, the East Caribbean Common Market, and the Caribbean Community. The guidelines for definitions resulting from this conference provided the basis for defining international travellers used by most countries today. The details of these guidelines as well as some caveats about unresolved difficulties may be found in the *Technical Handbook on the Collection and Presentation of Domestic and International Tourism Statistics*, published by the WTO in 1981. A summary of the terms recommended by the WTO and the associated definitions follows:

International visitor: an individual entering a country that is not his usual place of residence and who is not:

1. Intending to emigrate or to obtain employment in the destination country;
2. Visiting in the capacity of a diplomat or a member of the armed forces;
3. A dependent of anyone in the above categories;
4. A refugee, nomad, or border worker;
5. Going to stay for more than one year;

but who is or may be:

6. Visiting for purposes of recreation, medical treatment, religious observances, family matters, sporting events, conferences, study, or transit to another country;
7. A crew member of a foreign vessel or aircraft stopped in the country on a lay-over;
8. A foreign commercial or business traveller staying for less than one year, including technicians arriving to install machinery or equipment;
9. An employee of international bodies on a mission lasting less than one year, or a national returning home for a temporary visit.

International visitors are to be divided into international tourists and international excursionists:

International tourists: visitors who spend at least one night in accommodation in the destination country;

International excursionists: visitors who do not spend at least one night in accommodation in the destination country. These include visitors who are passengers on board cruise ships who may visit the same port of call over several days but who return to the ship to sleep. Excursionists do not include in-transit passengers such as airline passengers who may touch down in a country but do not officially enter by clearing customs.

Domestic travel

There has been less progress towards consensus on definitions of domestic travel than for international travel. This is a reflection of the great difference in needs and priorities of the many domestic travel industries and public agencies around the globe. While recognizing the need for flexibility in definitions for domestic tourism and the impossibility of imposing international conventions on such definitions, the WTO (1981) has suggested several guidelines for domestic tourism definitions. They urge national tourism organizations to:

1. Include both citizens and foreign nationals in their country as domestic travellers;
2. Exclude travel associated with the pursuit of employment, such as commuting;
3. Make a distinction between extended or permanent migration and short-term migration or travel;
4. Make a further distinction between stays of more than 24 hours (or overnight) and less than 24 hours (or not involving overnight stays).

These guidelines have often been consulted by national tourism organizations, although the resulting definitions do not always reflect all four concerns. Some typical definitions used by different jurisdictions include the following:

World Tourism Organization

The WTO defines a *domestic tourist* as a traveller visiting a destination in his country of residence for at least 24 hours but less than one year for the purposes of recreation, holidays, sport, business, meetings, conventions, study, visiting friends or relatives, health, mission work, or religion. A *domestic excursionist* is a visitor travelling in his country of residence for any of the reasons given for tourists, but who stays less than 24 hours at the destination.

United States

1. The National Tourism Resources Review Commission (1973) recommended that *tourist* refer to anyone who travels away from home for at least 80 km (50 miles) one-way for any purpose other than to commute to work, regardless of the duration of the trip.
2. The US Travel Data Center and the US Bureau of the Census define a *visitor* as anyone who travels at least 160 km (100 miles) one-way away from home, except for purposes of commuting to work, and regardless of the length of stay (Bureau of the Census 1978).
3. Several states suggest that *visitors* or *tourists* (the word is used interchangeably sometimes at the domestic level) must travel 80 km-one-way for any purpose other than commuting. Florida, however, defines a tourist as someone from out of state who visits for at least one night for recreation or a vacation (Lundberg 1980).

Canada

1. Statistics Canada and Tourism Canada use a minimum distance of 80 km for including a respondent in their Canada Travel Survey. These individuals are referred to simply as *travellers*. The Canada Travel Survey does collect information about the duration of the trip as well as whether the trip occurred as part of a vacation, so more precise distinctions can be made as an analyst desires.
2. Ontario uses a 40 km (25-mile) one-way distance criterion for defining a *tourist* (Ontario Travel Survey 1983), whereas British Columbia defines a *visitor* or *tourist* as an individual travelling away from his usual place of residence who stays away for at least one night. No specific distance is used to define 'away'. Distinctions are made between those who live in British Columbia (*resident travellers*) or elsewhere (*non-resident travellers*) and between *business* and *pleasure travellers*. British Columbia also recognizes *excursionists* as those individuals who travel away from their place of residence for less than one day (BC Ministry of Tourism and Small Business Development 1980).

United Kingdom

The British Tourist Authority (1980) defines a *tourist trip* (rather than a tourist) as a 'stay of one or more nights away from home for holiday, visits to friends or relatives, business, conferences, or any other purpose except such things as boarding education or semi-permanent employment'. Heely (1980) has argued, however, that tourist trips should not include any form of business travel but should include trips of less than 24 hours if they are away from home and are motivated by a desire for recreation. His arguments have had little effect on the collection of British tourism data, although the English Tourist Board (1983) did commission surveys in 1981 and 1982 on same-day travel for leisure.

Obviously there is no consensus on a comprehensive definition of the various types of travellers, tourists, and excursionists. Table 2.1, however, represents a classification system that approximates the suggestions of many different authors. The population of travellers may first be divided into those of interest to the tourism industry and those not of interest. Those identified as not being of interest are excluded largely because their travel is very short, usually does not

Table 2.1 Common classification of travellers

I. *Travellers relevant to the tourism industry*
- A. Tourists (trips lasting for more than 24 hours)
  1. International
     - (a) Intercontinental
     - (b) Intracontinental
  2. Domestic
     - (a) Interregional
     - (b) Intraregional
- B. Excursionists (trips lasting less than 24 hours)
  1. International
  2. Domestic
  3. Passengers and crews of airlines and cruise ships stopping for a few hours in a port of call, or who spend the night aboard the cruise ship and visit the port of call only during the day

II. *Travellers not relevant to the tourism industry*
- A. Business-related
  1. Commuters
  2. Migrant workers and those searching for work
  3. Refugees
  4. Military personnel
  5. Crews of airlines and commercial ships (sometimes included as a type of excursionist)
- B. Students travelling to an educational institution (study trips are often considered as part of tourism)

involve patronage of tourism businesses (with the exception of some transportation companies such as taxis and intra-urban buses), is not influenced by tourism promotions, or is for the purpose of long-term relocation of a household. This latter category of travellers, such as workers moving to new residences closer to jobs, does have potential for future tourism development. Visiting friends and relatives is traditionally one of the major travel purposes. The separation of family and friends by individuals or households moving for schools or jobs can be an important generator of new tourism business.

Travellers of interest to the industry are usually classified into those whose travels require the use of overnight accommodation and those whose trips last less than one day. As can be noted in the WTO definitions, these groups are further divided into international travellers and domestic travellers. A major reason for this distinction is that most nations are especially interested in developing tourism as an export industry. Export industries promote national economic development by generating new wealth for the state. Domestic tourism may be important for local or regional development, but many economists suggest it usually has the effect of merely shifting wealth from one region to another, and not of contributing to actual net growth in the gross domestic product of a country.

Some national tourism organizations have found it useful to make a further distinction between intercontinental travel and travel between adjacent countries. Trips between adjacent countries such as the Netherlands and Belgium, or between the USA and Canada are typically simpler, cheaper, and of shorter duration than travel between, say, UK and Australia.

A parallel distinction is sometimes made for domestic travel. Separate accounts might be kept for travel between the eight Discover America Travel Organization (DATO) travel regions in the USA and travel between states within one region.

Finally, there may be value in classifying crews of commercial carriers such as airlines or cruise ships as excursionists when they visit a port of call as part of their work. The passengers of cruise ships who stay on board the ship at night but visit a port during the day, even for several days in a row, may also be considered excursionists because they do not use local accommodation.

Describing the person

Once a researcher has developed a definition of the type of individual he is studying, it is necessary to determine what type of personal characteristics are important to measure. These are selected, of course, to conform to the purposes of the specific problem being analysed. Many of the personal characteristics chosen include the more common socio-economic variables. Table 2.2 is a summary of some of the more useful variables and levels of measurement for tourism research. This table is based on recommendations developed by the Tourism Research Planning Committee (1975) as well as on the author's review of tourism surveys. Other variables that have been found useful by some researchers include attitudinal and motivational questions and the use of specific types of information sources, such as travel agents. These variables are used in studies of tourist decision-making (some of the methods used for modelling decision-making are described in Ch. 4). Other data that are often desired include the mode of transportation, length of stay, and type of accommodation. These variables have been classified here as pertaining to the individual rather than the trip; this distinction, however, is largely arbitrary and made for convenience only.

Table 2.2 Suggested socio-economic characteristics for tourism analysis

Variable	Levels of measurement
1. Age	Collect by single years. It may be convenient to summarize by age cohorts
2. Sex	Male/female. Age–sex cohorts may also be useful.
3. Education	Given the diversity of educational systems in North America, a basic four-part classification may be most useful: elementary, secondary, post-secondary non-university, and university. It may be useful in other circumstances to distinguish between completion of secondary or post-secondary programmes and partial work (drop-out before completion)
4. Occupational status	Categories can include employed full-time, employed part-time, retired (some reference to former occupation may be desired), homemaker, student, unemployed. If employed, refer the respondent to the next question, 'occupation'
5. Occupation	This is best determined through an open-ended question. Responses can be summarized according to the *Occupation Classification Manual* or other comparable national statistical coding system such as the *Canadian Classification and Dictionary of Occupations*. These codes refer to the type of industry in which the traveller is employed
6. Annual income	This is an especially sensitive subject; some of the concern over reporting income can be reduced by using income categories. The specific categories should be based on those used in the most recent national census. Household income is often the most relevant measure of income, although the respondent's income may be useful in special circumstances

Table 2.2 (continued)

Variable	Levels of measurement
7. Family composition	This can be an especially important variable if the purpose of study includes some analysis of the effect of travel party composition on travel behaviour. One possible classification is: Single individual living alone Husband–wife family No children under 18 years No children at home or no children at all Adult children living at home or other adult relatives With children under 18 years With no other adult relatives With other relatives Single-parent families Male head Female head All other families
8. Party composition	This is closely related to the previous variable for many travelling parties Levels include: One person alone One family with children Two families with children Organized group One couple Two or more couples Group of friends (unorganized group) Other

Source: After the Tourism Research Planning Committee of the Canadian Federal – Provincial Conference on Tourism 1975.

Defining the trip

Although there is an obvious difference between a tourist (or visitor or excursionist) and a trip, their operational definitions are inextricably linked. If a tourist is someone who makes a one-way trip of 160 km (100 miles) or more, then a trip is defined as a journey made by an individual who has travelled 160 km or more one-way. An important use of the distinction between a person and a trip is that it permits the researcher to focus on trips as the unit of analysis rather than the traveller. Thus if the same individual takes three vacation trips a year, he may still be one traveller, but he has produced three person-trips. A couple making three trips is still only two people, but they represent six person-trips. For most analytical and planning purposes the number of trips or person-trips is more relevant than the number of people who travel.

A *trip* is generally considered to occur each time an individual or a group leave their place of residence, travel at least a specified distance, and return home. It may involve one or more destinations, several side-trips, or a circuit with no single destination. Different modes of transportation may be used, and the motivations for travel may include one or several reasons. Trips are normally defined to be less than one year in length, sometimes less than six months. They may, in practice, occasionally be longer. A *vacation* is a trip taken primarily for pleasure and lasting at least four consecutive nights (OECD Tourism Committee 1973). Some researchers, though, allow respondents to define 'vacation' for themselves, allowing for inclusion of 'mini-vacations' lasting perhaps for only a three-day weekend.

Person-nights are the product of the number of nights a party stays away from home and the number of people in the party. *Person-days* may be measured for day visitors (excursionists) or tourists. The length of a trip in person-days for a tourist is one day more than the length in person-nights: a trip of one night is considered to last two days. Person-nights are usually more relevant to analysts concerned with accommodation usage than person-days; person-days may be more useful to those interested in excursionists and their activities.

Trips are sometimes broken into segments. A *segment* of a trip changes when the traveller changes location, mode of transportation, or type of accommodation. Airline travel is sometimes divided into *legs*, which are the spaces between consecutive stops on a given flight. Trips originate at *origins* and often lead to *destinations*. Those that do not lead to a particular destination are *touring trips*. Arrival at a destination or the crossing of a border into a region of study is a *visit*. These terms, however, are not universally recognized. A traveller going to London from Toronto, and return, with a change of aircraft in New York might be considered as having made one trip if his entire travel pattern is considered or two trips if the intercontinental segments are counted separately. If separate emplanements or border crossings are counted, he has made four trips. And if each departure and arrival are counted separately, as they might be because of conventions governing the recording of international travel, he might be registered on eight trips!

Describing the trip

A great variety of information may be collected about trips. The variables can include descriptors related to the physical characteristics of

Table 2.3 Suggested trip characteristics for tourism analysis

Variable	Levels of measurement
1. Season or trip period	Calendar quarters: January to March April to June July to September October to December If the trip overlaps two or more quarters, the following convention is often used. For household surveys, use the quarter in which the trip ends. For exits or re-entry surveys, use the date of the survey It is sometimes desirable to distinguish weekend trips from other trips
2. Trip duration	Both days and nights are used as the unit of measurement. The number of nights is usually one less than the number of days; a three-day weekend lasts 'two nights'. The actual number of days or nights up to one week is often collected. Periods longer than one week are often measured as ranges, e.g. 8–15 days (or 7–13 nights).
3. Trip distance	This should be based, in part, on the threshold distance required for definition of a trip. Narrow ranges for lowest levels are desirable to permit aggregating or exclusion of data so that comparisons can be made between surveys using different distance thresholds. A possible classification would be: 25– 49 miles 50– 99 miles 100– 499 miles 500– 999 miles 1000–1499 miles More than 1500 miles (2400 km) Metric conversion is usually necessary for international comparisons; however, international travel is normally not measured by distance
4. Purpose of trip	Very simple classifications are used, such as business versus pleasure. This dichotomy is normally inadequate for analytical purposes and is too simplistic to represent the purposes of many trips. More precise classifications would include: Conventions or other business meetings Buying, selling, installation, or other business Recreation/vacation Touring/sightseeing Attending cultural/sporting events Participating in cultural/sporting events Visiting friends or relatives Other family or personal matters Shopping Study tour Health/rest Many trips involve more than one purpose, so it may be useful to specify 'primary' purpose

Table 2.3 (continued)

Variable	Levels of measurement
5. Mode of transportation	Private automobile Rental automobile Bus/motor coach Train Scheduled airline Chartered airline Private aeroplane Boat/ship (additional categories for ferries, cruise ships, private boats may be added as necessary) Some trips involve multiple modes, such as a combination of scheduled airline and rental car. These combinations may be specified or a primary mode may be requested
6. Expenditures	Transportation (broken out by mode, if desired) Accommodation (including camping fees, but not park entrance fees) Food and beverages (restaurant meals may be separated from food purchased at a store) Convention or registration fees Admission fees and other entertainment, including park admissions, licence fees for hunting and fishing Souvenirs Other purchase
7. Type of accommodation	Hotels and inns Motels and motor inns Resorts Campgrounds Hostels Commercial cottages Institutional camps Private cottages Bed and breakfast/tourist home Homes of friends or relatives Other Additional classifications could be based on size of accommodation, price, public versus private ownership, function (e.g. fishing camp; ski resort), type of location (e.g. airport strip; downtown) availability of liquor, and so on

Source: Tourism Research Planning Committee of the Federal–Provincial Conference on Tourism, 1975.

trips such as their duration and the distance covered as well as descriptors more closely associated with the traveller, such as the purpose of travel. Table 2.3 is a summary of many of the more common variables used to describe trips. Again, this table is based on both recommendations by the Tourism Research Planning Committee and the author's review of tourism surveys.

Data on trips are usually obtained from two major sources: household surveys and on-site surveys. Household surveys are typically conducted among the general population to identify broad social travel patterns. They may be based on personal interviews, mailed questionnaires, or telephone surveys. Regardless of the method employed, many of the respondents selected in a general household survey will not have made a trip during the survey period. This can be a desirable feature if the purpose of the study is to learn more about non-travellers and potential travellers as well as active travellers. If the purpose, however, is to focus on travel patterns alone, a household survey may not be the most efficient method of collecting the desired information. Further, most household surveys are designed to elicit information about travel patterns for the previous quarter or even the previous year. Some information, such as whether the respondent took a vacation trip or not, may be reliably obtained from recall. Information about short trips to local attractions is more difficult if the period of recall is several months or longer. And valid information about expenditures is virtually impossible to obtain from a household survey. Many travellers do not keep accurate records of all of their expenditures, nor calculate total expenditures by the categories tourism researchers are interested in. Even if the traveller can recall total costs, it may be impossible to break them down into specific categories if the travel was part of a tour package.

As we will see in Chapter 9, there are some other definitional matters to resolve when assessing travel costs. Certainly variable costs associated with accommodation and direct travel costs such as gasoline or airline tickets should be included. It is less clear whether some prorated costs of a motor home or a boat should be allocated as trip costs. Investments in photographic equipment, recreational equipment, luggage, and other travel goods might also be included if some of the methodological problems associated with collecting reliable estimates of expenditures can be resolved.

On-site surveys refer to interviews conducted at tourism locations. These include visitor surveys at attractions, user surveys for accommodations, in-flight surveys, and exit surveys. The information may be obtained through face-to-face interviews or through the use of a drop-off questionnaire. The data obtained from on-site surveys tend to be more reliable than that collected through household surveys because of the immediacy of the data. Some information, though, cannot always be obtained on-site. For example, questions concerning psychological satisfactions may elicit misleading temporary emotions – extant at the time of the survey, but which could be significantly different from the overall feelings associated with the completed trip. Further, on-site surveys are normally specific to a particular visit, not an entire trip. A respondent can answer questions about his visit to a specific national park where the park staff is conducting a user satisfaction survey, but these data indicate nothing about other visits made to other attractions on the same trip. One important exception to this is the use of a travel diary. A travel diary is a record book or log the traveller maintains for the duration of his trip, at the request of the surveyor, and which is turned over to the surveyor for analysis at the end of the trip.

Some useful information may also be obtained from administrative data. Administrative data refer to information collected by a business or organization as part of its day-to-day operations. Although the purpose of this information is not explicitly for tourism research, it can become a useful secondary data source. Examples of administrative data include records of admissions or registrations, receipts, inventories of sales, and taxes collected. Great care must be taken in using administrative data to ensure that the units of measurement and the associated definitions are clearly understood. Accommodation records may be kept in terms of rooms, room-nights, person-nights, or beds. Camp-ground records may refer to single parties or to the number of people in the parties. Length of stay may be noted in days or nights. Airline departure information indicates the number of people flying from airport to airport, but cannot indicate anything about real origins or ultimate destinations.

Defining tourism

Once you have operational definitions and measures for the basic phenomena of tourism, tourists, and trips, it is easy to assume that the field of tourism itself has been defined. Some authors, indeed, appear to make this assumption because they never offer a definition of tourism distinct from their definitions of tourists and trips. The lack of a precise definition for tourism may not pose problems in certain situations, but it is a serious shortcoming when one is involved with questions such as measuring the magnitude of tourism as an industry. The lack of a precise definition of the field is also a challenge when one attempts to identify the range of business operations and other activities that will become the basis for data collection. It would be unwise to develop a data bank for tourism planning and analysis without first deciding the types of variables and the range of phenomena that should be included in data collection efforts.

A major barrier to the development of a broadly acceptable definition of tourism is the fact that planners and analysts will always need to formulate operational definitions specific to their needs. Tourism, as such, does not have a real, objective, precise, and independent existence that is waiting to be discovered and described. It is, to a significant degree, whatever we decide it will be. Thus a sociologist studying the effects of tourism development on a Third World country will be likely to define tourism differently from a marketing executive hired to promote tourism in a large Western city.

Despite the need for flexibility in the creation of definitions for different purposes, there is still value in having a generally accepted definition for policy and planning purposes. Whether one wishes to compare tourism to other forms of regional development, to speak of tourism as one of many industries, or to evaluate tourism as a social and economic force in a community, the credibility of the field and of tourism research itself will benefit greatly from the use of an objective, verifiable, and defensible operational definition.

Several definitions have been proposed that begin to suggest a possible industry definition. One of the earliest was offered by a United Nations conference on tourism (UNCTAD 1971):

> the tourist sector or the tourism industry . . . can be broadly conceived as representing the sum of those industrial and commercial activities producing goods and services wholly or mainly consumed by foreign visitors or domestic tourists.

These industrial and commercial activities include: commercial passenger transportation; travel agents; tour operators; accommodation and food services; recreation and attractions; manufacturers of souvenirs and crafts; and governmental organizations involved with regulating or monitoring the tourism industry.

Other agencies have offered similar definitions, such as that proposed by the US Senate Committee on Commerce, Science, and Transportation (1978: 217)

> The interrelated amalgamation of businesses, organisations, labor, and governmental agencies which totally or in part provide the means of transport, goods, services, accommodations, and other facilities, programs, and resources for travel and recreation.

Powell (1978: 1) suggested:

> Tourism is both an industry and a response to a social need. . . . Its product includes all the elements that combine to form the tourism consumer's experiences and exists to service his needs and expectations.

And Leiper (1979: 400) concurs:

The tourist industry consists of all those firms, organizations, and facilities which are intended to serve the specific needs and wants of tourists.

These definitions share two common features. First, they are supply-side definitions. That is, they focus on the production of commodities, not on the demand for those commodities. This approach is consistent with that used by other industries to define themselves. Second, these definitions have the same weakness: each suggests including businesses such as restaurants that serve the needs of tourists as well as local residents as part of the tourism industry. This may make sense conceptually, but in practice the majority of receipts at most restaurants are derived from residents, not travellers. Some recognition needs to be incorporated into any operational definition of the fact that some businesses are virtually 'pure' tourism while others are only partially tourism. Failure to make this distinction would result in a consistent overestimate of the magnitude of tourism as an economic force, thus contributing to the continued lack of credibility of the field.

One solution to this problem has been suggested by the (Canadian) National Task Force on Tourism Data (1985). Their definition, like the others given above, is a supply-side definition: the tourism industry is the aggregate of those retail goods and services businesses that serve the needs of people travelling outside their home community. The definition, however, goes one step further. Tourism businesses are divided into two tiers (see Fig. 2.1). Tier 1 firms are those that would not exist in the absence of travel. Examples include hotels, airlines, cruise ships, and travel agents. Tier 2 firms are those that would continue to exist in the absence of travel, but only in a diminished form. These businesses include taxis, restaurants, rental car agencies, gift shops, and attractions and events. Such businesses derive a significant portion – but less than 100 per cent – of their revenues from tourists. Empirical evidence suggests that most tier 2 businesses obtain between one-fourth and one-third of their income from tourism.

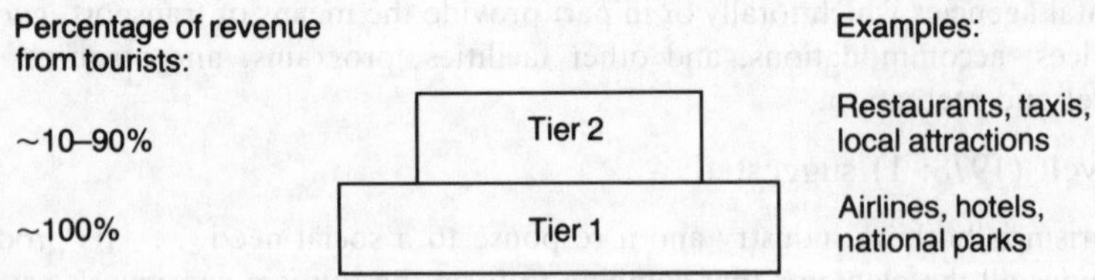

Fig. 2.1 A supply-side definition of the tourism industry

The inclusion of particular businesses in either tier 1 or tier 2 depends on the scale of analysis as well as regional characteristics of the tourism industry. Some restaurants located in popular tourism destinations may derive virtually all of their revenues from visitors. In such cases, and in the context of a local tourism industry, these restaurants would be included as tier 1 firms. If the level of analysis is national, restaurants will belong to tier 2. Grocery stores, drugstores, and other common retail establishments in cottage communities may properly be classified as tier 2 businesses at a local scale, whereas they would not be considered as tourism businesses at all nationally.

It should be emphasized that this definition depends on a sense of reasonableness and the ability to overlook minor inconsistencies. The case of hotels is a good illustration of this need. Although hotels are tier 1 firms because they exist to serve the travelling public, many will also derive some revenues from local residents who might eat or drink in the hotel, or who might check in for a 'get-away' weekend. The point is not to insist that if a business makes even $1 from local consumers, it cannot be classified as tier 1. Every industrial definition has certain operational problems or exceptions associated with it. The issue is one of degree and agreement. The definition proposed by the Task Force provides several important advantages.

1. It is consistent with definitions of other industries. The steel industry, agriculture, health care, and all other industrial fields are defined in terms of the commodities they produce. Defining tourism in terms of the motivations or other characteristics of travellers would be like trying to define health-care professions by describing a sick person. If tourism is to be treated equitably and credibly as the major industry it is, it must be defined in terms compatible with other industries.

2. The definition permits relatively easy measurement of the magnitude of the tourism industry. Many governments regularly collect business receipts data from all firms. These firms are also classified into reasonably precise groups, such as the SIC series. Table 2.4 lists some of the more important industries in both tiers by their US and Canadian SIC codes. The proposed definition permits the aggregation of the total receipts for all tier 1 firms and weighted or discounted receipts of tier 2 firms (weighted to reflect the relative proportion of gross receipts attributable to tourism) to obtain an estimate of the total spending on tourism. This information can then be incorporated into existing national income accounts and macro-economic models to estimate the economic multiplier for tourism and, with proper data, the employment-creation effect of new tourism businesses. The major

Table 2.4 US and Canadian SIC codes for tourism businesses

	USA (rev. 1972)	Canada (rev. 1980)
Tier 1		
Accommodation		
Hotels and motor hotels	7011	8011
Motels	7011	8021
Fishing/hunting camps; residential camps	7032	8031
Campgrounds; trailer parks	7033	8031
Transportation		
Air passenger and freight service	4511	4511
Inter-urban buses	4131	4921
Charter and sightseeing buses	4119	4929
Rail passenger service	4011	4611
Ferries	4452	4711
Passenger ships; sightseeing boats	4459	4711
Travel services		
Travel agents	4722	8231
Tour operators	4722	8232
Travellers' aid centres	8231	n/a
Tourist bureaux, local	n/a	7031
Tourism development programmes, provincial	n/a	7028
Tourism promotion programmes, federal	n/a	7018
Tier 2		
Transportation		
Automobile rental	7512	3042
Taxis	4121	4922
Limousines; caleches	4119	4929
Food services		
Licensed restaurants	5812	8111
Unlicensed restaurants	5812	8121
Fast food; snack bars	5812	8131
Bars; taverns; nightclubs	5813	8141
Recreation facilities		
Golf-courses	7992	8221
Ski resorts	7011	8221
Theme parks	7996	8228
Marinas	7999	8221
Other facilities	7999	8221
Culture/entertainment		
Commercial museums and galleries	7922	7541
Non-profit museums and galleries	8411	7541
Commercial zoos and botanical gardens	7999	8229
Non-profit zoos and botanical gardens	8422	8229
Theatrical companies	7922	8219
Theatres (as properties)	6512	4022
Race-tracks	7948	8219
Professional sports clubs	7941	8211

Table 2.4 (continued)

	USA (rev. 1972)	Canada (rev. 1980)
Tier 2		
Retail		
Gift and souvenir shops	5947	8799
Camera and photographic supplies	6946	8799
Gasoline stations	5172	1041
Sporting goods	5941	8791
Liquor, beer, and wine shops	5921	0231
Luggage	5948	8799

Sources: US Office of Management and Budget; and Statistics Canada.

problems associated with this type of analysis are technical, not conceptual. For example, original surveys may be necessary to derive estimates of what proportions of total receipts are derived from tier 2 businesses. Some SIC codes are rather broad, combining tourism and non-tourism activities into the same category. An example of this problem is the Canadian SIC code for airlines: 4511. This number includes both passengers and freight receipts. It is conceptually and technically possible to separate passenger receipts from freight receipts. All that is needed is the political will to push for such refinements.

3. The definition recognizes, in spirit, the distinction between tourists and excursionists as suggested by the WTO. Tier 1 businesses serve almost exclusively those travellers who traverse significant distances and stay away from home overnight. Tier 2, on the other hand, serve both these types of travellers as well as those who stay closer to home and do not remain away overnight. Although the data-reporting procedures required by most national governments with respect to income tax and other business surveys do not permit separation of receipts from tourists versus excursionists, the definition does allow for the distinction.

Some of the methods that can be used to measure the local magnitude of tourism are described in Chapter 10. An example of how the supply-side definition can be applied to the tourism industry is seen in Fig. 2.2 (Simard and Hill 1986). This figure illustrates some preliminary estimates of the tourism-related revenues for various industry segments. These segments do not represent the entire scope of tier 1 and 2 firms, but rather those firms for which data were readily available. Based on a combination of assumptions about the nature of certain businesses as well as available surveys of consumer spending

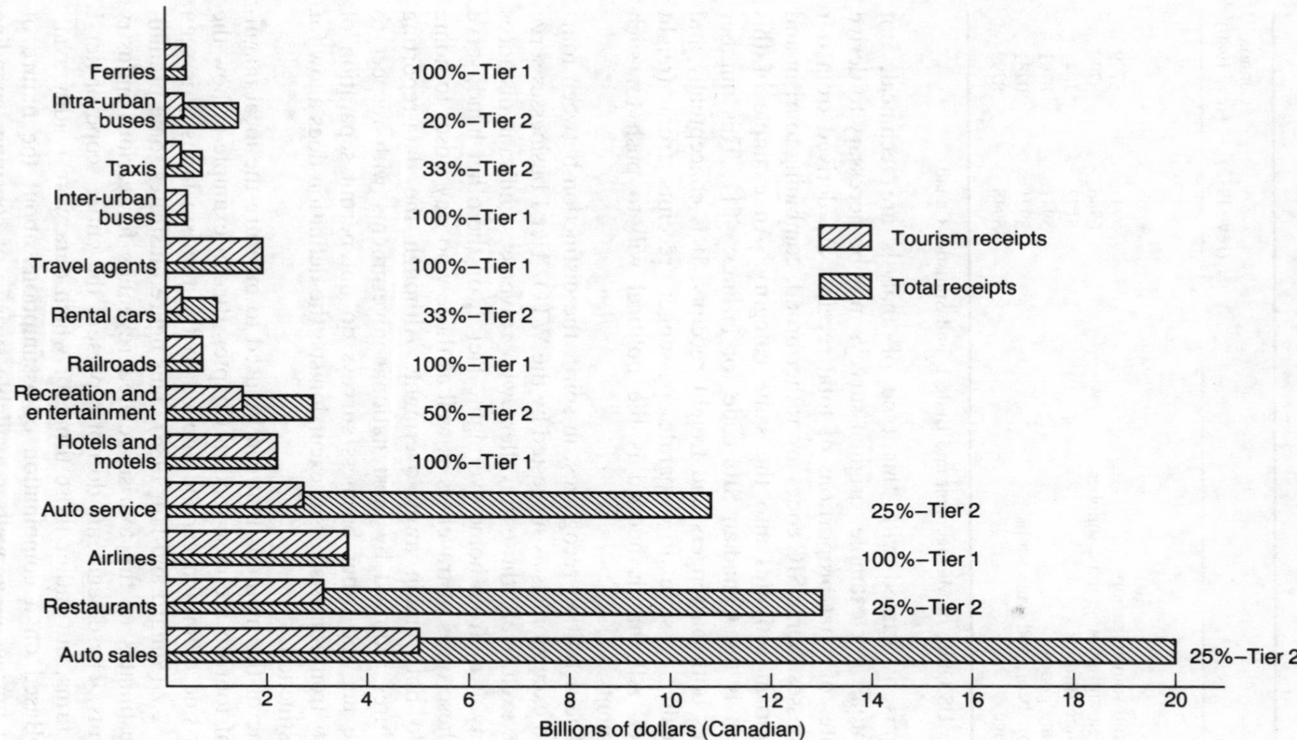

Fig. 2.2 Examples of tier 1 and tier 2 industries: preliminary estimates of tourism-derived revenues, 1981

habits, approximate ratios between total receipts and tourism-related receipts for each sector or business category were obtained. These range from a low of about 20 per cent for intra-urban buses to a high of 100 per cent for ferries, inter-urban buses, and travel agents as well as several other sectors. The magnitude of the tourism industry, in terms of total receipts, can be obtained by summing the receipts associated with tourists from all sectors. The estimated total, using these preliminary data from 1981, was about $22.3 billion (Canadian).

Summary

There are many difficulties in defining the words, tourist, trip, tourism, visitor, and similar terms. These difficulties become especially apparent when one begins to compare the definitions used by various governments. Progress has been made towards consensus of international definitions, but there is still much variation in domestic tourism terminology. Tourism analysis may emphasize either the traveller or the trip, depending on the particular problem being studied. Some common descriptors for both the traveller and the trip have been presented in this chapter; many more can be selected by analysts as needed.

The definition of tourism as an industry is more than a list of definitions of the phenomena to be studied. A separate definition is required for the industry. A supply-side definition based on the types of products and services offered by businesses serving travellers is proposed. This definition is consistent with that used by other industries and permits relatively simple quantification of the magnitude of the industry at a national level.

Further reading

Britton R 1979 Some notes on the geography of tourism. *Canadian Geographer* **23**(3): 276–82.

Chadwick R 1981 Some notes on the geography of tourism: comments. *Canadian Geographer* **25**(2): 191–6.

Cohen E 1974 Who is a tourist? *Sociological Review* **22**(4): 527–53.

Dunstan P J 1980 Tourism in Australia. *World Tourism* **154**: 43–4.

Frechtling D C 1978 A brief treatise on days and nights. *Journal of Travel Research* **17**(2): 18–19.

Gee C Y, Choy D J L and **Makens J C** 1984 *The travel industry*. AVI Publishing, Westport, Conn.

McIntosh W and **Goeldner C** 1985 *Tourism: principles, practice, philosophies*, 5th edn. Grid Publishing, Columbus, Ohio.

Metekla C J 1985 *The dictionary of tourism*. Merton House, Wheaton, Ill.

Miecskowski Z T 1981 Some notes on the geography of tourism: comments. *Canadian Geographer* **25**(2): 186–90.

Pearce P L 1985 A systematic comparison of travel-related roles. *Human Relations* **38**(1): 1001–11.

CHAPTER 3

Segmenting the tourism market

Introduction

Diversity among people and places is a fact of life. Variety adds colour and excitement to all aspects of life, but it also confounds easy understanding and simple solutions to problems. A tendency among some social scientists is to deny diversity. This may be done explicitly by assuming homogeneity among consumers and producers as neoclassical economists do, or by defining 'average' individuals as many sociologists, psychologists, and geographers do. Other researchers have found, though, that they cannot deny or hide the diversity among people in their studies without risking the loss of validity in their findings. They attempt to find some workable compromise between denying the great heterogeneity of the world and being overwhelmed by that same heterogeneity. One strategy to do this is segmentation.

The potential for segmentation to bring some degree of order at an acceptable cost into marketing studies was first stated by Smith in 1956. His basic argument was that groups of consumers could be defined in such a way that their purchasing behaviour would be relatively homogeneous. If a business person could identify these segments, he might be able to design products and advertising messages in such a way to increase sales over what would be expected if the product or the promotion were designed for the general population. Since Smith's pioneering article, tens of thousands of marketing studies have been completed that have used and improved concepts of segmentation.

The logic of segmentation resembles in some ways the logic of regionalization. The analyst's task is to define groups of people that are relatively similar with respect to some internal criteria and yet that are relatively different from other groups. The definition of groups is essentially a classification exercise and, as we shall see in Chapter 7, many of the issues involved in regionalization have their counterparts in segmentation. Both processes may be either agglomerative or deglomerative; both are done for some practical purpose beyond just the definition of groups; and methodological issues concerning how groups are defined and how many groups are to be formed are central to both processes.

In practice, it is not always possible or necessary to define market segments. Any of three population patterns may exist for a particular segmentation analysis. First, everyone may have such similar qualities that, in effect, everyone belongs to the same segment. Alternatively, everyone has unique characteristics. Concentrations of similar people do not exist, at least to the degree that meaningful segments may be identified. Finally, several concentrations of similar consumers do exist, but are relatively distinct from other concentrations. This latter pattern is the requisite condition for segmentation analysis.

This chapter begins with an examination of some of the critical issues associated with segmentation as an analytic tool and as a marketing tool. Two basic segmentation procedures are then described. Finally, some guidelines for the use of segmentation in tourism research are provided.

The literature on segmentation is vast. Some references that can help you get deeper into the tourism literature are provided at the end of this chapter. The interested reader is strongly encouraged to consult these.

Issues in segmentation

Types and uses of segmentation

An analyst beginning to work his way through the segmentation literature will soon become aware that not only are there many different types of segmentation methods, there are a great many ways of describing the types of segmentation methods. Wells (1975) describes five separate categories of psychographic segmentation; Young, Ott, and Feigin (1978) present three separate forms of benefit segmentation; Wind (1978) sees four different approaches; while Engel, Fiorillo, and Cayley (1972) derive a hierarchy of approaches.

While the outlines of the authors (and of many others not cited here) are informative and can shed light on different aspects of the segmentation exercise, a simple two-part classification will be sufficient for our purposes. Segmentation methods in tourism may be generally described as being either *a priori* or as *factor-clustering*. The charac-

Table 3.1 Some common types of descriptors used in segmentation studies

Social class
Occupational status
Ethnic background
Demographic characteristics
Motives for buying
Personality characteristics
Psychographic characteristics
Geographic characteristics of residence
Price sensitivity
Brand loyalty
Frequency or volume of purchasing
Cash versus credit purchaser
Product use patterns
Images or perceptions of product

teristics and differences of these two approaches will be discussed in detail in a subsequent section.

Segmentation is a multivariate technique, but the common distinction between dependent and independent variables rarely applies in segmentation work. The task is not to predict or explain some form of human behaviour, but rather to describe groups. As a result, the actual task becomes one of finding those variables that work well as descriptors for the particular segmentation problem at hand. Table 3.1 contains a list of some of the more common types of descriptors used in segmentation studies. In addition to these descriptors, tourism analysts have employed some less common but still very useful variables. These include vehicle preferences (Hawes 1978), mode of transportation (Thomson and Pearce 1980), casino game preferences (Dandurand 1982), and choice of near-home versus distant vacation destinations (Etzel and Woodside 1982).

An important reason for the diversity of potential descriptors is the fact that segmentation may be undertaken for many different reasons. Although most segmentation research is conducted for business-related purposes, it is also a legitimate research tool for academic enquiry into consumer behaviour. In the case of business, the major reasons for doing segmentation research are to improve either the market share of a business or its profitability. Segmentation can help achieve either of these goals in several ways. Given an appropriately defined set of segment descriptors, segmentation research can provide applied information on:

1. The reasons different groups of people buy a product or visit a destination;

2. How big these groups are;
3. The spending patterns of these groups;
4. Their loyalty to name brands or destinations;
5. Their sensitivity to price changes;
6. How they respond to changes in advertising, distribution, or pricing strategies;
7. How to design an advertising message or a new product to generate sales in specific markets;
8. Whether a new product should be introduced, or an existing product can be redefined, or an established product should be discontinued.

Academic researchers may be interested in these matters from a theoretical perspective. For example, segmentation methods can define life-style characteristics for the sociological study of a wide range of subpopulations such as consumers of the performing arts, families that take vacations, or people that participate in outdoor recreation. Segmentation can also provide psychologists and social psychologists with insights into the motivations and other relevant characteristics of people who have particular political orientations, such as being pro-tourism development or anti-tourism. These methods could also be used to define groups who share common sets of values and can assist in the analysis of important social trends by providing relatively homogeneous groups on which models might be tested.

Running through all these reasons for segmenting people are several assumptions. These assumptions are, in effect, a summary of the beliefs shared by all analysts who do segmentation research. First, of course, is the belief that people differ from each other. This is balanced by the belief that differences tend to be differences in degrees and that some people are more alike than others. Further, these differences are related in some way to other aspects of people's lives, especially their market behaviour. Next, these differences can be objectively measured so that relatively homogeneous and meaningful groups of people may be defined. The use of segmentation implies a belief in the possibility of balance and compromise. As noted previously, an analyst often finds himself stretched between two extremes: the temptation to oversimplify by denying all differences among people and the temptation to give up looking for any generalities by seeing every individual as unique. Practical segmentation is the search for a workable compromise.

Special questions

Unit of analysis

Most social scientists study the individual. Even when population aggregates are studied, their characteristics are usually conceived in terms of multiples of the individual. The fact is, of course, that much consumer behaviour actually reflects some type of group decision-making, frequently that of a household. The choice of a vacation, for example, typically involves negotiations (both explicit and implicit) among the various members of a household. A husband and wife will come to some agreement about whether to vacation together and, if so, about where they shall go. If they have children living at home, the preferences of the children may be sought or at least given tacit weight by their parents as they evaluate alternatives, budgets, time available, and past experiences. More formal types of negotiations come into play when groups of unrelated adults work out a mutual vacation.

There are several reasons why the analysis of group decisions is rare in social science. First is intellectual inertia. There are few successful models available for simulating group decision-making. Lacking good examples about how such research can be done, most analysts are reluctant to try it themselves. If they are willing to try, three questions must be answered. The first concerns the choice of the relevant group members. Just who is to be considered part of the group making the decision – all family members or just certain ones? Answering this question alone can be a formidable task. Next, one must decide how to define the decision reached by the group. There are actually a number of aspects of any decision regarding a vacation or other travel experience. Choices must be made about destination, mode of transportation, timing of trip, selection of accommodation, and activities. Different combinations of individuals may be responsible for different aspects of the total travel plan.

Once this has been worked out, there is the final problem of specifying the critical variables that must be considered when trying to model the group decision. Does one consider characteristics of each individual, characteristics averaged over all individuals, group characteristics, or some combination.

The continuing lack of experience by researchers in answering these questions means that, in practice, most segmentation studies will focus, in the foreseeable future, on the individual.

Working definitions

This is a perennial research issue. Every variable to be used as a descriptor or as a basis for defining a segment must be operationally defined. If you define segments on the basis of 'heavy half' and 'light half' consumption patterns, are the halves defined in terms of frequency of purchase, frequency of use, value of total investment, total number of purchases made in a specified period of time, or percentage of all purchases of some type of good that is a certain brand? Should you use actual values or some form of scaling? Should the data be based on recall or on diary information? Such issues must be worked out for every variable that you will be using.

Reliability

Reliability refers to the measurement quality that states that the same information will be obtained every time it is collected or that the same results will be obtained every time the same set of data are analysed. Although reliability is a desired quality in segmentation research, it is rarely verified. Most researchers just assume that their data and conclusions are reliable as long as they seem reasonable.

In practice, the issue of reliability can arise in different places. The data collected to be used in segmentation must be reliable. Certain types of variables tend to be more reliable than others. Objective characteristics, such as the sex or age of a respondent, are more reliable than questions about motivations or beliefs. Standard test – retest or split-half samples can be used to estimate the reliability of data collected for segmentation studies.

Reliability also applies to the structures identified during a segmentation analysis. This is especially important with segments defined with factor-clustering techniques. A simple way to illustrate the problem is to ask whether the same factors and clusters would have been derived if a different sample from the same population had been drawn. A useful but infrequently employed method to ensure structural reliability is to replicate the analysis on randomly drawn halves of the same sample and to retain only those solutions that are identical for both halves.

Validity

As with reliability, this issue concerns both original data and segment structure. In the case of original data, do your variables truly measure what they are designed to measure? If you want to measure 'adventureness', does a question concerning the degree of advanced planning a respondent puts into a vacation really tell you anything about this quality? With regards to structure, do the segments you have defined exist in the larger population or they just artefacts of your analysis? Few validity studies have been published (Massy, Frank, and Lodahl 1968 and Frank 1972 are two examples). In most cases it is difficult to determine with any degree of certainty whether the data or the segments are valid. Possible methods for checking the validity of data include correlating variables selected for use in a segmentation study with other variables that have been accepted by other researchers as valid indicators of the concepts you are attempting to measure. A high degree of correlation does not guarantee validity, of course. It may only mean both measures are invalid in the same way; still, such correlation does provide some tentative evidence of validity.

If the segments are eventually to be used to predict market shares or other types of objective market-place performance, you can use the accuracy of those predictions to estimate the degree of validity of the segments. However, such uses of segmentation results and the translation of those results into quantitative predictions are also rare.

Stability

Market segments may be reliable and valid, but if they are not stable they may still be useless for practical applications. Stability, in this context, means at least one of the following: (1) the characteristics that define a segment remain constant over a reasonable period of time; (2) the individuals who constitute a segment tend to remain associated with that segment; and (3) the size of the segment remains relatively constant. The most important type of stability is the first. If the existence and character of segments is relatively constant, a manager can develop various strategies to improve market performance on the basis that those strategies will not become quickly dated as the segments disappear or change unrecognizably. The other two forms of stability are less critical from a manager's perspective, although they may still be of interest. For example, a sales manager might be especially interested in knowing which segments show potential for growth and which are likely to remain stagnant or decline. Actual individual membership as well as membership change may be of theoretical interest, but generally the identities of specific individuals in various segments are unimportant to marketing applications – as long as an acceptable number of consumers is always present in the segment.

As with reliability and validity, stability is an oft-neglected topic in segmentation studies. There are even fewer guidelines concerning how long a period one might hope or expect stability in segments – six months, five years, or what? Bass (1977) and Calantone and Sawyer (1978) are two studies that have examined stability in segmentation studies.

Homogeneity

Market segments are characterized as relatively homogeneous groups of individuals, yet this ideal is not necessarily matched by reality. A lack of homogeneity on important characteristics is a special risk with *a priori* segmentation methods (to be described later in this chapter). In the case of *a priori* segmentation, two or more segments are defined on the basis of a particular characteristic, such as whether or not they have previously visited a destination. Once the general population has been divided into these two groups, the segments are 'analysed' by evaluation of the means of a series of demographic and social variables such as sex, age, and income. The intent of the researcher is to identify those variables that distinguish the two segments from each other. Often, however, the variability in demographic and social variables is such that there is no significant difference between the segments.

Generalizability

The final issue of concern to any analyst working on a segmentation study is the generalizability of the results. This is very much a matter of the adequacy of the sample and sample design. Segmentation is not done simply to describe a sample but to provide information that may be generalized to a larger population. Whether you conduct your own survey, rely on a professional survey organization, or tap a secondary data source, you need to ensure the representativeness of your sample. Advice concerning adequate sample sizes, reliable sampling designs, and sources of potential bias can be found in any of a large number of survey methods books available in any good research library.

A priori segmentation

Description

A priori segmentation is a procedure in which the analyst selects at the outset the basis for defining the segments. The basis may be an intuitive belief of the researcher about how people should be grouped, but segmentation is more commonly tied to the use of one objective variable the researcher believes is critical for understanding travellers' behaviour. Heavy-half/light-half segmentation is one such method. It utilizes some measure of consumption such as the number of days spent on vacation or the value of purchased package tours. Individuals or travelling parties are then ranked and bisected at the median. Those who spent less than the median on the commodity are described as the 'light half'; those who spent or consumed more are the 'heavy half'. A business will often wish to develop marketing strategies or product designs that have a special appeal to the heavy half – those consumers who account for the greatest volume of sales.

A priori segmentation may be based on many other variables besides heavy half/light half comparisons. In the context of tourism you might find purpose of travel, mode of travel, use of travel agents, use of package tours, type of accommodation, destinations, distance travelled, and duration of vacation useful descriptors. The choice should be made on the basis of whatever descriptor is of the greatest relevance to the marketing issue prompting the segmentation. Although we examine heavy-half/light-half segmentation here, the general logic and procedures will be similar for other types of *a priori* segmentation.

Procedures

1. Develop a sampling procedure to obtain data representative of the population you wish to study. Heavy-half/light-half methodology examines only those people who have actually purchased a product, so the sampling design will reflect the subpopulation of consumers rather than the general population.
2. Select the variable on which the segmentation is to be made (the segmentation base). This will be some measure of participation, purchasing, or usage behaviour such as the number of trips made. Operationally define the variable to be examined in each segment. These may include socio-economic characteristics or benefits sought from a travel experience.
3. After collecting data from the sample population, order the observations with reference to the segmentation base. Identify the median value and divide the sample into two halves.
4. Calculate the percentage split between heavy-half and light-half users for nominal and ordinal characteristics. For example, you might want to note the ratio of males and females in each half. Calculate means for each half for those variables that have interval or ratio scale properties such as age and income.

Appropriate significance tests can be used to test the observed differences.

5. Identify those variables for which there are significant differences between the two halves and which might be used to guide the promotion or design of vacation packages and other tourism commodities. Finally, interpret the results to develop specific recommendations for promotional and design strategies.

Example

An illustration of this type of segmentation can be found in Stynes and Mahoney (1980). The authors were interested in segmenting the active downhill ski market in Michigan (USA) to develop guidelines for marketing ski resorts.

They began by conducting a series of telephone interviews with a random sample of 671 households in selected Michigan cities. This procedure identified 229 active skiers who were then sent a mail questionnaire. The questionnaire included items concerning the number of days spent skiing in the previous year, socio-economic characteristics, participation characteristics, and preferences for ski area attributes. Respondents were ranked according to the number of days spent skiing and then divided into halves at the median, 7.5 days. All those who skied 7 days or less were assigned to the light half; those who skied 8 days or more were put into the heavy half. The light half accounted for only 17 per cent of all days skied; the balance of 83 per cent was attributable to the heavy half.

Once the skiers were assigned to one of the two segments, comparisons were made between the segments with reference to other characteristics of the skiers. Tables 3.2 to 3.6 provide a summary of the authors' results. As can be seen from these tables, there were few significant differences between the two halves. It would be difficult to develop a marketing strategy that would differentially reach heavy-half skiers because they were similar in most respects to the light half. The major differences related to equipment ownership, frequency of ski vacations, and membership in ski clubs. Promotional material for ski resorts might be distributed through equipment shops, through direct mail aimed at names on lists of ski club memberships, and through displays at equipment shows to ensure reaching the frequent skier. The authors also discussed the potential advantage of on-site advertising and the development of high-quality, challenging slopes to attract frequent skiers.

Stynes and Mahoney noted several limitations in their work that

Table 3.2 Socio-economic characteristics of heavy- and light-half skiers

Socio-economic characteristics	Light half (N=116) (%)	Heavy half (N=113) (%)	Chi-square statistic	Significance level
Sex			0.000	0.980
Male	60.3	61.1		
Female	39.7	38.9		
Marital status			0.730	0.694
Single	56.9	59.3		
Married	38.8	34.5		
Divorced/widowed	4.3	6.2		
Have children[†]			0.509	0.475
Yes	74.0	65.2		
No	26.0	34.8		
Age			5.644	0.343
18–19	16.5	20.4		
20–24	35.7	33.6		
25–29	20.9	15.0		
30–39	10.4	17.7		
40–49	8.7	9.7		
50+	7.8	3.5		
Occupation			0.861	0.835
White collar	46.6	44.2		
Blue collar	12.9	14.2		
Homemaker	5.2	8.0		
Student	35.3	33.6		
Income[‡]			0.355	0.986
Less than 10 000	47.4	44.0		
10–14 999	11.4	12.8		
15–19 999	7.9	7.3		
20–24 999	9.6	10.1		
25 000+	23.7	25.7		

Source: Stynes and Mahoney 1980.
[†] Figures are the percentage of married respondents.
[‡] Students and homemakers are included in these percentage figures.

illustrate some common limitations in segmentation work. First, their sample was drawn only from major marketing areas. This is a practical and efficient method of obtaining data, but it means that skiers from out of state were not represented. These skiers may have important differences when compared to the population sampled for the study. The sample was also drawn from individuals 18 years of age and over, who had telephones, and who agreed to respond to a mail questionnaire. This sampling design ensured a high response rate, so non-response was, at worst, a minor problem. On the other hand, this

Table 3.3 Preferences for ski area attributes: comparison of heavy and light half skiers

Ski area attributes	Mean important ranking[†] Light half $N = 96$[‡]	Heavy half $N = 97$[‡]	*F* ratio	Significance level
After ski entertainment	5.55	5.34	0.535	0.465
Lodging facilities at the ski area	5.05	5.07	0.008	0.931
Restaurant facilities at the ski area	5.32	5.22	0.385	0.536
Amount of crowding at lift lines	2.33	2.60	1.894	0.170
Slope quality	2.14	1.58	14.147	0.002[§]
Price of lift tickets	4.08	4.34	1.307	0.254
Driving distance from home to the area	3.52	3.80	1.352	0.246

Source: Stynes and Mahoney 1980.
[†] One being the most important and seven being the least important ski area attribute.
[‡] Only those heavy and light half skiers who returned a mail questionnaire are included in these percentage figures.
[§] Difference is statistically significant at the 95% confidence level.

Table 3.4 Slope attribute preferences: comparison of heavy- and light-half skiers

Slope attributes	Mean ranking[†] Light half $N = 96$[‡]	Heavy half $N = 97$[‡]	*F* ratio	Significance level
Steep runs	5.55	4.70	12.685	0.001[§]
Moguled (banked or curved) slopes	5.85	4.99	19.057	0.001[§]
Uncrowded slopes	2.74	3.20	4.285	0.039[§]
Well-groomed slopes	3.01	3.10	0.178	0.673
Slopes of varying degrees of difficulty	2.58	3.52	11.446	0.001[§]
Long runs	3.07	2.84	1.134	0.288
Lighted slopes for night skiing	5.15	5.60	3.655	0.057

Source: Stynes and Mahoney 1980.
[†] One being most important and seven the least important slope attribute.
[‡] Only those heavy- and light-half skiers who returned a mail questionnaire are included in these percentage figures.
[§] Difference is statistically significant at the 95% confidence level.

Table 3.5 Willingness to pay and travel: comparison of heavy- and light-half skiers

Variable	Light half $N = 96$	Heavy half $N = 97$	F-ratio	Significance level
Distance travelled				
Number of hours usually driven (one way) to reach a ski area for an overnight/weekend trip	3.6	3.9	1.495	0.2230
Maximum number of hours willing to drive (one way) to reach a ski area for an overnight/weekend trip	5.1	5.4	1.422	0.2345
Price of lift ticket				
Amount usually paid for a daily lift ticket	9.50	10.00	2.679	0.1033
Maximum amount willing to pay for a daily lift ticket	11.75	12.60	3.095	0.0802

Source: Stynes and Mahoney 1980.

design excluded young skiers, who are an important market for ski resorts in Michigan.

The profiles of the segments represent, within certain limits, the population of active skiers. They do not necessarily represent the profiles of skiers at a specific resort. The authors were unable to make any forecasts about the changes in skier profiles that might occur over the next few years.

Finally, Stynes and Mahoney defined preferences for the attributes of ski resorts and ski slopes in terms of overnight ski trips. It is conceivable that different patterns would be discovered if attention were directed to day trips.

The failure to find significant differences between the two segments meant that there was little value in developing elaborate marketing strategies to target on heavy-half skiers. Simpler strategies based on providing resort material at locations frequented by all skiers is probably more feasible. If, on the other hand, major differences had been discovered, the authors would then have considered the relative profitability of marketing to one segment and would have compared this increase in profitability with the costs of developing a targeted market strategy. If the heavy-half segment were too small, did not have adequate potential for further growth, or were too costly to reach,

Table 3.6 Participation patterns: comparison of heavy- and light-half skiers

	Light half $N = 116$ (%)	Heavy half $N = 113$ (%)	Chi-square statistic	Significance level
Weekend/weekdays			4.048	0.025†
Weekends	56.5	71.7		
Weekdays	43.5	28.3		
Overnight/day trips			7.3165	0.007†
Overnight trips	22.4	39.8		
Day trips	77.6	60.2		
Equipment ownership			16.310	0.001 †
Rent (all or a portion)	36.2	12.4		
Own	63.8	87.6		
Skill level			39.978	0.001†
Beginner	30.2	2.2		
Intermediate	44.8	47.8		
Advanced	22.4	42.0		
Expert	2.6	8.0		
Ski club membership			0.196	0.658
Belong	12.9	19.5		
Do not belong	87.1	80.5		
Participated in a ski vacation	16.4	46.4	22.614	0.001†

Source: Stynes and Mahoney 1980.
† Difference is statistically significant at the 95% confidence level.

there would be little merit in using this segment as a target for promotion.

Factor – cluster segmentation

Description

Factor–cluster segmentation is a more complex method of defining segments. It requires familiarity with factor analysis and clustering procedures. Unlike *a priori* segmentation methods in which the analyst specifies the number and identity of the segments, factor–cluster segmentation produces segments analytically. The analyst still has some degree of control over the formation of segments through selection of variables and the particular computer algorithms used, but this control is much less direct than with the *a priori* method.

Factor–cluster segmentation, as the name implies, is a two-step procedure. The first step involves the definition of important characteristics of the segments through factor analysis of a large number of descriptive variables. These characteristics are then used to cluster individuals into statistically homogeneous segments. This creation of homogeneous clusters is one of the major advantages of factor–cluster segmentation over the *a priori* method.

A special concern when using this method is the question of the stability and reliability of the segments. As discussed previously, the use of split-half replications can verify whether the segments defined are reasonably reliable or if they are merely statistical artefacts. This type of replication, of course, will indicate nothing about stability over time or the generalizability of the results to other populations. Still, it can be of help by indicating whether your results have any basis in reality as opposed to statistics.

As we have noted, the purpose of segmentation is not just to define groups; the groups must be useful for some larger purpose. One of the criteria to be used in evaluating the segments should be whether they are 'reachable' for marketing purposes. In other words, is there any quality about the groups that would allow a marketing expert to contact and communicate effectively with the groups? Characteristics that permit contact include a high concentration of readership in certain magazines or high viewer ratios for particular television programmes. A tendency to live in certain geographical areas might allow the development of an efficient direct mail campaign. On the other hand, if there are no characteristics that permit the marketing message to be delivered more effectively than a general, population-wide campaign, there would probably be no point in pursuing further segmentation work.

Procedures

There may be value, before beginning to describe the specific steps associated with this method, to review briefly the two analytic procedures upon which factor–cluster segmentation is based: factor analysis and cluster analysis. Factor analysis is a general term that refers to both traditional factor analysis and principal components analysis. The technical and conceptual distinctions will be noted later, but for most purposes factor analysis can be interpreted to include both methods.

Factor analysis is a procedure that identifies a hidden structure in a set of data. This structure is composed of a number of statistically independent factors or variables. For example, if you were to study a set of socio-economic characteristics of a population, you would probably find that there are a number of significant correlations between some variables. Voting preferences and religious affiliations might be correlated. People who chose certain types of vacation may be especially likely to participate in certain forms of recreation. Income, education, and occupation are often related. All these regularities may represent a fundamental structure in the population that is not immediately apparent. Income, education, and occupation may reflect a social class factor; certain combinations of vacation and recreation patterns may represent life-styles; political party and religious affiliations may reflect personal or social values. Factor analysis is a statistical procedure that can be used to identify and measure these hidden structures quantitatively.

Factor analysis begins with the construction of a correlation matrix in which the values of each sampled individual on each variable are compared to their values on all other variables. The form of the matrix is a square with the rows and columns representing the variables. The correlations between pairs of variables range from −1.0 (perfect inverse correlation) to 1.0 (perfect direct correlation). Most values are not very close to either extreme, indicating some degree of imperfect correlation. The diagonal of a correlation matrix is usually a vector of 1.0s because each variable is perfectly correlated with itself. This diagonal is replaced in factor analysis by communality estimates, which are measures of the correlation between each variable and the set of all other variables. If communality estimates are not available, you can retain the values of 1.0 in the diagonal as a preliminary estimate. The replacement of 1.0s in the main diagonal of a correlation matrix is a feature of factor analysis that distinguishes it from principal components analysis (which retains the 1.0s). Principal components analysis produces final communality estimates that can be examined upon completion of the analysis.

After the correlation matrix is computed, factor analysis examines the pattern of correlations to find the best combination of variables that will summarize that pattern. A new set of variables, called factors, is defined. Each factor is a set of the original variables multiplied by weights, called loadings, that represent correlations between the original variables and the newly defined factor. Each factor is statistically independent of every other factor. There are as many factors produced by factor analysis as there were original variables, but only a small number of these are meaningful. You must use some guideline to determine which are worth keeping for further analysis. In the case of traditional factor analysis, you specify *a priori* the number of factors to be extracted. If there is no theoretical basis on which to specify the number of factors, statistical guidelines may be used. The use of theory as opposed to statistics is another characteristic separating factor analysis from principal components analysis.

The most common statistical guideline is the use of eigenvalues. An eigenvalue is a measure of the explanatory power of each factor in comparison to the original variables. The first factor explains much more of the total variance in the data set than the original variables did individually; subsequent factors are less powerful or meaningful. As a result, the first factor will have an eigenvalue above 1.0, indicating its greater explanatory power. Each additional factor will have a lower eigenvalue, reflecting their lower power. All those factors having eigenvalues above 1.0 explain more of the overall variance than the 'average' original variable; a factor with an eigenvalue of 1.0 is comparable to the 'average' original variable. Factors with eigenvalues less than 1.0 are not as meaningful as the typical original variable and thus are usually ignored. Typically, only those factors with eigenvalues above 1.0 are retained for segmentation work or other analytical purposes.

After the factors have been selected, you try to name them. Factor names or identities are selected on the basis of the pattern of loadings produced for each factor. High loadings indicate a high degree of correlation between certain original variables and the factor. These original variables can be examined to see if their names suggest any particular identity for the new factor.

The initial factor solution, however, often produces many high loadings on the first factor, with succesively fewer high loadings on subsequent factors. A clearer pattern – for the purposes of identifying the factors – can be obtained through a statistical procedure called 'rotation'. The most common form of rotation is varimax rotation. This forces the loadings to approach ± 1.0 or 0.0 as closely as possible on each factor while retaining the same level of explained variance obtained in the initial factor solution. This forced dichotomization of loadings often makes interpretation of the factor structure easier.

The next step in factor analysis is to calculate the factor scores for each individual for each of the new factors. To calculate a factor score, you multiply the loading of each variable on a factor by the individual's original value for that variable. This is repeated for all variables on the factor for that individual. These are then summed to give a preliminary score. The process is repeated for all other factors for that same individual. Next, this process is repeated for all other individuals.

Finally, all scores are standardized to a mean of 0.0 and a standard deviation of 1.0. The factor scores are recorded in a factor score matrix where the rows are the individuals and the columns are the factors.

Since each of the factors is statistically independent of each other, they can be interpreted as defining a multidimensional mathematical space. For example, two orthogonal axes on a piece of graph paper define a two-dimensional space; three orthogonal axes define a three-dimensional space. Although it is impossible to visualize, four, five, or more factors similarly define a four-, five-, or more dimensional space. The set of factor scores for each individual locates that individual in space, just as latitude and longitude 'scores' can locate a traveller on the surface of the earth. The more similar two individuals are in terms of their overall factor scores, the closer they will be to each other in this mathematical space. Factor scores, therefore, can be used as a measure of similarity. People who have similar scores will tend to be located relatively closer to each other while located further away from people who have very different factor scores. Groups of similar individuals can be identified using cluster analysis.

There are several different types of clustering analysis used in social science research. The specific type used in factor–cluster segmentation is hierarchical clustering. Hierarchical clustering produces succesively larger and more inclusive clusters by combining smaller clusters. An individual belongs to one and only one cluster, but the number of clusters depends on how general or precise you wish to make them. Clusters are defined from factor scores by measuring the distance between each individual in the mathematical space defined by the factor structure. The actual procedure for doing this begins with a generalized form of the Pythagorean theorem. It can be summarized by the following steps:

1. Calculate the distances between all pairs of points, using the Pythagorean theorem generalized to n-dimensions.
2. Identify the smallest distance. Replace the pair of points associated with that distance by a new point midway between them.
3. Recalculate distances between all points, including the new point (but excluding the two points that were replaced).
4. Continue to some termination point.

This procedure begins by considering every individual as a cluster of one and continues until everyone is grouped into a single cluster. These two extremes are rarely useful solutions. Some compromise balancing numerous highly homogeneous clusters with very few and highly general clusters is normally desired. One technique for finding a good solution is to plot the error sum of squares or other measure of the increasing variance in each cluster (based on statistics produced by most computer clustering programs). When this measure is plotted against the decreasing number of clusters, you will often find a sudden large jump in the plot. This indicates the combination of two relatively disparate groups, creating a sudden increase in the level of variance. The clustering solution just before this may be a good choice.

With this background in mind, we can now examine how factor analysis and clustering may be used to define market segments.

1. Develop a sampling design to obtain data representative of your study population. The data may include both tourists and non-tourists and may be comprised of socio-economic variables, attitudinal data, buying behaviours, and many other personal characteristics that might be useful. Since factor analysis is based on regression analysis, the variables should be measured on an interval scale or recorded as dichotomous variables (yes/no). Be sure to attach an identification number to each respondent's data record (but do not, of course, use this number as a variable in the factor analysis).

2. Organize the data into a matrix with the rows representing respondents and the columns representing variables. Reduce this matrix through factor analysis. The conventions of varimax rotation and an eigenvalue cut-off of 1.0 are usually appropriate. Check the communality estimates for each variable and eliminate any variables that have low communalities. The definition of 'low' is a matter of judgement, but many researchers use a threshold of 0.3 or 0.4 to retain a variable.

3. Repeat the factor analysis if any variables have been removed. You may also find it desirable to experiment with different solutions based on different numbers of factors.

4. Once you have decided upon a particular factor solution, identify each factor by examining the patterns of high loadings. Obtain the factor scores for each respondent.

5. Cluster the individual respondents using a hierarchical clustering program.

6. Once the clusters have been formed, begin to characterize each one. Sort through each cluster to obtain the identification numbers of the respondents assigned to each cluster. Determine the average factor scores for those individuals on each factor. Large factor scores (greater than $\pm$ 1.0) indicate factors that may be important in determining the identity of a cluster. Calculate *F*-ratios and *t*-tests for each factor in each cluster. The *F*-ratio is a measure of the variance in each factor;

the *t*-test is a measure of the difference between the clusters on each factor. Ideally, you want to find those factors that have high mean scores, low *F*-ratios, and high *t*-test scores.

7. Finally, once all clusters have been formed and identified, note their relative sizes. Interpret the results and make recommendations for application to the marketing problem at hand.

Examples

This type of procedure was employed by Smith and Smale (1982) in their analysis of the demand for performing arts and cultural activities. Using a survey of 13 400 adult Canadians with over 60 variables related to participation in various cultural, artistic, and sports activities and socio-economic characteristics, the authors produced a 12-factor model that summarized about 80 per cent of the original variance in the data. The factors were identified as a series of activity specializations plus three social factors: (1) reading; (2) visiting art and cultural facilities; (3) viewing educational television; (4) listening to popular recorded music; (5) viewing popular television; (6) 'life cycle I'; (7) listening to popular radio programmes; (8) listening to recorded classical music; (9) viewing televised sports; (10) 'life cycle II'; (11) education; and (12) participating in sports. A clustering routine was then employed to group the individual respondents on the basis of their factor scores. A 12-segment solution was defined. Mean component scores, *F*-ratios, and *t*-test values were calculated and segment descriptions derived (Table 3.7).

Table 3.7 Identification of 12 clusters by Smith and Smale

Cluster	Number of respondents	% of sample	Description
1	18	3.6	Predominantly singles and students who watch a lot of television. Some tend to listen to a lot of popular radio. They are average in the amount of reading for pleasure, their attendance at performing arts, and in the frequency of listening to classical music at home
2	62	12.4	Educated professionals, primarily. Their cultural interests and activities are relatively homogeneous with the rest of the population
3	34	6.8	Average socio-economic group, with typical family structures and cultural interests and rates of participation except for an apparent strong dislike of classical music

Table 3.7 (continued)

Cluster	Number of respondents	% of sample	Description
4	82	16.4	Perhaps the most typical group. Average and relatively uniform cultural interests and rates of participation. Slightly more smaller families and two-income families than in most other groups
5	41	8.2	A diverse group of respondents in terms of age, marital status, and household size. They are alike in shared interest in playing sports, watching television frequently and an apparent lack of interest in popular radio
6	76	15.2	Another group of average individuals. These are distinguished by an apparent dislike for televised sports and a strong preference for listening to music on records and tapes
7	37	7.4	Homemakers and non-professional heads of households. They read more than average. They are quite diverse in terms of interests in listening to classical music and in attending performing arts
8	62	12.4	A generally average and uniform set of respondents who are unusual only in that they report watching very little, if any, television
9	32	6.4	Older, married people with average cultural interests, except for below-average viewing of educational television. A few also report frequently listening to records and tapes
10	47	9.4	A diverse group socially, who are alike in that they listen to the radio more than they do to anything else
11	4	0.8	A small group of primarily homemakers and non-professional workers, with below-average education, who do not read much, but spend a lot of time watching educational television and listening to classical music
12	5	1.0	A small, highly diverse group. They tend to be older, retired people. They generally read little, but go to performing arts frequently and watch televised sports regularly

Source: Smith and Smale 1982.

Smith and Smale then examined demographic, occupation, social, and participation trends to develop rough estimates of likely changes in each segment. They also defined a set of 'cultural elasticities' that indicated the change expected in participation in each activity given a 1 per cent change in the size of any segment. The author's use of segmentation may be viewed as a conceptual application of segmentation. Their interest was primarily on the development of a forecasting model based on the concept of 'cultural elasticities' rather than on actual marketing techniques. Had the authors included descriptors such as exposure to and use of specific mass media, it may have been possible to develop recommendations on how to reach those segments that showed potential for significant growth in participation in particular activities.

A more marketing-oriented study was conducted by the same research team that provided us with our *a priori* example: Stynes and Mahoney (1980). They identified seven general ski area attributes on the basis of a factor analysis of the same data set described previously: (1) after-ski entertainment, (2) lodging facilities, (3) restaurant facilities, (4) lift-line crowding, (5) slope quality, (6) lift-ticket price, and (7) driving distance from home. The authors then clustered their respondents and identified a set of five clusters. These clusters are identified in Table 3.8.

Stynes and Mahoney also examined the actual skiing patterns of their clusters as well as some of their socio-economic characteristics. They could then develop some marketing implications of the various segments. For example, ski areas that are distant from major markets can successfully attract the 'quality-conscious' and the 'price-conscious' segments by emphasizing quality and value in their advertisements. A ski resort close to the market can successfully tap the large 'crowding-conscious' segment by restricting the number of skiers allowed on the

Table 3.8 Identification of five clusters by Stynes and Mahoney

Cluster	% of sample	Description
1	16.0	'Quality conscious' – emphasis on slope quality and availability of restaurants and accommodation
2	33.6	'Crowding conscious' – emphasis is on crowding at lift lines and on distance travelled
3	7.7	'Price conscious' – emphasis is on price, even if it means travelling far distances or enduring crowds. Also least concerned about slope quality and most concerned about after-ski entertainment
4	24.3	'Strictly skiing conscious' – emphasis is on slope quality, crowding, and price
5	18.1	'Travel conscious' – emphasis is on travel distance, and moderately concerned with price levels

Source: Adapted from Stynes and Mahoney 1980.

slopes, opening additional runs and lift lines, and perhaps through the use of differential pricing schedules to encourage off-peak-time use.

Summary

Market segmentation can improve the efficiency of advertising aimed at different groups of potential consumers and by increasing the appeal of advertisements or products developed for specific groups. Segmentation can also be a tool for other analytical projects such as the development of forecasting models for different social groups or for the study of the motivations and behaviours of different types of individuals. There are two basic types of segmentation methodology: *a priori* and factor-clustering. The first is based on the arbitrary choice of one or more variables by the analyst to develop the segments. Factor–cluster segmentation, on the other hand, produces statistically based segments. Factor–clustering produces more objective results than *a priori* segmentation, but it requires more data and statistical ability. And even though factor-clustering is more objective, the results can still be influenced by modifications to the specific factoring and clustering routines used.

Regardless of which method is chosen to define segments, there are several criteria any good segmentation should satisfy:

1. *Accessibility*. The researcher or market planner must be able to reach the segments through existing information channels; ideally, the channels should allow the message to reach only or predominantly the target audience and not other groups which are not likely to respond to the message. If the target segments cannot be reached within the limits of the available advertising budget, or if they cannot be singled out for a focused campaign, there is little point in identifying them.
2. *Size*. The segments must be of a size sufficient to make them economical to reach. In other words, they must be big enough to justify the cost and effort of a directed marketing campaign. This is a special concern with factor–cluster segments. A solution of many small segments might make statistical sense, but could be meaningless in practical terms.
3. *Measurability*. The segments must be defined in such a way that you can obtain adequate information about their market behaviour to monitor the effectiveness of a marketing campaign. This is also a concern when segments are being defined to be used in forecasting models (as in the case of Smith and Smale).

The characteristics used for defining the segments must be those for which adequate trend data are available for forecasting.

4. *Appropriateness*. Certain products are generally not appropriate for segmentation. Specialized products like large main-frame computers for research will be purchased by a small number of institutions. The number, nature, and needs of these institutions are so limited that there is usually no need to segment them. Other companies will enjoy a monopoly in a geographical region; such as newspapers in a one-newspaper town. With no competition, there can be no competitive advantage to be gained from segmentation. On the other hand, such firms would use segmentation procedures to develop specialized products or product characteristics that cater for the different population segments they are serving.

Further reading

Abbey J R 1979 Does life-style profiling work? *Journal of Travel Research* **18**(1): 8–14.

Crask M R 1981 Segmenting the vacationer market: identifying the vacation preferences, demographics, and magazine readership of each group. *Journal of Travel Research* **20**(2): 29–34.

Graham J and **Wall G** 1984 American visitors to Canada: a study in market segmentation. *Journal of Travel Research* **16**(3): 21–4.

Hawes D K 1977 Psychographics are meaningful, not merely interesting. *Journal of Travel Research* **15**(2):1–7.

Hawes D K 1978 Empirically profiling four recreation vehicle market segments. *Journal of Travel Research* **16**(4): 13–20.

McQueen J and **Miller K E** 1985 Target market selection of tourists: a comparison of two approaches. *Journal of Travel Research* **24**(1): 2–6.

Solomon P J and **George W R** 1977 The bicentennial traveler: a lifestyle analysis of the historian segment. *Journal of Travel Research* **15**(3): 14–17.

Thomson C M and **Pearce D G** 1980 Market Segmentation of New Zealand package tours. *Journal of Travel Research* **19**(2): 3–6.

Woodside A G and **Jacobs L W** 1985 Step two in benefit segmentation: learning the benefits realized by major travel markets. *Journal of Travel Research* **24**(1): 7–13.

Woodside A G, Moore E M, Bonn M A and **Wizeman D G** 1986 Segmenting the timeshare resort market. *Journal of Travel Research* **24** (3): 6–12.

CHAPTER 4

Understanding the tourist

Introduction

Tourism marketing problems often require answers to questions about what tourists are thinking and how they make decisions. The owner-operator of a small resort may want to know, 'Are my customers satisfied with my housekeeping?' An airline marketing director may wonder, 'Are we stressing the right issues in these advertisements to compete successfully?' A restaurateur might ask, 'Are my menu selections and prices attractive?' These types of questions require specialized instruments to probe the minds of tourists and potential tourists to better understand their attitudes, tastes, motivations, and decision-making criteria. Such topics are so complex that entire books are devoted to the methodologies developed for their measurement and analysis. The purpose of this chapter is to provide an overview of some of the major concepts of attitude measurement and related topics and to examine in detail two procedures commonly used to obtain a better understanding of tourists' attitudes and actions.

Before beginning our overview of basic concepts, a few words about definitions may be helpful. An *attitude*, as the term is used in this chapter, is a predisposition of an individual to act or otherwise respond to an object or stimulus. It is not the actual response, but rather the tendency towards a consistent response. This definition implies that attitudes persist over time, changing slowly, if at all. They tend to produce predictable behaviour, although circumstances often cause an individual to act contrary to his normal predispositions.

Attitudes also imply some form of preference or evaluation regarding a stimulus. For example, some people tend to prefer restaurants that emphasize low price. Their attitude may be one of an emphasis on 'value' or 'fiscal conservatism' in matters of personal finance. They will tend to patronize those restaurants that offer them opportunities to save money on meals or that offer good value for the price. As previously suggested, however, there will be circumstances that temporarily override the tendency to patronize inexpensive restaurants – such as the desire to celebrate an anniversary by sharing an especially nice meal at a fancy restaurant with a spouse.

Stimuli that are more directly tied to overt behaviour, such as the decision to go to a gourmet restaurant, may be termed *motivations*. They are related to attitudes, but are usually conceived as being expressed more directly in actual behaviour. They tend to be goal-directed, and are operative for a shorter period of time than attitudes. The motivation for going to an expensive gourmet restaurant to celebrate an anniversary ends once the anniversary is over. The attitudes about money and about the importance of celebrating family events, though, endure.

Tastes are more closely tied to sensory stimulation than attitudes. You may have a taste for Bordeaux wines or rare roast beef. You can have a taste for high-quality service in hotels or for flying first class. If you cannot afford these, however, you do not indulge your tastes. Tastes represent preferences for certain types of products or services, but they are not necessarily linked to actual behaviour. The ability to satisfy your tastes depends on the availability of the products you desire and on your ability to afford them. The question of taste also arises if you are asked to evaluate the quality of a product or service, such as when you receive a questionnaire about the quality of service during your stay at a hotel. The issue is not one of your attitudes or motivations affecting your decision to come, but rather how well the hotel met your tastes or standards.

Researchers, managers, and planners are interested in all three concepts: attitudes, motivations, and tastes. The first two, though, are generally of greater importance for marketing and planning. Regardless of the particular quality you want to measure – attitude, motivation, or taste – the task is to design an instrument that will allow you to infer conclusions objectively and accurately about the mental processes or states of tourists and potential tourists.

Some may object, at this point, that we can never measure anything for certain about what other people are thinking or feeling. This is, in fact, true. The point of attitude (or motivation or taste) measurement is not literally one of measuring attitudes; rather it is a matter of counting the number of people who respond a certain way to certain types of questions. The questions asked about attitudes usually are designed to generate structured answers; that is, they use scales for respondents to indicate their answers. At this point, therefore, we should begin our overview by looking at the different types of scales that may be used in tourism analysis: nominal scales, ordinal scales, interval scales, and ratio scales.

Types of scales

The most primitive type of scale, the *nominal scale*, is the use of numbers as labels. Identification codes, such as 001, given to each respondent in a survey are an example of this type of scale. Labels can also be given to groups or classes of respondents or objects. All male respondents could be labelled '1', while those who are female can be labelled '2'. In such cases, the only arithmetic sign or manipulation that can be meaningfully applied is the equality sign, '='. Everyone who has a value of 1 is the same; everyone who is a 2 is the same. No other operations will produce meaningful results.

Ordinal scales possess nominal scale properties as well as the property of indicating order or rank. For example, a listing of preferred vacation destinations, from 1 to 10, or most preferred to least preferred would be an interval scale. The relative ranks between any two destinations, say 1 and 5, do not indicate anything about the absolute difference between the attractiveness of the two destinations. The ranks indicate nothing more than the relative attractiveness of the two. You can perform monotonic transformations on ordinal scale data. A monotonic transformation changes the magnitude of the original numbers while retaining their relative positions. A special type of monotonic transformation is conjoint measurement, an analytical tool we will examine later in this chapter.

Interval scales retain the properties of nominal and ordinal scales plus indicating the distance between objects ranked on the scale. You do not know, however, anything about the absolute magnitude of the objects. A flight that leaves at 12 noon leaves six hours later than a flight that leaves at 6 a.m., but you cannot say that the noon flight leaves 'twice as late' as the early morning flight. Ratios of interval scales are meaningless. Interval scales remain invariant under most arithmetic transformations. For example, you could transform the flight times into minutes by multiplying each hour by 60. Certain types of attitude scales are expressly designed to have interval scale properties, such as Thurstone's differential and case V scales.

The most powerful scale is the *ratio scale*. This scale measures some phenomenon with respect to an absolute zero value. The number of tourists, the price of tourism commodities, the distance between an origin and a destination are all examples of ratio scales. Virtually all types of analyses are possible with ratio scales.

You need to be careful about applying appropriate methods when working with different scales. Obviously, it would be nonsense to add 1 and 2 to obtain 3, if 1 refers to the USA, 2 to Canada, and 3 to Mexico. It is less obvious, though, whether one can take the average of ordinal scale data to obtain an average ranking of a series of attitude measurements. Nor is it obvious whether it is legitimate to perform a simple regression analysis using Pearson's product-moment correlation coefficient to compare ordinal attitude scores with income (a ratio scale variable). Traditional statisticians would suggest the answer is 'no' to the last two questions. One can argue, however, that the potential gain from conducting some limited analyses on carefully selected 'questionable' scale data may outweigh potential problems. These issues have not been adequately addressed in the tourism field, but they are persistent questions. One statistician, Nunnally (1967) suggests that some analyses treating ordinal data as interval data may be acceptable and produce correct conclusions. His view has been challenged by Wilson (1971) who argues that there is too much potential for abuse of analysis and for falling into logical traps if ordinal data are treated like interval data. It is clear, at least, that the debate about which analyses can be applied to ordinal data is unresolved. The subject is also reviewed by Sonquist and Dunkelberg (1977: 255–6).

Scaling techniques

Psychologists have developed many different types of scales for attitude measurement, motivational analysis, personality assessment, and marketing applications. Many of these have, at best, only a remote application to tourism analysis. Most scale development work in tourism is based on some version of five well-established techniques: ranking, Thurstone's differential, Thurstone's case V, Likert, and semantic differential.

Ranking

The simplest of all scaling techniques for attitude measurement is ranking or rank ordering. A respondent is given a list of items, such as hotel attributes, and asked to rank them in order of preference. The ranking can be done directly if there are relatively few items to consider, or it can be done in stages if there are many items. A typical procedure for ranking many items is to first sort them into low, medium, and high ranks. Each item in these general ranks is then ranked within its category. The highest-ranked item in one category is compared to the lowest-ranked item in the category above it to ensure consistency in ranking. When the final ordering for each category is determined, the categories are placed in proper order to obtain overall rankings.

Individual respondents may also be asked to repeat the ranking process two or more times to check for reliability. Although the resulting ranks are an ordinal scale only, most researchers will calculate arithmetic averages of the ranks of multiple respondents to obtain an overall ranking for their study population.

Thurstone differential scales

The basic Thurstone differential scale (Thurstone 1927) consists of a series of statements which a respondent is asked to review. He then indicates which statements he agrees with. Each statement carries a ranked score, not known to the respondent; the respondent's overall score is the mean or median score of those statements with which he has agreed.

Consider the following statements regarding vacations:

1. Vacations are a proper reward for anyone who has worked hard throughout the year. (4.0)
2. Vacations are absolutely essential for everyone's mental health. (5.0)
3. Vacations are a luxury that most people cannot afford. (1.0)
4. Vacations should be a human right guaranteed by the government. (7.0)
5. Vacation expenses should be subsidized through government or employer-sponsored programmes. (7.0)
6. Vacations are a nice reward, but only after years of hard work and careful savings. (3.0)

These statements express a variety of possible attitudes towards vacations; the score reflecting the degree of positive feelings towards vacations is given in parentheses (which are normally not shown to the respondent). The stronger the positive evaluation, the higher the number. If a respondent indicated he agreed with statements 1 and 2, his score would be the average of 4.0 and 5.0, or 4.5.

As you can see, this type of procedure is quite simple for the respondent. The real work lies in the development of the scale and the associated values. The analyst begins by formulating a large number of statements expressing a range of attitudes towards a particular subject, ranging from very positive views to very negative. These statements are then presented to a panel of judges who are asked to group the statements into 7, 9, or 11 categories reflecting their perception of the positiveness or negativeness of each statement. The distribution of each statement is reviewed, and those that received a wide range of rankings are discarded. The items that remain are then combined into a survey instrument for administration to the sample population. The ranking associated with each statement is based on the judges' consensus about the degree of favourableness of the statement.

As the name indicates, this is a differential scale. That means that each respondent indicates simply whether or not he agrees with each statement. An important explicit assumption behind this type of scale is that the attitudes and the statements intended to describe those attitudes are normally distributed and have interval scale properties. The significance of these assumptions is more obvious in the development of a Thurstone's case V scale, which is described later. Details about developing the Thurstone differential scale are described in Edwards (1957); a critique of these scales is in Nunnally (1967). His primary criticisms of differential scales include the laboriousness of developing the scale, although this is somewhat offset by the simplicity of the scale from the respondents' perspective. Moser and Kalton (1974) disagree about Nunnally's perception of the difficulty in developing a differential scale and suggest the work is not overly demanding.

In comparison to the other scales presented here, Thurstone scales are relatively rare in tourism research. There is, though, significant potential for their application. One example of their use in a tourism project is Lopez's (1980) analysis of the effects of different tour leaders' styles on the satisfaction of tour members with their trip. One key element in assessing leadership style was the measurement of the degree of authoritarianism of each leader. Lopez used an 80-item Thurstone scale developed by Ezekial (1970) consisting of 40 statements tending towards an authoritarian position and 40 statements tending towards non-authoritarianism. The leaders were asked to fill out the instrument confidentially, checking off all statements with which they agreed. The scores of the leaders were then correlated with the expressed levels of satisfaction provided by the tour members who had travelled under the leader.

Thurstone scaling lends itself well to measuring certain attitudinal characteristics of travellers or potential travellers, such as attitudes towards certain vacation styles. Scales could be developed to assess individuals' desires for excitement, for relaxation, for security, or for careful vacation planning. A Thurstone instrument could also be derived to examine the relative influence or dominance levels of husband and wife with respect to vacation decision-making. Such an instrument might list a series of specific tasks or decisions such as where to go, how much to spend, how to travel, and how long to stay. The spouses would then check off those tasks for which they believed they were responsible. A comparison of the total number of checked statements as well as the identify of those statements could yield useful information about how different couples prepare for vacations.

Thurstone's case V

Thurstone's early work on measuring attitudes led to his development of the law of comparative judgement. This law attempts to explain the inconsistency surrounding the selection of which of two items is preferred by an individual or a group. The following example may help to illustrate how the law is intended to work and how it can be used to develop a scale that is of particular value to tourism researchers.

Consider three resorts, A, B, and C. If we ask a group of individuals to evaluate the attractiveness of each resort on a scale of 1 to 10, we will get a range of rankings for each resort. Thurstone's law of comparative judgement is based on the hypothesis that if we were to ask a large sample of people to rank those resorts, their rankings would form a normal distribution around some mean for each resort.

Assume that resort C has the lowest mean, A has the next highest, and B has the highest, as shown in Fig. 4.1. Some individuals, however, gave resort A a higher ranking than B, as can be seen from the overlap of the curves for A and B.

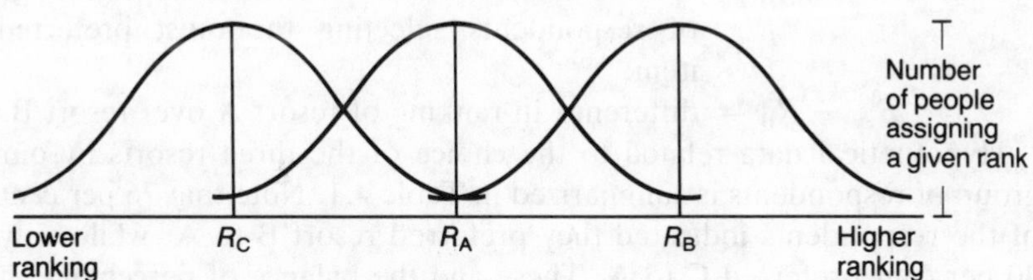

Fig. 4.1 Hypothetical distribution of rankings of three resorts under assumptions of Thurstone's law of comparative cognitive judgements

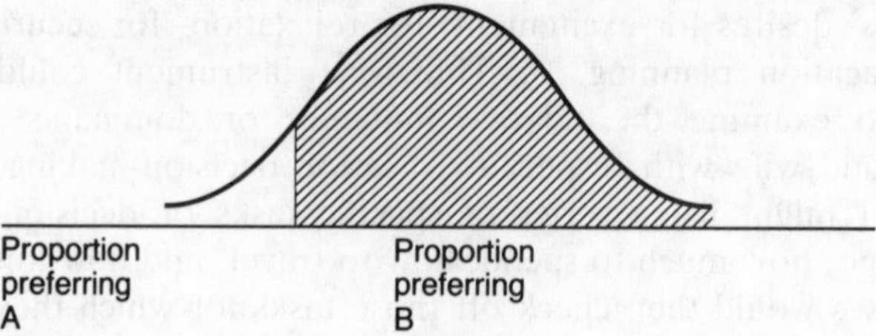

Fig. 4.2 Distribution of differential responses for two resorts as implied in Fig. 4.1

If these same individuals were asked to compare pairwise the three resorts, we would find a high proportion of people selecting B over A. Some, however, would prefer A over B. This pattern of responses can also be represented in the form of a normal distribution curve, as in Fig. 4.2. This figure has a curve resembling the curve shown in tables of standard normal variables. And in fact, the standard normal variable, Z, becomes an integral part of the calculation of Thurstone's case V scale.

Case V is a simple version of the application of the law of comparative judgements. It requires only that: (1) the percentage of respondents choosing each item in a series of pairs be known; (2) that the pattern of responses around the means, as shown in Fig. 4.1, be identical for each item; and (3) the correlations between the choice processes of the same set of judgements be zero (Green and Tull 1975). Under these conditions you can calculate the discriminal or perceived difference between pairs of items, such as resorts A and B, by the equation:

$$R_A - R_B = Z_{AB}\sqrt{2} \quad [4.1]$$

where: Z_{AB} = the standard normal variable for the percentage of respondents selecting the most preferred item;

$R_A - R_B$ = difference in ranking of resort A over resort B.

Hypothetical data related to the choice of the three resorts by our group of respondents is summarized in Table 4.1. Note that 76 per cent of the respondents indicated they preferred resort B to A, while only 40 per cent preferred C to A. These and the balance of percentage in Table 4.1 were converted to Z values by consulting Table A.1 in the Appendix. The results are shown in Table 4.2. Only percentages equal to or greater than 0.50 are used in this calculation. For percentages less than 0.50, the Z value for the complementary percentage is used, but given a negative sign:

Table 4.1 Percentage of respondents preferring resort shown at top of table to resort shown at side of table

	A	B	C
A	–	0.76	0.40
B	0.24	–	0.05
C	0.60	0.95	–

(– = not applicable)

Table 4.2 *Z*-values for Table 4.1

	A	B	C
A	–	0.70	−0.25
B	−0.70	–	−1.64
C	0.25	1.64	–
ΣZ_x	−0.45	2.35	−1.90

(– = not applicable)

Note: These are derived from Table A.1 in the Appendix in the following way. The largest proportion in any pair of resorts is identified (this will be equal to or greater than 0.50). This number is then subtracted from 1.00. For example, 76% of respondents preferred resort B over resort A, so 1.00 − 0.76 = 0.24. The value closest to 0.24 is then located in the body of Table A.1. This particular value is '24 196' in the row labelled '0.7' and in the column labelled '0.00'. The *Z*-value for 76% is thus about 0.70. The *Z* value of 24%, the number of respondents favouring resort A over B, is the negative value of *Z* for 76%, or −0.70.

$$R_B - R_A = -Z_{AB}\sqrt{2} \qquad [4.2]$$

Thus *Z* for 76 per cent, the proportion of people choosing B over A, is 0.70; the associated value for 24 per cent, those who choose A over B, is −0.70.

The scale value for each resort can now be calculated using the equation:

$$R'_X = \left(\frac{\sqrt{2}}{N}\right)\Sigma Z_X \qquad [4.3]$$

where: R'_X = scale value for the item being evaluated;
ΣZ_X = column total of *Z* values for the item being evaluated (see Table 4.2);
N = number of items.

Table 4.3 Scale values for three resorts

Resort	Value
A	−0.212
B	+1.108
C	−0.896

Applying equation [4.3] to our data produces the results shown in Table 4.3. These values are an interval scale of the relative attractiveness of each resort as derived from the percentages of a sample population indicating their preferences for each pair of resorts – an ordinal judgement. Scores calculated with this methodology can then be used in subsequent analyses requiring interval level data.

Likert scales

A Likert scale (Likert 1932) requires that the respondent indicate the degree to which he agrees or disagrees with each statement, rather than simple agreement or disagreement as in a Thurstone scale. The degree of agreement is often summarized on a five-point scale, ranging from strongly agree to strongly disagree, with a neutral position in the middle. The analyst designing a Likert scale should seek to ensure that the statements presented cover a wide range of attitudinal positions so that respondents have a reasonable chance of differentiating themselves. There is little value in having a series of statements that are so bland (or extreme) that everyone agrees (or disagrees) with them.

Once a series of statements has been developed, the analyst gives them to a sample of individuals who are representative of the larger group he is studying. These individuals act as judges who indicate their own degree of agreement with each statement (unlike the development phase for a Thurstone scale in which the judges assess only the degree of favourableness of a statement and not their own attitude). A total score for each judge is obtained by summing his responses over all questions (you must make sure that the scoring spectrum is consistent; that is, all negative attitudes should receive low values while all positive attitudes receive high values, or vice versa). The preliminary results are then looked at in detail. Identify, for example, any statements that fail to discriminate between the highest- and lowest-scoring groups of judges. Statements that correlate poorly with the total score of respondents or that fail to contribute to the distinction between high and low scores are eliminated. A list of 20 to 25 statements is desired in the end.

Once the instrument has been developed, it may be administered to the study population. Its scoring is conducted as with the judges: means of individual statements as well as overall scores can be determined and studied. Such analysis – it should be noted – is based on the assumption that Likert scales have interval properties. Strictly speaking, there may be no basis for this assumption. The interval between agree and strongly agree is not necessarily the same as the interval between neutral and agree or between disagree and strongly disagree. As Moser and Kalton note, however, Likert scales, even when treated as interval scales, have shown themselves to be fairly reliable in obtaining reproducible results. They are also simpler to construct and are perhaps the most frequently used scale in tourism research.

Two examples will help to illustrate the uses to which Likert scales are put. These two examples, though, do not represent the entire range of problems to which Likert scales have been applied in tourism.

Shih (1986) assessed the market position of the state of Pennsylvania by providing a group of respondents with 36 vacation criteria. These criteria included qualities such as 'safe to visit', 'friendly people', 'reasonable prices', 'fishing', and 'beach resorts'. Each respondent was asked to indicate the importance of each quality on a five-point scale, ranging from very important to very unimportant. The respondents were also asked to indicate how well Pennsylvania and the surrounding states provided each quality or service on a five-point scale, ranging from excellent to poor.

Shih then assigned each respondent to one of nine life-style categories defined by the Value and Life-styles (VALS) typology developed by SRI International. Those life-style groupings with the most favourable impressions of Pennsylvania were noted, along with their socio-economic characteristics. The information obtained by Shih confirmed the merits of Pennsylvania's promotional theme, 'You've got a friend in Pennsylvania'. He also provided advice about the best mix of images and advertising media to reach the life-style groups with the greatest potential for taking a Pennsylvania vacation.

Wall and Knapper (1981) applied Likert scaling to their analysis of attitudes of Canadians concerning art galleries. A questionnaire containing 25 statements about art and art galleries was distributed to visitors to the Art Gallery of Ontario during the Tutankhamun exhibit in 1979. Typical statements included, 'An art gallery should add enjoyment to people's lives', and 'Art galleries are for university professors and other élite groups'. The responses to these statements were factor analysed to reveal eight basic structures that describe attitudes towards art galleries. These included an 'education' component, a 'public involvement' component, 'preservation and conservation', plus five others. Individuals' scores on each factor were examined to identify correlations between other personal characteristics, actual visitation patterns at art galleries, and other leisure activities. The authors concluded that visitors who came to the King Tut exhibit were, as predicted, supportive of art galleries. They were also generally better educated and more socially 'upscale' than the general public. Wall and Knapper also found evidence that the visitors who had come to the Art Gallery of Ontario for the first time to see the Tutankhamun exhibit represented a potentially important market for future visits if the proper types of programmmes and shows could be mounted. Further, these individuals could be a small but attractive market for tourism promotions developed by the city of Toronto emphasizing the artistic attractions of that city.

Semantic differential

Developed by Osgood, Suci, and Tannenbaum (1957), the semantic differential examines respondents' attitudes towards one specific topic in terms of a number of bipolar adjective pairs. The pairs are typically separated by a scale with five or seven points. Examples include:

Strong ____ : ____ : ____ : ____ : ____ Weak
Bad ____ : ____ : ____ : ____ : ____ Good
Cold ____ : ____ : ____ : ____ : ____ Hot
Friendly ____ : ____ : ____ : ____ : ____ Unfriendly

Respondents are presented with these statements and asked to indicate their feelings about the topic under study by placing a check mark at the appropriate point on each scale.

Osgood, Suci, and Tannenbaum found that attitudes towards many topics consisted of three factors: potency (e.g. strong – weak), evaluation (e.g. bad – good), and activity (e.g. cold – hot). Analysts often use these three factors as guides for the development of specific adjective pairs for their research. They also include other pairs relevant to their particular problem. Thus a study of attitudes towards air travel might include 'cheap – expensive', 'reliable – unreliable', and 'safe – dangerous'.

If a single dimension, such as evaluation, is used to select the adjective pairs, a summation system can be used to calculate an individual's score as in Likert scaling. If several independent dimensions are used, separate scores could be calculated for each. You may also find it useful to examine the mean rankings of the sample population on each adjective pair. So, for example, the ranking of a group of business travellers' perceptions of the reliability of a particular airline could be determined and compared to their perceptions of other airlines.

An example of the use of the semantic differential is LaPage and Cormier's (1977) assessment of the images of camping. They constructed a semantic differential instrument specific to issues of concern expressed by industry analysts. These included pairs such as 'interesting–boring', 'fun–work', 'clean–dirty', and 'expensive–inexpensive'. A national sample of non-campers, current campers, and former campers was contacted for the survey. Each respondent was also asked questions about his socio-economic characteristics. The responses to the semantic differential items were summarized for each of the three groups. The authors discovered that the camping industry suffers from many negative images among non-campers and former campers. They viewed the activity as being expensive, dirty, crowded, and inconvenient. LaPage and Cormier concluded by offering suggestions about how the industry should respond to these image problems to reverse the decline in North American camping participation rates.

The subject of attitude theory and measurement is a very large field. It is impossible to do any more than just touch on some of the major concepts and basic techniques relevant to tourism in this chapter. If you are interested in pursuing the subject of attitude measurement in greater detail, one useful reference is Guilford's 1954 text, *Psychometric methods*. Green and Tull (1975) also provide a useful overview of scaling procedures in marketing research. At this point, we must move on from the subject of measuring attitudes and examine some models that can be used to study how people make decisions. Again, these methods do not represent a complete listing of all the techniques that are available. They are, however, important ones for tourism research. Additional methods may be found in the supplemental list provided at the end of the chapter.

Expectancy-value models

Description

Expectancy-value models represent the single largest group of consumer decision-making models used in tourism analysis. Most are based on the Fishbein model (described below). Engel, Blackwell, and Kollat (1978) have noted, in fact, that Fishbein models accounted for more research in consumer behaviour in the 1970s than any other subject. They continue to be important into the 1980s as well.

Two names are normally associated with expectancy-value models: Rosenberg (1956) and, of course, Fishbein (1963, 1966, 1967). Although neither author's models were originally intended to be applied to marketing research, their formulations have proven to be important sources of market research hypotheses, especially with reference to modelling consumer decision-making.

Rosenberg's model describes a predicted relationship between the attractiveness of some object or action, A_j, and two variables: (1) the importance of specified characteristics or 'values' associated with the action or object; and (2) the perceived 'instrumentality' of those characteristics. The concept of instrumentality as articulated by Rosenberg is a difficult one, but it can be thought of as the degree to which an object or action provides the benefits a consumer associates with particular object (or action) characteristics. The mathematical form of the model may be expressed as

$$A_j = \sum_{i=1}^{N} (V_i)(I_{ij}) \qquad [4.4]$$

where: A_j = attractiveness of some object or action, j;
V_i = importance of the ith value or characteristic;
I_{ij} = instrumentality of alternative j with respect to i;
N = total number of characteristics.

In the context of tourism, A_j might refer to different cruise packages; V_i would represent the importance a potential cruise passenger attached to the various characteristics of the cruise package, such as ports of call or total price; I_{ij} would be an assessment of the degree to which the various packages available to the consumer were seen to provide access to the ports of call or the degree to which they met the desired level of price.

Rosenberg suggested using a 21-point Likert scale to measure V_i, with values ranging from 'gives me maximum satisfaction' to 'gives me maximum dissatisfaction'. He also proposed using an 11-point scale to measure I_{ij}, with the ranks ranging from 'values are completely attained' to 'values are completely blocked or unavailable'. Respondents would be asked to assess the importance of a range of characteristics and their associated instrumentalities for each of a series of alternatives. Each individual's assessment of each alternative is a function of the sum of his scores over all characteristics. The relative attractiveness of the alternatives is determined by the relative scores for each alternative.

Fishbein's model is quite similar to that of Rosenberg. Although some authors, such as Sheth (1972) argue that there are important differences between the two, these differences are subtle and of questionable relevance. For example, there are some methodological differences in how the two authors suggest developing their scales. Further, Fishbein's model was developed with reference to examining beliefs about the qualities of an object and the associated attitudes people held towards the object, whereas Rosenberg's model was applied to examining beliefs about whether an object would lead to the attainment of certain goals. For most tourism applications, though, these are probably distinctions without a difference.

In any event, Fishbein's model combines two variables, 'belief' and 'affect', to predict the attitude or opinion a person holds about a particular choice:

$$A_j = \sum_{i=1}^{N} (E_i)(B_{ij}) \qquad [4.5]$$

where: B_{ij} = belief about whether a particular object or action, j, possesses a given quality, i;
E_i = evaluation of the desirability of the ith quality;
other variables are as defined previously.

The Fishbein model in its original form is rarely used in tourism research because it was designed for attitudinal research and not analysis of consumer intentions. A modification of the Fishbein model, a model that is actually a hybrid of Fishbein and Rosenberg, is normally used:

$$A_j = \sum_{i=1}^{N} (V_i)(B_{ij}) \qquad [4.6]$$

where: A_j = intention to select (or the probability of selecting) any particular alternative product, j;
V_i = importance of characteristic i;
B_{ij} = the degree to which alternative j provides characteristic i.

Despite the popularity of the expectancy-value model in the research literature over the last decade and a half, it does have several weaknesses. Many of these are related to the fundamentally weak connection between the intention to buy, which these models are designed to predict, and actual buying behaviour, which is of the greatest interest to most marketers. Another limitation is that the context of the decision to buy is normally excluded from consideration in expectancy-value models. Experience and research have shown that the context of the actual decision greatly influences ultimate behaviour. The problem of context may be handled by specifying precisely the situation to which the model is intended to apply. For example, respondents might be presented with a carefully constructed description of the full context of a particular vacation decision, including the time of year, the motivations for taking the vacation, the available budget, the length of time available, and the nature of the travelling party.

Another problem, related to the issue of context, is the potential influence of family and friends on the actual decision to make a purchase. An individual consumer has his own preferences and opinions about the importance of various product characteristics and the degree to which various products possess these, but peer pressure from significant others who do not share these perceptions may force a decision contrary to the individual's own beliefs.

Expectancy-value models also fail to account for variations in the availability of the supply of a product or of the financial resources available to the consumer at the time of decision. The intention to make a particular purchase could be real and strong, but the lack of funds or a shortage of the desired product could circumvent the intention.

Other weaknesses in these models are related to certain assumptions that must be made in their development. First, these models are normally constructed as a linear combination of variables. The weighted characteristics of each choice are summed to obtain an overall score for each alternative. This implies that there are no significant interactions among the characteristics – such as between price and the quality of service. Schuler and Prosperi (1977) have found tentative evidence that interaction effects are minimal on many consumer decisions, but the issue should still be considered open for tourism research.

Expectancy-value models use untransformed data. In the situation of distance perceptions, at least, there is strong evidence that travellers do not respond to differences in distance according to simple linear arithmetic, but rather to a logarithmic transformation of those differences. Whether such transformations should be applied to other types of characteristics remains inadequately researched in tourism. It should be noted, though, that Fechner's law (Fechner 1889) that states that psychological responses to physical stimuli vary in direct proportion with the logarithmic magnitude of the change in the intensity of the stimulus suggests that some types of transformations may be important in modelling perceptual responses to product stimuli.

Finally, as we shall see in the next section, the development of the weights for each characteristic and the assessment of the degree to which each alternative product possesses those characteristics require the use of ratio scales. Special effort is required to ensure that the data obtained from respondents reasonably approximate ratio data if the results are to be trusted.

Procedures

1. Identify a number of destination characteristics that are likely to have a significant influence on the perceived attractiveness of the destinations being considered. This may be done through a review of other studies, by obtaining expert opinion, or by conducting a series of focus group interviews with potential respondents. There is no absolute minimum or maximum number of characteristics needed for analysis, but more than 20 or 25 often taxes the concentration of the respondents. With fewer than four or five, you have probably overlooked some important qualities.

2. Establish a sampling design and a set of respondents appropriate to your problem.

3. After drawing your sample, collect the data required for the model as described in equation [4.6]. First, ask each respondent to indicate the relative importance of each attribute. Because this measure of importance will be used as a weighting factor, it must have ratio scale properties. A simple way to achieve this is to have the respondents assign a total of 100 points to all attributes so that the number of points any attribute receives represents its proportional significance.

4. Next, have each respondent indicate the degree to which he believes each commodity possesses each attribute. This is usually done on a Likert scale, with 7 points ranging from '6 – possesses to a great degree' to '0 – does not possess at all'. It is worth emphasizing again that this scale must have ratio scale properties. This point could be explained to respondents so that they understand that, for example, a rating of 4 implies that the alternative has twice as much of some characteristic as an alternative with a rating of 2.

5. Multiply the weight assigned by the first respondent to the first

attribute by that respondent's ranking of the attribute. Repeat for all other attributes. Sum these products to get a commodity or alternative weighting for the first respondent.

6. Repeat step 5 with all other respondents. Add and average all their scores for the first commodity to obtain an overall measure of the perceived attractiveness of that commodity.

7. Repeat steps 5 and 6 for all other commodity alternatives. The results define the attractiveness of each commodity as perceived by all respondents as a group.

Once you have obtained the relative attractiveness of each commodity, you can estimate the expected market share of each, if you desire. To do this, sum all A_js, the relative attractiveness of all commodities, to obtain an aggregate measure of the total attractiveness of the entire set of commodities being studied. Divide each alternative's A_j by this total. The quotient indicates the proportion of the total attractiveness (or utility) of all alternatives associated with each alternative. Applying the logic of the Luce choice theorem (Luce 1959), one can hypothesize that the proportional attractiveness of an alternative also represents the expected market share of that alternative:

$$S_j = \frac{A_j}{\sum_{i=1}^{N} A_j} \qquad [4.7]$$

where: S_j = expected market share of commodity j;
A_j = proportional attraction of commodity j;
N = number of commodity choices.

Here S_j may be interpreted as either the market share of a commodity alternative or as the probability that the average respondent would select choice j from among all alternatives considered.

Examples

The following hypothetical example will help clarify the calculations involved in the procedure. The example uses only three destinations (A, B, and C) and three attributes (X, Y and Z). Normally, many more would be considered. Table 4.4 is a summary of the responses of a set of hypothetical respondents. The numbers in the matrix represent the score for each attribute–destination pair. The vector of

Table 4.4 Use of the scaling method to model individual locational choices: hypothetical data

	Attributes		
	X	Y	Z
Destinations A	5	4	4
B	1	3	3
C	4	0	4
Weights	50	20	30

	Relative attractiveness
$A_A = 5(50) + 4(20) + 4(30) = 450$	1
$A_B = 1(50) + 3(20) + 3(30) = 200$	3
$A_C = 4(50) + 0(20) + 4(30) = 320$	2

$$S_A = \frac{A_A}{A_A + A_B + A_C} = \frac{450}{450 + 200 + 320} = 0.46$$

$$S_B = \frac{200}{450 + 200 + 320} = 0.21$$

$$S_C = \frac{320}{450 + 200 + 320} = 0.33$$

three numbers beneath the matrix contains the weights (out of 100 points) assigned to each attribute.

The individual attractiveness of each destination is calculated with equation [4.6] from the data in Table 4.4. In this case, destination A is the most attractive, followed by destination C, and then B. This predicted order could be compared, if desired, to the order actually expressed by the respondents. Expected market shares were also estimated using equation [4.7]. Destination A is predicted to receive 46 per cent of all visits, while C should receive 33 per cent and B 21 per cent. As noted previously, these percentages may also be interpreted as indicating the probability that an average respondent will choose any particular destination: 46 per cent chance of selecting A, 33 per cent of selecting C, and 21 per cent for B.

Goodrich (1978) provides a similar example of the application of an expectancy-value model in an actual tourism situation. He selected nine destination regions: Hawaii, California, Florida, Mexico, the Virgin Islands, the Bahamas, Jamaica, Barbados, and Puerto Rico. Ten 'tourist attracting attributes' such as 'availability of facilities for water sports' were identified through discussions with travel professionals. A sample of 900 American Express Card customers was drawn. They were sent a questionnaire asking them to rate the importance of each attribute as a factor influencing their choice of destinations on a seven-point scale and the degree to which the nine regions possessed these qualities, again on a seven-point scale. Goodrich also asked his respondents to directly compare the relative attractiveness of the nine destinations.

Two hundred and thirty questionnaires were returned for analysis (a 25 per cent response rate). Goodrich followed the procedure described above to estimate the attractiveness of each region. He also used Thurstone's case V method to analyse the direct evaluations of the attractiveness of the nine destinations. Finally, he compared the scaled attractiveness values of the destinations as determined through the case V method with the values predicted through the expectancy-value model. He found a very close correlation.

The results of this study support the utility of using an expectancy-value model. Goodrich did note three limitations in his study that are relevant for similar projects. First, he cautioned against generalizing too far from the results of his study. His respondents were relatively affluent travellers living only in New York and who carried American Express cards. Second, many other variables such as cost, advertising, availability of time, and the desire for a change influence the ultimate choice of a destination. Some of these are specific to the destination and might be added as additional characteristics in the model. Others are specific to the decision-maker or are exogenous, and thus not easily accommodated in the model. Finally, Goodrich's questionnaire was quite lengthy and required significant effort to fill out. He suggested this was a major factor contributing to his poor response rate. The potential for simplifying the questionnaire for any form of an expectancy-value model is quite limited, so this latter problem is likely to remain one of the major drawbacks to its widespread application.

Conjoint measurement

Description

Consider the following choices for a vacation:

- Two weeks in a rented cottage at a beach during the summer. The cottage costs $800 per week, The only recreational activities available are those you can provide for yourself. Residents of neighbouring beach cottages are predominantly families with two or three children.

Or

- One week in a ski lodge in the mountains during the winter. A room in the lodge costs $500 per week. Recreational activities include skiing, skating, sauna, bar, games room, and indoor pool. The other people in the lodge are predominantly single and in their late twenties and early thirties.

Which would you choose?

The choice you make between these two reflects your own preferences for vacations in certain seasons, the type and range of recreational activities, and the type of other people you are likely to meet. Different people will make different choices, and those who select the same vacation may do so for different reasons. The selection of an alternative requires the implicit weighting of each variable (time of year, location, type of accommodation, length of stay, activities, cost, and nature of other people) to reflect the importance of that variable. The combination of weighted variables is then compared, probably implicitly, to determine which alternative will be likely to give the greatest satisfaction.

This conceptualization of how a choice is made is similar to that behind expectancy-value models. In practice, of course, people do not normally assign explicit weights; they are conscious only of having made a choice. Since the choice may be the only reliable, observable phenomenon accessible to the researcher, there is a challenge to take the observed choices and to deduce from them: (1) the relative weights implicitly assigned to each variable; and (2) how they are combined in the consumer's mind to arrive at the ultimate expressions of preference.

Shepard (1957, 1962), Luce and Tukey (1964), and Kruskal (1965) developed a method known as conjoint measurement that allows a researcher to begin with simple rank orders, such as the expressed order of preferences for a series of vacation packages, and to analyse these choices to determine the weights the individual consumer appears to assign to each quality.

An important feature of conjoint measurement is that it presents the choice problem to respondents in a format that is more realistic than that used in expectancy-value models. Each respondent is given a profile of several commodity choices similar to those introduced at the beginning of this section. He is then asked to rank them in order of preference. This avoids the unrealistic task of presenting the respondent with a series of discrete commodity characteristics and asking him to assign ratio scale weights to each.

The profiles presented to the respondents consist of several specific variables, such as price, and some specified level for that variable, say $100. Each profile contains the same list of variables but different combinations of levels. Conjoint measurement allows the researcher to produce a series of coefficients, called 'part-worths', from the overall rankings of the set of profiles. A separate part-worth is estimated for each level of each attribute. These values represent the relative importance of each attribute and its associated levels in terms of its contribution to the overall attractiveness of any particular choice.

Conjoint measurement is based on three assumptions. First, it is assumed that an individual's preference for certain products is based on the trading-off of different characteristics. Second, and closely related to the first assumption, is that the individual's preference for any product is determined by the summation of the preferences for the various individual attributes of the product. Third, the intention to buy a product is closely correlated with the objective attributes of the product.

Conjoint measurement also has a number of limitations. One of the more frequently cited is that most conjoint models do not allow for the possibility of interactions between variables. For example, the combination of excellent quality food and superior service in a restaurant may contribute more to the overall attractiveness of a restaurant than the simple sum of the importance of either attribute by itself. The extent to which interaction effects influence the validity of conjoint measurement results is still debated. Many researchers are confident that interaction effects are present in human behaviour, but several empirical studies have shown that their importance in conjoint measurement models is negligible. Johnson (1973, 1974, 1976), Green and Devita (1973), Green and Wind (1975) and Green and Srinivasan (1978) have found that the simple additive model, without interaction effects, provides a level of accuracy in conjoint measurement that is comparable to that of more complicated interaction models.

Another limitation in conjoint measurement is that the results are relevant only for the specified attribute levels. If one attribute is price and the specified levels are $100, $200, and $300, it is not possible to interpolate to obtain part-worths for $150 nor is it possible to extrapolate to $400.

Conjoint measurement requires the use of objective product attributes, but those attributes need not be quantitative. Brand names, qualitative conditions, styles, and other types of attributes may be used if they can be described in objective terms. The choice of the attributes is an important aspect of the development of a conjoint model. The researcher must identify the most salient features to be used in the product profile. Further, these features should often be those the designer of the product can influence. If, for example, a particular corporate name must be associated with a certain product, there is little point in using different brand names as part of the product profile. On the other hand, different model names for the same product could be tried to see if one has an especially desirable effect on increasing the attractiveness of the product.

Since the introduction of conjoint measurement to market research by Green and Rao in 1971, hundreds and perhaps thousands of applications have appeared in the marketing literature. Its use in tourism is much more limited; increased use, though, is likely. As a result of its current scarcity in tourism research, it may be difficult for some analysts to obtain the software necessary to do a conjoint measurement. The algorithm of choice is monotonic analysis of variance (MONANOVA), but if this is not available there are alternatives. Cohen (1968) and Green and Srinivasan (1978) have demonstrated the functional equivalence of different forms of analysis of variance, including monotonic analysis of variance, with general linear models. Empirical tests have shown that differences in the numerical results begin to appear, if at all, only in the third decimal place. This usually is not significant in conjoint measurement work. Such findings mean that dummy variable regression – a general linear model – may be employed to produce results virtually identical to those obtained with the more specialized MONANOVA. Dummy variable regression, besides being more generally accessible to researchers, also has the advantage of providing significance tests and a measure of the level of explained variance that MONANOVA does not provide.

Procedures

1. Develop an appropriate sampling framework to select respondents for your study.

2. Identify a set of objectively defined destination or product attributes and associated levels for each attribute. As noted, these do not need to be quantitative, but they must be described clearly and precisely. The attributes must also be expressed as a series of discrete levels or categories. The attributes chosen should reflect those variables that are the most important influences on a tourist's choice of a tourism product. If the research is being done for management or planning purposes, it may also be useful to concentrate on those specific attributes that can be manipulated by the manager or planner.

A balance must be struck with respect to the number of attributes included in the profile. Three separate characteristics are usually a minimum for designing a realistic profile. The use of more than five or six, however, raises difficulties. Very complex descriptions can cause confusion on the part of the respondents as they attempt to make trade-offs. Further, the number of required profiles increases dramatically as the number of attributes increases. The same effect of greater complexity is also experienced as the number of levels for each attribute is increased, as explained in the next step.

3. Prepare a set of destination or product profiles composed of different levels of the attributes. These profiles provide the basic information on which conjoint measurement operates, so they must be developed with care. This step is not only one of the most important, it is one of the most difficult. If you have only three attributes with two levels each, it is easy to develop profiles showing all possible combinations. However, as the number of attributes and levels increases, the possible combinations increase exponentially. For example, a set of five attributes of four levels each produces $5^4 = 625$ combinations. This is an impossible number for your respondents to compare.

Fortunately, alternative research designs exist in the form of Latin squares, Latin–Graeco squares, balanced incomplete block designs, and partially balanced incomplete block designs. These designs allow a researcher to consider only a small fraction of the total number of combinations that would otherwise need to be considered. The trick here is in the choice of combinations. As an illustration, consider the choice of an airline for a trip between New York and London. The profile consists of three levels of price, three levels of connections, and three levels of service. A 3 × 3 × 3 Latin square of the following format could be used to design the profiles:

	Level of service		
	Full meal and complementary alcoholic beverages	Full meal and charge for alcoholic beverages	Snacks and charge for alcoholic beverages
Non-stop	$250	$350	$450
One stop in Gander, Newfoundland, with no plane change	$350	$450	$250
One stop in Gander, Newfoundland, with a plane change	$450	$250	$350

The distinguishing feature of this type of design is that each level of the third attribute, price, occurs once and only once in each row and column. With this design you can limit your survey to nine profiles; without this design you would be forced to use $3^3 = 27$ profiles, a number that is too large for most respondents to compare efficiently.

More complex designs are possible for problems involving more than three attributes and for attributes having different numbers of levels. The design of these formats is a complex task, requiring advanced training in the design of multi-factorial experiments or the advice of a statistician. Some basic references you can consult for background information include Plackett and Burman (1946), Bose and Bush (1952), Cochran and Cox (1957), Addelman (1962), and Winer (1971). Green (1974) provides a helpful, non-technical review of some research designs developed specifically for conjoint measurement.

As a rule, 20 to 25 profiles are the maximum most respondents can compare. A larger number can be accommodated through the use of a two-stage ranking procedure as described earlier.

4. Once the profiles have been developed and ranked, the rank orders are analysed using conjoint measurement. As noted, the most common algorithm used is MONANOVA, developed by Kruskal (1965). The analysis may be done for each individual respondent or it may be done for the 'average' respondent through analysis of mean rankings. Analysis of average rankings is usually not a good idea, though, for the initial examination of your data. Subgroups of respondents might have significantly different values and preferences with respect to their product choices. This potentially useful information would be lost if all responses were aggregated through averaging. A more useful strategy might be to conduct conjoint measurement of each respondent and then examine the patterns of results. Individuals with similar response functions or other similar personal characteristics can then be grouped for further analysis.

5. One measure of the validity of the conjoint measurement function is Kruskal's stress test. This measure, provided as part of the output of most MONANOVA programs, is a type of residual sum of squares that describes the goodness of fit between the original rank order data and the ranks predicted by the analysis. No test of significance is available for Kruskal's stress test, so the author (Kruskal 1964) has suggested the following qualitative guidelines:

Stress (%)	*Goodness of fit*
20	Poor
10	Fair
5	Good
2·5	Excellent
0	Perfect

6. The part-worths produced by MONANOVA are of special interest. They indicate the relative importance of each level of each attribute in terms of its contribution to the overall worth of a destination. You may examine these values to make conclusions about how alterations in a destination's or product's attributes would affect its perceived attractiveness and thus its probable market share.

The part-worths can also be generalized in such a way to indicate the relative overall importance of each attribute with respect to other attributes, without reference to the individual levels of those attributes. To do this:

(a) Subtract the lowest part-worth for an attribute from its highest part-worth to determine the total range of part-worths for that attribute.
(b) Sum the ranges to get a measure of the total variation in utility (overall worth) of all destinations or products.
(c) Divide the range for each attribute by the total variation obtained in the previous step. The result indicates the relative importance (as a percentage) of each attribute with respect to the total utility of a product.

Example

June and Smith (1987) undertook a conjoint measurement of the variables influencing the choice of restaurants and the role different social contexts play on the relative importance of the restaurant characteristics. Four separate contexts were defined for meals:

1. An intimate dinner with a friend or spouse;
2. Dinner with a group of friends to celebrate a birthday party;
3. Lunch with a group of business associates; and
4. Dinner with the family.

Five restaurant attributes and associated levels were also defined, and are listed in Table 4.5. Because this number of attributes and

Table 4.5 Restaurant attributes and associated values

Attribute	Level	Values
Price	a	Less than $10 for entrée
	b	$10–$15 for entrée
	c	More than $15 for entrée
Service	a	Inattentive servers
	b	Moderately attentive servers
	c	Very attentive servers
Atmosphere	a	Little privacy
	b	Moderate privacy
	c	Great deal of privacy
Quality	a	Average quality food
	b	Above average quality food
	c	Excellent quality food
Liquor licence	a	Not licensed
	b	Licensed

Table 4.6 Experimental design for evaluations of restaurants

Profile	Price	Service	Atmosphere	Liquor licence	Quality of food
1	a	a	a	a	a
2	a	b	b	a	b
3	a	c	c	a	c
4	b	a	b	a	c
5	c	a	c	a	b
6	b	b	c	a	a
7	c	c	b	a	a
8	b	c	a	a	b
9	c	b	a	a	c
10	a	b	b	b	a
11	a	c	c	b	b
12	a	a	a	b	c
13	b	b	c	b	c
14	c	b	a	b	b
15	b	c	a	b	a
16	c	a	c	b	a
17	b	a	b	b	b
18	c	c	b	b	c

levels produces 324 possible combinations, an orthogonal design was employed to reduce the total number of comparisons for the respondents to make. The orthogonal design is summarized in Table 4.6. A series of cards was prepared with one of the 18 different profiles on each card. Profile 9, for example, contained the following description:

Price: More than $15
Service: Moderatively attentive servers
Atmosphere: Little privacy
Food: Excellent quality food
Liquor: Not licensed

The cards in each deck were randomly sorted, and the four decks (one for each context) were presented in a random order to a panel of 50 respondents.

The rankings provided by the respondents for each context were analysed using a conjoint measurement program. The resulting part-worths are summarized in Table 4.7. The 'stress' associated with each model was under 4 per cent, indicating a good fit. The values of 0.00 reported for one level for each attribute are a 'reference level' required by the particular algorithm used. The size of the part-worth indicates the relative importance of each level of each attribute towards the overall attractiveness of a restaurant. Because the rankings begin with '1', the most preferred profile, and end with '18', the least preferred, smaller or negative part-worths indicate more desirable attribute levels

Table 4.7 Part-worths for each level of each context

Attribute	Context 1 (intimate dinner)	Context 2 (birthday dinner)	Context 3 (business lunch)	Context 4 (family meal)
Price				
Less than $10	0.74	−0.13	−0.07	−0.48
$10–$15	0.00	0.00	0.00	0.00
More than $15	0.78	2.57	3.16	3.89
Service				
Very attentive	−1.50	−1.44	−1.68	−1.99
Moderately attentive	0.00	0.00	0.00	0.00
Not attentive	3.80	4.29	5.27	4.79
Atmosphere				
Privacy	−1.29	−1.10	−0.97	−1.02
Moderate privacy	0.00	0.00	0.00	0.00
Very little privacy	0.22	−0.64	0.28	−0.54
Liquor licence				
Available	−6.21	−6.24	−2.68	−3.21
Not available	0.00	0.00	0.00	0.00
Quality of food				
Average	1.70	1.22	1.32	1.80
Above average	0.00	0.00	0.00	0.00
Excellent	−0.87	0.30	−0.16	−0.09

than larger or positive numbers. A price under $10 for a birthday party, with its part-worth of −0.13, for example, is thus more desirable than a price over $15, with its part-worth of 2.57.

A preference function for a restaurant can be determined by specifying the pertinent attribute levels and then summing the part-worths associated with those levels. In the context of intimate dining, restaurants with entrées less than $10, very attentive service, with a private atmosphere, licensed, and average-quality food would have the following preference function:

$$0.74 - 1.50 - 1.29 - 6.21 + 1.70 = -6.56 \qquad [4.8]$$

An alternative restaurant with entrées costing over $15, inattentive servers, very little privacy, no liquor licence, and excellent food would be summarized by the function:

$$0.78 + 3.80 + 0.22 + 0.00 - 0.87 = 3.93 \qquad [4.9]$$

The first restaurant, with its large negative score is more preferred than the second restaurant with its relatively large positive score. Similar calculations may be done for any combination of restaurant attributes, whether or not they correspond to the original 18 profiles.

The individual part-worths can guide management decisions and product development. For example, consider a restaurateur concerned about compensating for a lack of privacy for intimate dining in the interior layout of his restaurant. If he cannot adjust the interior design at an acceptable cost, he faces a loss of utility of 1.51 units of utility in comparison to an identical restaurant offering significant privacy (0.22 − (−1.29) = 1.51 units). This could virtually be offset by improving service from being only moderatively attentive (if that were the case) to being very attentive – an increase of 1.50 units of utility.

It should be noted that the units of utility do not have any physical meaning. They are simply coefficients that have been estimated at those values which will allow the original ranks to be reproduced as closely as possible. The significance of the part-worths is in their relative size, not absolute magnitudes.

An alternative way of examining the importance of the part-worths is to determine the proportion of total product attractiveness attributable to each characteristic in the profile. In the case of a restaurant serving business lunches, how important is service in comparison to price or other attributes? This question is answered by following the tasks described in step 6 of the procedures. The relative importance of each attribute for each context in Smith and June is summarized in Table 4.8. Service and the availability of liquor are generally the most

Table 4.8 Relative contribution of each attribute to the total attractiveness of the average restaurant

Attribute	Intimate dinner	Birthday celebration	Business lunch	Family dinner
Price	0.018	0.151	0.207	0.245
Service	0.324	0.320	0.446	0.381
Atmosphere	0.092	0.097	0.080	0.088
Liquor	0.379	0.348	0.172	0.180
Food	0.157	0.085	0.095	0.106
Total	1.000	1.000	1.000	1.000

important qualities, accounting together for more than 50 per cent of the total attractiveness of a restaurant in each context.

Summary

Although there are many models available for analysing and simulating consumer choice behaviour, the two methods presented here, expectancy-value and conjoint measurement, illustrate many of the important issues in consumer research and are two of the most important models in their own right, Both models are based on the assumption that the choice process is rational and that rationality can be adequately represented by an equation. Empirical testing of consumer-choice models indicates that this assumption has some basis in fact. This is, of course, a fortunate finding, but the objective modelling of rationality still poses some unique challenges for tourism analysts. For example, many tourists return to the same location year after year because of habit. This is rational from the perspective of the people doing it, and it certainly represents predictable behaviour, but the problem is a trivial one for studying destination choice. In contrast, other people seek new places for vacations each year. They desire novelty, uniqueness, and perhaps a touch of adventure. Their choice, too, is rational given their values. Rather than being a trivial problem, this aversion to doing the same thing two years in a row makes for an exceedingly difficult modelling challenge. In still other cases the choice of a tourism destination is influenced by the preferences or expectations of people whose values are normally not included in a tourist-choice model. Thousands of people spend their holidays each year in places innocent of any touristic appeal because their families or friends want them to visit.

All these locational decisions can probably be explained in retrospect on a case-by-case basis; but it would be difficult to develop a predictive model that can accommodate equally those who decide by habit, those who seek constant novelty, those whose decisions are made by others, and those whose choices are based on a rational weighting of product attributes. And of course, the same person may employ each of these criteria at different times.

Both models are designed to explain preferences or behavioural intentions, rather than actual behaviour. The use of stated preferences allows the analyst to measure responses to a wider range of alternatives than normally possible if he limited himself to actual behaviour. Preferences can also be obtained for combinations of destination attributes that may not even exist in the real world, but that may still offer valuable theoretical insights. On the other hand, statements of preferences are often made without any real frame of reference or the need actually to commit oneself to following through on such a statement. The correlation between what people say and what they do is notoriously low. Inclusion of some description of the context of a purchase decision, as in the June and Smith example, can help to rectify this weakness (Kakkar and Lutz 1975), although it does not eliminate it.

The use of overt behaviour may be a better indication of 'real' preferences, but that behaviour may reflect variable forces other than preferences – such as the availability of alternatives.

An important difference between the two models concerns how the weights of the variables or attributes are determined. Goodrich's (1978) use of a Fishbein model illustrates the self-explicated approach. The analyst asks a series of respondents to assign their own weights to the attributes. This is simpler than the statistical derivation of weights, as with conjoint measurement, but the results may be questioned. The self-explicated approach assumes that potential consumers are able to consider product attribute separately and consistently as they assign weights to each. The large body of empirical research based on Fishbein models would suggest there is merit in this assumption, but the approach is still quite removed from how consumers really choose among products. The use of profiles and an analytic or decompositional approach (where choices are 'decomposed' to arrive at weights), represented by conjoint measurement, appears to reflect more closely the actual decision-making process. As a result, this latter approach may give generally more valid results.

No single choice model is appropriate for all circumstances. Ultimately you will need to sort out the relative merits and costs associated with the various models and their modifications, and then match them to the problem you are studying. If possible, the best approach is to experiment with several different models to determine which provides the most accurate, reliable, and useful results.

Further reading

Ajzen I and **Fishbein M** 1980 *Understanding attitudes and predicting social behavior*. Prentice-Hall, Englewood Cliffs, NJ.

Alpert M I 1971 Identification of determinant attributes: a comparison of methods. *Journal of Marketing Research* **8**: 184–91.

Beckwith E and **Lehman N R** 1973 The importance of differential weights in multiple attribute models of consumer attitude. *Journal of Marketing Research* **10**: 141–5.

Bettman J R, Capon N and **Lutz R** 1975 Multivariate measurement models and multiattribute theory: a test of construct validity. *Journal of Consumer Research* **1**: 1–15.

Cattin P and **Wittink D R** 1982 Commercial use of conjoint measurement: a survey. *Journal of Marketing* **46**: 44–53.

Cohen J R, Fishbein M and **Ahtola O T** 1972 The nature and uses of expectancy value models in consumer attitude research. *Journal of Marketing Research* **9**: 456–61.

Cosper R and **Kinsley B L** 1984 An application of conjoint measurement to leisure research: cultural preferences in Canada. *Journal of Leisure Research* **16**: 224–33.

Hansen F 1969 Consumer choice behaviour: an experimental approach. *Journal of Marketing Research* **6**: 436–43.

Johnson B and **Meyer R** 1984 Compensatory choice models of noncompensatory processes: the effect of varying contexts. *Journal of Consumer Research* **11**: 528–41.

McCullough J and **Best R** 1979 Conjoint measurement: temporal stability and structural reliability. *Journal of Marketing Research* **16**: 26–31.

Ryan M J and **Bonfield E H** 1975 The Fishbein extended measurement model of consumer spatial behaviour. *Regional Science Perspectives* **7**(2): 12–34.

Scott D R, Schewe C D and **Frederick D G** 1978 A multi-brand/multi-attribute model of tourist state choice. *Journal of Travel Research* **17**(1): 23–9.

Var T, Beck R A D and **Loftus P** 1977 Determination of touristic attractiveness of the touristic areas in British Columbia. *Journal of Travel Research* **15**(3): 23–9.

CHAPTER 5

Forecasting tourism demand and market trends

Introduction

This chapter introduces two important concepts for tourism analysis: forecasting and demand. Both are common words, but the relationship between them as tourism concepts may not be immediately apparent. Forecasting, of course, refers to the task of making predictions. In practice, most of the predictions made by tourism analysts concern the demand for tourism commodities. An understanding of the concept of demand and of its various connotations can help deepen your understanding of the practice and problems of forecasting tourism trends. Conversely, an appreciation of the nature of forecasting can shed light on how demand is studied and measured. The chapter begins by describing the nature of forecasting and some of the general issues associated with selecting a forecasting model. The nature of demand is then considered, with special attention given to both the definitions of demand and the forces that cause demand to change. Finally, four different forecasting models are described in detail that illustrate some of the more common approaches used in forecasting tourism trends.

Nature of forecasting

Virtually all policy analysis and planning problems in tourism require forecasts of future conditions. Estimates of future levels of demand for different commodities, travel volumes, the market share of various destinations or businesses, household incomes, interest rates on loans, changes in consumer tastes, and many other economic and social variables are vital to managing and planning tourism development. Forecasting can give you an idea of what future conditions may be like if you fail to take corrective action, and it can provide you with an assessment of the possible outcomes of alternative courses of action.

The challenges of successful forecasting are more than just the technical difficulties of developing an accurate model. Forecasting models must be developed with a clear understanding of both the nature of the problem for which forecasts are desired and of the resources available to the analyst charged with making the forecast. Stynes (1983) identifies four factors that should be considered when developing a forecasting model: (1) the organizational environment; (2) the decision-making situation; (3) existing knowledge; and (4) the nature of the phenomenon being studied.

The organizational environment

Each organization has resources, structures, ways of operating, and objectives specific to it. These characteristics influence the goals and types of forecasting the decision-makers in that organization want. An agency that prides itself on being politically neutral and on producing objective, high-quality forecasts will have very different standards for forecasting from an organization devoted to the lobbying of a predetermined political position. The availability of resources such as data banks, computers, software, statisticians, and other technical experts will also influence the type of forecast that can be developed. The forecaster needs to be aware of all of these aspects of the organizational environment in order to design a model that will function effectively within that environment.

The decision-making situation

This is related to the organizational environment. Some organizations need to make decisions quickly for their immediate future; others work with a more distant planning horizon and have a longer time period available for developing their model. The level of precision required for a decision is also important in selecting the appropriate forecasting technology. Generally, the greater the precision required, the more complex the model and the longer the lead time required. Another aspect of the decision-making situation is the level of accuracy required. Whereas precision refers to the amount of detail, accuracy is a measure of the correctness of the forecast. For example, a forecast that the demand for international air travel between the UK and the USA will increase next year by 98.76 per cent is precise, but probably not accurate. On the other hand, simply saying that the demand will increase may well be accurate, but it is not precise. As with precision, greater accuracy usually requires more resources and a longer lead time for model development.

Existing knowledge

Scientific forecasts are based on information about past and current conditions. Some types of forecasting models, such as trend extrapolation or systems simulation models require significant amounts of historical data. Other methods, such as the Delphi technique, require less data. The issue of existing knowledge also refers to the forecaster's understanding of theoretical issues associated with the phenomenon being forecast and his familiarity with the forecasting technology. A match must be made between the theoretical and technical requirements of the problem and the abilities the forecaster is able to bring to the problem.

Nature of the phenomenon being forecast

Certain phenomena show a high degree of stability. The percentage of Canadians taking vacations has remained virtually unchanged at about 55 since the early 1970s. Other phenomena exhibit dramatic changes from year to year in response to fads, local crises, or other forces. The former, by their very nature, are much easier to predict than the latter. The forecaster will also need to consider whether the phenomenon being modelled is best studied with a stochastic model (which predicts percentages or probabilities) or a deterministic model (which predicts absolute numbers). A choice between a linear and a non-linear model will also depend on the nature of the phenomenon. More general knowledge of the forces that have affected the past behaviour of the phenomenon can assist in the selection of the most useful variables and perhaps even the best model structure.

Nature of forecasting models

Forecasting models in tourism may be classified as belonging to four categories: (1) trend extrapolation models; (2) structural models; (3) simulation models; and (4) qualitative models.

Trend extrapolation models, as their name suggests, rely on the extrapolation of a historical series of data into the future. One of the simplest such models is a manual plot of data on a graph. The vertical axis on the graph is some measure of tourism demand or market activity, while the horizontal axis contains units of time, such as years. A line is visually fitted to the data and then extended beyond the observed data to a desired point in the future. More sophisticated models are available to accomplish the same task. These include simple regression models, exponential models, logistic models, quadratic equations, and harmonic analysis. Despite the differences in the statistical complexity of each and the shape of the extrapolation curve, the forecaster assumes in each model that the observed trend will continue for some reasonable period of time into the future.

Structural models depend on the identification of the relationship between some measure of tourism demand and a series of causal variables, such as price, income, distance, or competition. These relationships are usually identified using multiple regression or analysis of variance and cross-sectional data. Once the model has been calibrated, estimates of future values of the causal variables are used in the model to make a forecast of future tourism demand.

Simulation models are a complex set of equations that typically combine both trend extrapolation and structural models into a more comprehensive systems simulation. Relationships between many variables, including feedback, synergistic, and dampening effects, are specified through a series of interrelated equations. These models also rely on historical data for model calibration. Forecasts are made by specifying expected values for the causal variables, and then solving the system of equations to arrive at predicted values of the dependent variables.

Qualitative models include a variety of techniques, including the use of intuition by a single decision-maker to anticipate future developments. The best known and most widely respected qualitative forecasting model is the Delphi technique. This procedure involves the formal and structured soliciting of expert opinion from a panel of knowledgeable individuals concerning a given forecasting problem. The results of their collective opinions are given back to the panel one or more times to encourage them to move towards a consensus of opinion about the timing and unfolding of future events.

The choice of the most appropriate model involves consideration of the four factors described earlier. The ultimate choice often requires trade-offs between a model that will provide the ideals of the greatest accuracy and precision possible and the constraints imposed by time, budget, and other resources. A summary of the requirements and characteristics of the four general model types is provided in Table 5.1. A review of the table illustrates the fact that no single model is best on all criteria. It is significant that two important criteria are not included on this table: accuracy and precision. All models are capable of producing good-quality forecasts if they are properly developed and applied, if adequate data are available, and if the problem being studied conforms closely to the assumptions implicit in the specific model. The degree to which the development and application of a forecasting model departs from these conditions ultimately determines the quality of the forecast.

Nature of demand

Demand is an ambiguous word with at least four definitions used by tourism analysts. The most traditional definition is that of neo-classical economics: demand is the schedule of quantities of some good or service that will be consumed at various specified prices. Higher consumption is usually associated with lower prices; lower consumption with higher prices. Demand, in this sense, can be described graphically as in Fig. 5.1. The downward sloping line, DD', reflects the inverse relationship between price and consumption. Consumption, in the context of tourism, refers to the purchase of some good or service, such as a hotel room; participation in some activity, such as a pleasure drive in a private automobile; or attendance at an attraction, such as visiting a historical site.

Demand is also used to refer to actual consumption. This definition of demand would be represented as a single point on DD' in Fig. 5.1. Such a point, labelled X, is the pairing of a specific price, P_1, and observed consumption, Q_1. This is arguably the most common use of the word 'demand', but it is of limited usefulness to tourism analysts because it tells us nothing about trends of levels of unmet demand. It is not, therefore, a useful definition for forecasting.

A third definition is that of unmet demand, which is also referred to as latent demand. Latent demand is a measure of the difference between the potential level of consumption and the observed level. The difference may be due to shortage of supply, excessively high prices, scheduling problems, or other barriers. Latent demand is of special interest to tourism planners because it represents the potential for market expansion.

Finally, demand is used to refer directly to a forecast of future consumption. This conception of demand is closely related to the neo-classical definition, but there are important distinctions. Demand in the sense of future participation is seen as a function of many variables, not just price. It also refers to the anticipated mix and values of those variables that affect demand. Demand as future consumption is thus both broader and narrower than the neo-classical definition. It includes more variables, but the focus is on estimating one single value, not a schedule of values.

Table 5.1 Summary of requirements and characteristics of forecasting models

	Trend extrapolation	Structural	Simulation	Qualitative
Technical expertise required	Low to medium	Medium to high	High	Low to medium
Type of conceptual knowledge or data required	Time series data	Cross-sectional data plus causal relationships	Time series, cross-sectional, causal relationships and change processes	Expert and experiential
Required data precision	Medium to high	High	High	Low
Computing resources required	Minor to moderate	Moderate	High	Nil
Appropriate forecast horizon	Short	Short to medium	Long	Long
Time required for forecast	Short	Short to medium	Long	Medium to long
Type of problem best suited for	Simple, stable, or cyclic	Moderately complex with several variables and known, stable relationship	Complex with known and quantifiable relationships and some feedback effects	Complex with known but qualitative relationships and strong elements of uncertainty

Demand shifters

The variables implicit in demand as future consumption are known collectively as demand shifters. These include consumer characteristics such as age, education, previous experience with similar products, and tastes as well as the effects of promotional efforts, product innovation, and new technology. The reason these variables are called demand shifters may be seen by reference to Fig. 5.1. Consider the demand for rooms at a given hotel. This demand, in the neo-classical sense, would be represented by curve DD'. If the hotel adds a new recreational complex, shuttle services to a nearby airport, or expands its conference and meeting facilities, the demand is likely to grow. This would be represented by shifting DD' to the right, to $D_1D'_1$. Consumers are willing to pay more, P_2, for the same level of consumption. They are also willing to consume more, Q_2, if the price remains at P_1.

If the hotel begins to deteriorate through poorer maintenance, a lessened quality of service, or unfavourable publicity about hotel problems, the demand can be expected to drop. This is reflected by shifting

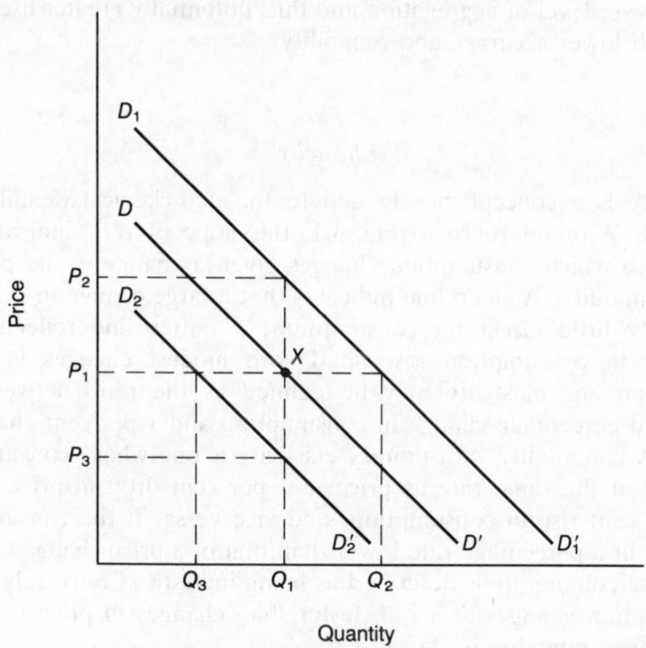

Fig. 5.1 The concept of demand

DD' to the ieft, to $D_2D'_2$. Consumers would be willing to purchase the original number of rooms only if the price drops to P_3. If prices do not change, total consumption will fall to Q_3.

Demand analysis, including forecasting, may focus on either an individual or a group. The patterns for individuals tend to be more complex and have a higher degree of variance, and thus are harder to predict accurately than demand patterns for groups. The main reason for this is the fact that large numbers of individuals tend to average out the idiosyncratic behaviour of single individuals. Large groups tend to display more stable patterns that cluster around a mean value. Young and Smith (1979) describe the effects of the level of aggregation on demand forecasting. Their work confirms the experience of many others who have noted that the reliability and accuracy of models increases as the level of aggregation increases. While this is desirable to a point, the most accurate models are often obtained at the most general levels of analysis – analysis so generalized and based on such highly aggregated data that the results have little value for policy and planning problems. As with the other issues surrounding the selection of a forecasting model, the analyst must make a trade-off between a highly accurate, highly aggregated, but less useful model and one that has a lower level of aggregation and thus potentially greater usefulness but with lower accuracy and reliability.

Elasticity

Elasticity is a concept closely tied to the neo-classical definition of demand. With reference to Fig. 5.1, the slope of DD' indicates the degree to which consumption changes given a change in the price of the commodity. A steep line indicates that a large change in price has relatively little effect on consumption; a flatter line reflects large changes in consumption associated with modest changes in price. Quantitatively, elasticity may be defined as the ratio between the observed percentage change in consumption and 1 per cent change in price. A commodity with unitary elasticity is one whose consumption changes at the same rate as price: a 1 per cent drop in price causes a 1 per cent rise in consumption, and vice versa. If the consumption changes at a percentage rate lower than that of a price change (a steep line), the commodity is described as being inelastic. Conversely, if the consumption changes at a rate faster than changes in price (a flatter line), the commodity is elastic.

Two major characteristics of commodities influence their degree of elasticity. Those that are necessities tend to be inelastic. Food staples such as bread and salt, modern necessities such as gasoline or telephone service, and life-supporting goods such as some prescription drugs show relatively little short-term variation in consumption due to changes in price. In contrast, the purchase of luxury goods, which include many tourism commodities, tends to be elastic.

Goods for which there are few substitutes are often inelastic whereas those for which we have ample substitutes will be more elastic. Thus one can find examples of intense price competition between gasoline stations, beer retailers (in those fortunate jurisdictions where beer sales are not a government or industry-controlled monopoly), soft-drink bottlers, and many other types of goods for which one brand is an acceptable substitute for another. Note that in the case of gasoline, the demand for gasoline as a generic product in the short run is relatively inelastic, whereas the demand for gasoline from specific dealers can be highly elastic. Consumer responses to price changes in the long run may exhibit different strategies from simple changes in the level of purchasing. The dramatic increases in fuel prices in the 1970s and early 1980s resulted in motorists shifting to more fuel-efficient cars and other forms of energy conservation.

Elasticity may also be examined from the perspective of income. This shift in perspective is of special value to tourism analysts because of the close relationship between the ability to pay for tourism experiences (measured by income) and the willingness to pay for them (measured by demand). If we replace price on the vertical axis of a demand curve by income, the slope of the demand curve becomes positive (see Fig. 5.2). Higher incomes are usually associated with higher levels of consumption. The degree of association, reflected by the slope of the line, is the income elasticity. Commodities that are purchased at only slightly elevated levels as incomes rise have low elasticity. Expenditures on other goods, however, rise at a rate faster than income rises. These high elasticity goods are known as superior goods. Commodities whose rate of consumption rises at the same rate as income increases have unitary elasticity (see Fig. 5.2). Finally, the consumption of other commodities may actually drop as incomes rise. These are known as inferior goods. These observations were first formally made by a German statistician, Ernst Engle, in the middle of the nineteenth century. Engle predicted that as incomes rise: (1) the percentage spent on food would fall; (2) the percentage spent on lodging and clothing would remain about the same; and (3) the percentage spent on all other goods would rise.

Current census information allows us to verify the accuracy of

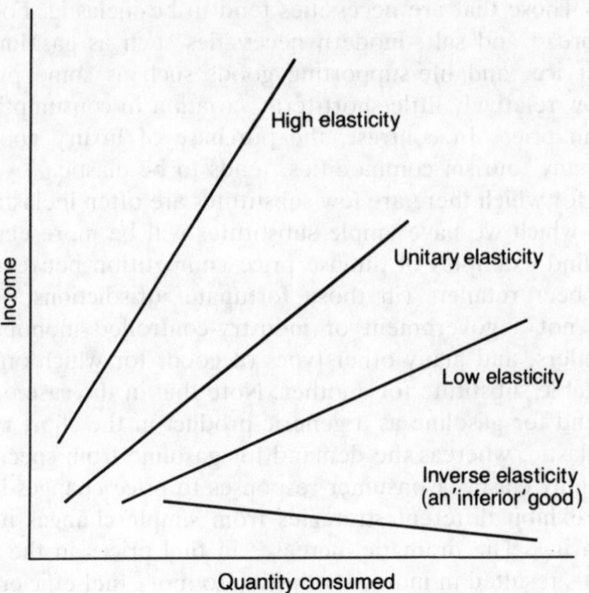

Fig. 5.2 Income elasticity curves for inferior, normal, and superior economic goods

Engle's law, as his observations have become known. Consider the data in Table 5.2. These figures are from a family expenditure survey conducted by Statistics Canada (1978). As Engle predicted, the percentage of income spent on food shows a clear decline with

Table 5.2 Expenditure data illustrating Engle's law

Household income ($)	Sector (%)				
	Food	Shelter	Clothing	Recreation	Transportation
<6 000	26.5	31.8	5.1	4.5	5.2
6 000– 7 999	25.0	27.1	6.4	3.9	9.2
8 000–11 999	21.5	23.2	6.5	4.1	10.3
12 000–15 999	19.0	19.2	6.3	4.3	11.9
16 000–19 999	18.1	18.0	6.7	4.5	12.0
20 000–24 999	17.1	17.0	6.5	4.8	12.3
25 000–29 999	15.4	16.0	7.0	4.9	12.0
30 000–34 999	15.0	15.7	6.4	4.7	11.2
>35 000	13.5	13.5	7.2	5.2	10.9

Source: Statistics Canada 1978.

increasing incomes. In fact, the proportion spent on food in households earning over $35 000 is only about half that spent on food in households earning under $6000. In contrast with Engle's predictions, the Canadian data suggest that housing is also an inferior good (the percentage declines with higher incomes) while clothing is a superior good. Those commodities that might be classified as 'recreation' indicate that recreation is also a superior good, although the trend is not strong. Finally, transportation appears to be a superior good for low- to middle-income households and an inferior good for upper-income households.

There is one other aspect of demand that is important for tourism analysis: consumer surplus. Consumer surplus refers to a method of interpreting an empirically derived demand curve to arrive at an estimate of the value of a tourism resource. Consumer surplus and its relationship to demand and resource valuation will be examined in greater detail in Chapter 9.

Trend extrapolation: simple regression analysis

Description

One of the simplest but most useful methods of trend extrapolation is simple regression analysis. Simple regression is a method for correlating two variables against each other. Both variables must be measured on an interval scale. The form of a simple regression model is

$$Y = a + bX \qquad [5.1]$$

where: Y = dependent variable;
a, b = coefficients to be estimated;
X = independent variable.

The dependent variable is some measure of tourism demand or consumption, such as a count of visitors to an attraction, total receipts, or the number of scheduled airline flights. The independent variable may be any of a wide variety of demand shifters such as income, or other aggregate variables such as total market size. One especially useful independent variable is time. Data related to levels of demand are collected for a number of specified units of time, such as years. If the change in business levels is fairly stable over time, a reasonably accurate forecasting model may be developed by correlating level of demand against time.

Regardless of the independent variable selected, the process of making a forecast is the same. The coefficients in equation [5.1] are

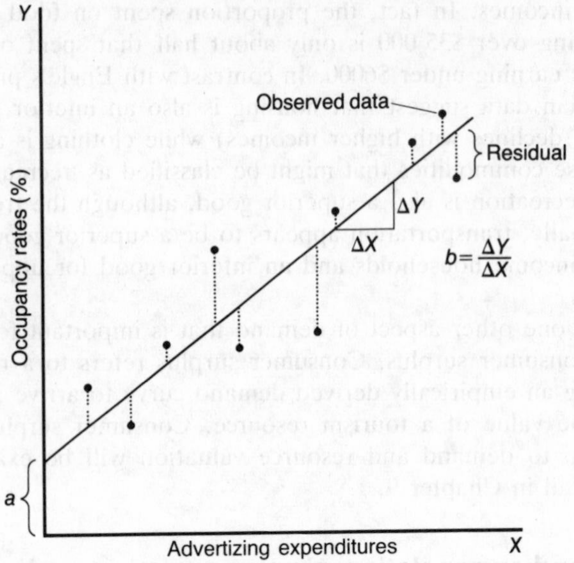

Fig. 5.3 Hypothetical regression line relating hotel occupancy rates with advertizing expenditures

estimated using a procedure known as least-squares estimation (described below) using historical data. Once the model has been calibrated, you substitute an expected future value of the independent variable (obtained from an independent forecast) into equation [5.1] and solve for Y. This new value of Y is the forecast value of future business levels.

The central problem in simple regression is the statistical definition of a linear function that best summarizes a set of data. The role of least-squares estimation can be described graphically. If a set of data describing two variables, say hotel occupancy and advertizing expenditures, is plotted on a graph (Fig. 5.3), least-squares estimation specifies the position of a line that best fits the scatter of points. The best fit is that line that minimizes the sum of the squares of the vertical distance between each point and the line. The line may also be interpreted as a plot of the predicted values of the dependent variable given any particular value of the independent variable. The position of the line is given by two separate pieces of information: the point where the line intersects the vertical axis and the slope of the line. The intersection of the line is the value a in equation [5.1]; the slope is specified by b. The equations for calculating a and b are given below. A more extended discussion of the theory and applications of regression analysis may be found in Draper and Smith (1966) or similar texts.

Procedures

1. Select the appropriate dependent variable and an independent variable, usually some unit of time. Designate the dependent variable as Y and the independent variable as X. Select appropriate units of analysis and collect data. A minimum of 10 to 15 observations is normally desirable.

2. Prepare a table similar to that in Table 5.3. The first column, X, will contain values of the independent variable; the second column, Y, lists values of the dependent variable. The third column is the product of X and Y. The fourth and fifth columns are X^2 and Y^2 respectively. Also obtain the sums of each column.

3. Calculate b with the equation:

$$b = \frac{n(\Sigma XY) - (\Sigma X)(\Sigma Y)}{n(\Sigma X^2) - (\Sigma X)^2} \qquad [5.2]$$

4. Once you have a value for b, the value of a is obtained from:

$$a = \frac{\Sigma Y - b(\Sigma X)}{n} \qquad [5.3]$$

where: n = number of observations.

5. The coefficient of correlation, r, is a measure of the goodness of fit between the estimated regression line and the data. It indicates the degree to which there is a linear relationship between X and Y. It is calculated with the equation:

$$r = \frac{n(\Sigma XY) - (\Sigma X)(\Sigma Y)}{\sqrt{(n(\Sigma X^2) - (\Sigma X)^2)}\sqrt{(n(\Sigma Y^2) - (\Sigma Y)^2)}} \qquad [5.4]$$

The sign of r will be the same as that of b, the slope of the regression line. A positive sign reflects a direct correlation between X and Y; a negative sign reflects an inverse relationship. A value close to zero indicates a horizontal line, or no correlation between X and Y. The values of r range from 1.00 to −1.00. These extreme values as well as the mid-point of 0.00 are easy to interpret, but intermediate values are more frequently obtained. One method of interpreting these is to square the value, obtaining r^2. This statistic may be interpreted as a measure of the explained variance attributable to the independent vari-

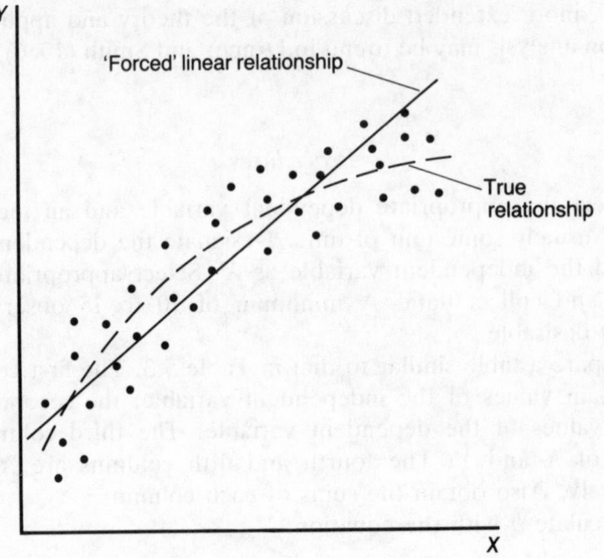

Fig. 5.4 Hypothetical curvilinear relationship

able. The extreme values of r^2 are 0.00 and 1.00. A value of 0.80 indicates that the independent variable explains 80 per cent of the variation in the dependent variable; a model with an r^2 of 0.80 would be considered four times as strong as one that produced an r^2 of 0.20.

The notion of explained variance is a statistical concept; it does not necessarily imply a causal relationship. A common misuse of r^2 is to interpret the existence of a high r^2 as proof of a true causal relationship. Whereas a low r^2 is evidence of a lack of any causal connection between X and Y, a high r^2 does not necessarily mean such a relationship exists. It is merely suggestive evidence that could be coincidental. The coefficient, r^2, is also a measure of the strength of the linear hypothesis implied by equation [5.1]. Two variables may be strongly related through a curvilinear function, but r^2 would fail to measure this because it is predicated on the assumption that the relationship is linear (see Fig. 5.4).

6. Once the regression model has been calibrated, select a value for the independent variable reflecting some anticipated future condition. Substitute this value for X in equation [5.1] and solve for Y.

If the values of X are years, a short cut is possible to simplify the calculations of a and b. The trick is to replace the values of X as years with values that will cancel out when summed. If the number of years is even, replace the years with the values: . . .,−3, −2, −1, 1, 2, 3, ... If the number is odd, use: . . ., −3, −2, −1, 0, 1, 2, 3, ... The equations for a, b, and r become:

$$a = \frac{\Sigma Y}{n} \quad [5.5]$$

$$b = \frac{\Sigma XY}{\Sigma X^2} \quad [5.6]$$

$$r = \frac{n(\Sigma XY)}{(\sqrt{n(\Sigma X^2)})(\sqrt{n(\Sigma Y^2) - (\Sigma Y)^2})} \quad [5.7]$$

A forecast is then made by extending the series of codes to the future year. If your data extended from 1980 to 1988, these years would be recorded as follows:

1980 = −4	1984 = 0
1981 = −3	1985 = 1
1982 = −2	1986 = 2
1983 = −1	1987 = 3
	1988 = 4

A forecast to 1990 would involve recoding 1990 as 6. The rest of the forecast would follow the procedure described previously.

Example

An illustration of the use of simple regression may be seen in the following model of worldwide air passenger traffic. Table 5.3 is a listing of total worldwide airline passengers for the years 1974 to 1982, inclusive (American Express 1985). The value of b was calculated using equation [5.2]:

$$b = \frac{n(\Sigma XY) - (\Sigma X)(\Sigma Y)}{n(\Sigma X^2) - (\Sigma X)^2}$$
$$= \frac{9(464\,834) - (702)(5932)}{9(54\,816) - (702)(702)}$$
$$= 35.6$$

This positive value indicates a positive relationship between the volume of air passenger flow and years, or more precisely, a pattern of increasing air travel over time.

The intercept, a, was then estimated using equation [5.3]:

Table 5.3 Forecast of worldwide air passenger traffic

Year	Millions of passengers			
X	*Y*	*XY*	X^2	Y^2
74	515	38 110	5 476	265 225
75	534	40 050	5 625	285 156
76	576	43 776	5 776	331 776
77	610	46 970	5 929	372 100
78	679	52 962	6 084	461 041
79	754	59 566	6 241	568 516
80	748	59 840	6 400	559 504
81	752	60 912	6 561	565 504
82	764	62 648	6 724	583 696
Σ = 702	5932	464 834	54 816	3 992 518

Source: American Express 1985.

$$a = \Sigma \frac{Y - b\ (\Sigma X)}{n}$$

$$= \frac{5932 - 35.6\ (702)}{9}$$

$$= -2117.7$$

Finally, r was calculated as

$$r = \frac{n\ (\Sigma XY) - (\Sigma X)\ (\Sigma Y)}{(\sqrt{n(\Sigma X^2)} - (\Sigma X)^2)(\sqrt{n(\Sigma Y^2)} - (\Sigma Y)^2)}$$

$$= \frac{9(464\ 834) - (702)\ (5932)}{\sqrt{(9(54\ 816)} - (492\ 804))\ \sqrt{(9(3\ 992\ 518)} - (35\ 188\ 624))}$$

$$= 0.962$$

This value is positive, as expected given a positive value for b. The value also indicates a strong linear relationship. If we calculate r^2, we obtain 92.5 per cent, which is quite strong. Given such results, we can reasonably feel comfortable using the model to forecast future airline travel. The forecast model is obtained by substituting the estimated parameter values into equation [5.1]:

$$\text{Passengers} = -2117.7 + 35.6\ (\text{year})$$

To make a forecast to 1984, we substitute 84 for 'year' and solve:

$$\text{Passengers} = -2117.7 + 35.6(84)$$
$$= 873\ (\text{million})$$

Data for 1984 are available and permit a check of the accuracy of our forecast. The actual value was 832 million passengers. This represents an error of about 4.9 per cent, which is not too bad for most marketing forecasts.

Gravity model

Description

The gravity model is a well-known structural forecasting model. As its name suggests, the gravity model is based on an analogy to Newton's law of gravitation. Newton's law states that the gravitational attraction between any two bodies is directly proportional to the masses of the two bodies and inversely proportional to the square of the distance between them:

$$I_{ij} = \frac{GM_iM_j}{D_{ij}^2} \tag{5.8}$$

where: I_{ij} = gravitation attraction between two bodies, i and j;
G = gravitational constant;
$M_{i,j}$ = masses of i and j;
D_{ij} = distance between the centres of i and j.

This rather simple formulation has been the inspiration for a growing body of travel and interaction models in the social sciences. Interaction here refers potentially to any form of exchange between two social groups. This may be financial flows, telephone calls, mail volumes, marriages, trips, and literally hundreds of other variables. The masses of the social groups may be expressed in terms of population, relative wealth, retail floor space, destination attractiveness, and many other variables. Distance is usually measured in terms of physical separation, but measures of travel time or social distance can also be used.

Crampon (1966) was the first to demonstrate explicitly the usefulness of the gravity model to tourism research. Crampon's basic model, as well as that of most other researchers who have used the gravity model is:

$$T_{ij} = \frac{GP_iA_j}{D_{ij}^a} \tag{5.9}$$

where: T_{ij} = some measure of tourist travel between origin i and destination j;

G, a = coefficients to be estimated;
P_i = measure of the population size, wealth, or propensity to travel at origin i;
A_j = attractiveness or capacity of destination j;
D_{ij} = distance between i and j.

As with other structural models, equation [5.9] must be calibrated with historical data before it can be used for forecasting. If this calibration is done successfully, not only do you then have a forecasting model, but the coefficients G and a may have some intrinsic interest. The value of a,for example, reflects the relative strength of distance as a deterrent to travel. The larger the estimated value of a, the greater the effect of distance on reducing the number of trips. The value of G is less easily interpreted. In Newton's model, G is a universal constant – one of the four universal constants that shape the structure of the universe. For tourism, G is a proportionality constant that adjusts the magnitude of the other variables so that they explain as closely as possible the observed level of tourism activity, T_{ij}. The relative values of G in different modelling situations might contain some meaning of use to tourism research, but the subject has not yet been fully addressed.

The most important reason for developing a gravity model is not to replicate observed travel patterns or to examine the magnitudes of a and G, of course, but rather to provide a forecasting methodology. Given estimates of future values of P_i and A_j, and assuming a, G, and D_{ij} are constant, you can predict future levels of tourism demand.

The gravity model is used to forecast trips between a single origin and a single destination within a specified time period. If you want to make a forecast for a system with multiple origins and/or multiple destinations, simply calibrate a gravity model for each origin–destination pair. Be aware, though, that the number of such calibrations can increase quickly. A comprehensive set of equations for the 50 states of the USA, the District of Columbia, and the 10 Canadian provinces (including intra-state travel) would require (61 origins × 61 destinations) = 3721 separate equations. This is a rather large number to work with by hand, but it can be easily handled on a computer. As we shall see in the procedures section, computers are normally used to calibrate gravity models because of the complexity of the calculations. Before we turn to the procedures section, however, we should consider some of the major limitations in gravity models as well as some of the modifications that have been proposed to overcome those limitations.

One weakness in the basic gravity model, as expressed in the form of equation [5.8], is that it is unconstrained. In other words, there is no upper limit on the number of trips that the model may forecast. If, for example, you were calibrating a model to forecast travel by residents of some state to a given state park, and if you were to use the number of campsites as the attraction component, your model would predict a doubling of visitors with a doubling of campsite numbers. If the capacity were to increase tenfold, your forecast would increase tenfold. Unlimited use increases are not realistic. There is some upper bound to the number of trips a given population can make in one year; yet the basic gravity model cannot reflect this fact. The solution to the problem is to develop a constrained gravity model in which a realistic upper limit is identified. This is usually accomplished by developing a two-stage model. The first stage estimates the total number of trips that can be generated under specified conditions; the second part allocates those trips to competing destinations. A common form of the trip-generation component of a constrained gravity model is a simple regression equation relating income, population size, or mobility to the total number of trips expected. Multiple regression equations might also be used to combine several independent variables in a more accurate and comprehensive model. The trip-distribution component then allocates the total number of trips to available destinations on a stochastic basis. An example of a trip-distribution model is described later in this chapter.

Another criticism of gravity models, whether in the unconstrained or constrained format, is that they have no theoretical basis. This criticism was historically correct but is irrelevant, and is no longer true. Stewart (1948) and Zipf (1946) who independently developed the concept of the gravity model based their formulations explicitly on an analogy to Newton's law of gravitation. Although their models had no theoretical basis, it has been shown empirically that their models and various modifications that developed were as successful or more successful in forecasting travel patterns than models developed directly from theory. Further, Niedercorn and Bechdoldt (1966) have derived the gravity model from existing economic theory. They demonstrated that the gravity model is a logical and theoretically sound solution for the problem of maximizing individual satisfaction subject to time or budget constraints.

Another reason that the gravity model continues to be a popular structural forecasting tool is that it allows for substantial refinement and modification. The history of forecasting recreation and tourism travel is, to a very great extent, the history of the development of gravity models. One part of the gravity model that has undergone extensive development and experimentation is the distance variable. This experimentation has stemmed from another weakness of most gravity models: a tendency to over-predict the number of very short trips and to under-predict the number of very long trips (Martin, Memmott, and Bone 1961). One of the first researchers to address this problem in recreation and tourism travel was Whitehead (1965). He suggested adding a second distance term to allow feedback between the distance travelled and the response to that distance (the willingness to travel further):

$$T_{ij} = G\Sigma\left[\frac{P_i P_j e^{-\lambda D_{ij}}}{D_{ij}^{b}}\right] \qquad [5.10]$$

where: $P_{i,j}$ = population of origin and destination zones, respectively;
e = natural logarithm base;
λ = coefficient to be estimated; other symbols are as defined previously.

Wolfe (1972), while agreeing with Whitehead on the problem, suggested a different strategy for overcoming the difficulty. Drawing again from physics for an analogy, Wolfe proposed incorporating an 'inertial' term in the gravity model. This term would have the effect of lowering the predicted number of short trips to reflect the 'inertia' of starting travel, while increasing the number of long trips predicted, reflecting the effect of 'momentum'. Wolfe's model was of the form:

$$T_{ij} = G\,\frac{P_i A_j}{D_{ij}^{b}}\left[D_{ij}^{[(\log D_{ij}/m)/n]}\right] \qquad [5.11]$$

where: m, n = coefficients to be estimated; other symbols are as defined previously.

A still more elaborate modification of the distance variable was proposed by Edwards and Dennis (1976). Their approach was to define a distance measure more generalized than physical distance alone:

$$C_{ij} = \left[\frac{(X_1)\,(X_2)(X_3) + (X_4)}{X_5}\right]X_6 \qquad [5.12]$$

where: C_{ij} = cost of travel between i and j;
X_1 = cost of gasoline per litre;
X_2 = litres consumed per kilometre;
X_3 = average kilometres travelled per hour;
X_4 = value of leisure (travel) time, set at 25 per cent of hourly wage;

X_5 = number of people per car;
X_6 = total travel time.

This variable was then incorporated into the model:

$$T_{ij} = P_i A_j \exp(-\lambda C_{ij}) \qquad [5.13]$$

Edwards and Dennis next proposed a modification of the recreation 'pull' or attractiveness component, A_j:

$$S_{ij} = A_j \exp(-\lambda C_{ij}) \qquad [5.14]$$

where: S_{ij} = pull of destination on travellers at origin i.

The total number of trips generated between all origins and all destinations is then defined as

$$T_{ij} = P_i S_i^b \qquad [5.15]$$

where: $S_i = \Sigma S_{ij}$; or if expressed as a constrained model:

$$T_{ij} = T_i \frac{S_{ij}}{S_i}$$

where: T_i = total number of trips to be generated at origin i.

Combining equations [5.12], [5.14], and [5.15]

$$T_{ij} = P_i S_i^b A_j \exp(-\lambda C_{ij}) \qquad [5.16]$$

The calibration of equation [5.16] involves statistical estimation procedures beyond the scope of this book. Edwards and Dennis's work, though, does illustrate how the simple gravity model can be the seed for increasingly sophisticated and powerful forecasting models, each improving on the previous generation of forecasts. Additional examples of the development of the use of gravity models in tourism and recreation trip forecasting can be found in Smith (1983).

Procedures

1. Specify the origin-destination pairs and a relevant time period for data collection. Collect data on: (1) the total number of trips from the origin to each destination; (2) the population of the origin; (3) the capacity or attractiveness of the destination; and (4) some measure of the distance between origin and destination.

2. Define the per capita trip rate for the origin's population:

$$k = \frac{\Sigma T_{ij}}{P_i} \qquad [5.17]$$

where: k = per capita trip rate;
ΣT_{ij} = number of trips to all destinations by residents of i;
P_i = population of i.

3. Calculate the total attractiveness of all destinations by summing the attractiveness measure of each destination:

$$A = \Sigma A_j \qquad [5.18]$$

where: A = aggregate attractiveness of all destinations;
A_j = individual attractiveness of each individual destination (or the same destination over a period of years).

4. Calculate the expected number of trips for all travellers from the origin to each destination under the assumption that distance has no effect:

$$V_{ij} = \frac{k\mathrm{P}_i A_j}{A} \qquad [5.19]$$

where: V_{ij} = expected number of trips; other variables are as defined previously.

5. Calculate the effect of distance on the expected number of trips by dividing the actual number of trips by the expected number:

$$T_{ij}/V_{ij}$$

6. Obtain a measure of the distance between the origin and each destination and carry out the following regression:

$$\log \frac{T_{ij}}{V_{ij}} = \log a + b\ (\log D_{ij}) \qquad [5.20]$$

7. Remove logs, substitute using equation [5.19], and let $G = \alpha k/A$ (where α = antilog a) to obtain:

$$T_{ij} = \frac{GP_iA_j}{D_{ij}^{b}} \qquad [5.21]$$

8. To make a forecast, substitute predicted values for P_i and A_j for the values used in calibrating the model. Solve for the predicted T_{ij}. This procedure may be used either for future travel patterns between an existing origin and destination, or the model may be calibrated using an existing origin and destination pair and then applied to a different but similar pair.

Example

The following example is an application of the gravity model to vacation travel by residents of Ontario, Canada, to other Canadian provinces. The initial step was to collect data on travel volumes between Ontario and the nine other provinces as well as intra-provincial travel for a recent year. These cross-sectional data, shown in Table 5.4, were obtained from Tourism Canada. Note that the number of trips to Newfoundland and Saskatchewan was too small to be released. Tourism Canada, as many other agencies, has policies prohibiting the release of data if the sampling variance exceeds some specified maximum. The purpose of this policy is to prevent the use of data whose sampling variance is so great that they are virtually worthless for scientific purposes. In the case of Tourism Canada, the maximum variance allowed is 33.3 per cent; Newfoundland and Saskatchewan's data had variances greater than this due to the small number of observations upon which the trip estimates were based.

Great circle distances between the centres of population of Ontario and every other province (D_{ij}) were obtained from maps. Distance for vacation travel within Ontario was estimated at an average of 200 km (125 miles) one-way. This information is also shown in Table 5.4. The attractiveness of the destinations, A_j, was assumed to be proportional to their population, reflecting the fact that the most popular reason for travelling in Canada is to visit friends and relatives. Population estimates were obtained and are presented in Table 5.4. The total attractiveness, A, is the sum of these.

Per capita travel, K, was calculated at 1.63 using equation [5.16]. Following the steps in the procedures, V_{ij} was estimated for travel between Ontario and every province. The ratio, T_{ij}/V_{ij} was then obtained for each province. Note that a value of 0.01 was used arbitrarily for Newfoundland and Saskatchewan, necessitated by the fact that T_{ij} is unknown. The actual value of T_{ij} is small, so the estimate of 0.01 is not likely to be too far in error.

Here T_{ij}/V_{ij} was regressed against D_{ij}. The results are summarized in Table 5.5. Following the substitution in equation [5.21], and after calculating the value of G, the following gravity model was obtained:

$$T_{ij} = \frac{1.32(P_i)\ (A_j)}{D_{ij}^{1.67}} \qquad [5.22]$$

where: T_{ij} = predicted number of vacation trips between Ontario and province j;

P_i = population of Ontario;

Table 5.4 Ontario vacation travel data used for calibrating a gravity model

	Trips T_{ij} † (000s)	Distance D_{ij} (km)	Population A_j (000s)	V_{ij} (000s)	T_{ij}/V_{ij}	Predicted T_{ij} (000s)
Newfoundland	‡	2100	579	341.61	0.01§	18
Prince Edward Island	67	1400	124	73.16	0.92	8
Nova Scotia	90	1300	853	503.27	0.18	61
New Brunswick	85	1200	708	417.72	0.20	58
Quebec	865	500	6314	3 725.26	0.23	2 222
Ontario	12 542	200	8547	5 058.66	2.48	13 939
Manitoba	185	1400	1029	607.11	0.30	65
Saskatchewan	‡	2100	971	572.89	0.01§	31
Alberta	50	2500	2083	1 228.97	0.04	50
British Columbia	58	3100	2642	1 558.78	0.04	44

† Data obtained from Canadian Government Office of Tourism.
‡ Data not reported due to high variance.
§ 0.01 used arbitrarily to avoid missing cases; actual value likely to be 0.01 or below.

$P_i = 8574$
$A = \Sigma A_j = 23\,877$
$k = \Sigma T_{ij}/P_i = 1.63$

Table 5.5 Calibration results for Ontario vacation travel gravity model

Dependent variable: $\log[T_{ij}/V_{ij}]$
Intercept (a) = 4.2876; antilog $(a) = \alpha = 19\,390.99$
b coefficient for log distance = −1.67
$r^2 = 0.99$
Standard error (as % of mean Y) = 24.3%

$$G = \frac{\alpha k}{A} = \frac{(19\,390.99)\,(1.63)}{23\,877} = 1.32$$

A_j = population of j;
D_{ij} = great circle distance between Ontario and j;

With this equation, it is possible to go back and calculate a predicted value for the number of vacation trips between Ontario and each province using our original data. This 'replication' will provide us with a measure of how accurately our calibrated model can reproduce the original data. The predicted results are also shown in Table 5.4. If we regress the predicted number of trips against the observed number in this case, we obtain an r^2 of about 98.9 per cent. This is a very high correlation coefficient – much higher than one might expect after a quick review of the data shown in Table 5.4. The reason for the very high r^2 is due, in part, to the extreme values associated with Ontario intra-provincial data. These values, approximately 10 times that of Quebec and 100 times larger than any other province, distort the value of r^2. A more meaningful comparison of the predicted and observed values may be obtained by examining the root-mean-square as a percentage of the mean observed number of trips. The root-mean-square error is a statistic produced by most regression programs. If we divide the root-mean-square error by the mean value of our dependent variable we can obtain an estimate of the standard error of estimate as a percentage of the mean number of trips. For our regression analysis, the root-mean-square error was 500.11 and the mean of the dependent variable was 2055.88. The ratio, 500.11/2055.88 = 0.243 or 24.3 per cent. This is a measure of the expected mean error produced by this model. Whether this level of precision is acceptable is for the analyst to decide on the basis of previous experience and the potential uses of the predictions. For the purposes of comparison, it is worth noting that a standard error of estimate of 20 to 25 per cent is common for tourism and recreational travel gravity models.

A forecast of future travel can now be made by using predicted values for P_i and A_j instead of the observed values. If we predict that the population of Ontario is likely to rise to 8.8 million in some particular year, and that of Alberta will become 2.4 million, we can predict the travel from Ontario to Alberta as

$$T_{ij} = \frac{(1.32)(8800)(2400)}{2500^{1.67}}$$
$$= 58.98 \text{ or about 60 000 trips.}$$

Note that the values of P_i and A_j are recorded in thousands, and that the model was calibrated using these figures reported in thousands.

This example helps to highlight several important issues. The first concerns our measure of distance. The use of great circle distances is convenient, but more sophisticated measures could be developed. For example, surface travel from Ontario to Prince Edward Island requires the use of a marine ferry. Some weight might be added to the distance estimates to those provinces to account for the added inconvenience of ferries. Quebec is a French-speaking province and Ontario is English-speaking. The cultural differences between the two provinces make Quebec an especially attractive province for some Ontario residents. On the other hand, the open hostility of some Quebecers, including certain Quebec laws, towards English-speaking individuals has made that province more 'distant' to many other Anglophones, including those in Ontario. Simple physical distance misses this reality. The pattern of the Great Lakes means that automobile travel from Ontario to the western provinces must make a major detour. The great circle distance from Ontario's centre of population to that of Manitoba is about 1400 km (840 miles) the actual road distance is closer to 2000 km (1200 miles).

The pattern of predicted versus observed numbers of trips clearly illustrates the tendency of the gravity model to over-predict short trips (Quebec and Ontario) and to under-predict long trips (e.g. the Maritimes and British Columbia). Modifications such as those suggested by Wolfe (1972) could help correct for this.

The use of population estimates as the sole measure of attractiveness is, of course, simplistic. Measures of the levels of tourism development, including accommodation, events, and attractions would probably add greater precision to the estimate of provincial attractiveness. If our forecast year for Alberta, for example, was to have been 1988, we would have wanted to add some additional measure to reflect the temporary but significant drawing power of the 1988 Winter Olympics held in that province. Chapter 8 includes a method that can be used to estimate the attractiveness of tourism regions using a variety of components; such an aggregate measure could be developed for each province.

Finally, this model is an unconstrained model. The potential problems associated with unconstrained gravity models have already been described. We have also looked at the concept of a constrained gravity model. One of the major components of a constrained gravity model is a trip-distribution model. A common form of a trip-distribution model is the probabilistic travel model, which we now examine.

Probabilistic travel model

Description

The probabilistic travel model is another example of a structural forecasting model in which a prediction about travel volumes is made on the basis of a hypothesized structure relating several travel variables. This particular model differs from the gravity model in that the forecasts are expressed in terms of probabilities or percentages of total trips rather than as numbers of actual trips. This model can be combined with a trip-generation model such as a trend-extrapolation model to develop a constrained gravity model.

The model described here is a derivation of a consumer choice model originally developed by Luce (1959) and applied to recreational travel by Wennergren and Nielsen (1968). The model is based on the argument that the probability a consumer will select a particular product such as a tourism destination is directly proportional to the 'utility' of that product with respect to all alternative products. An important advantage of this model for tourism is that it allows the analyst to avoid the unrealistic assumption that a tourist will always go to the most desirable destination and that all other destinations will be totally ignored. The model accommodates the fact that the same traveller may go to different destinations and that many travellers will go to all available destinations in varying numbers. Specifically, the model assigns a probability estimate to each destination expressing the odds that the average traveller will select that destination. Since the probabilities total to 1.00 for all destinations in a set of competing destinations, the probabilities may also be interpreted as the expected market share of each tourism product or destination.

The central issue associated with the use of this model is the definition of utility. Utility reflects more than just attractiveness; it also includes the effects of cost or access limitations. Although many destination characteristics affect utility, you are limited to those that can be measured on an interval scale. Wennergren and Nielsen, in their analysis of boaters' choices of reservoirs, used reservoir surface area and travel distance. Although the authors recognized that other variables influenced a boater's choice of a reservoir, these two variables were believed to be the most important and the most reliably measurable. The results – a model that explained 80 per cent of the variance in boater attendance patterns – suggests their reasoning was not unjustified.

Before we examine the procedures to be followed in developing a probabilistic travel model, it will be helpful to identify several assumptions implicit in such models. First, the model is based on the assumption that travellers from any origin are homogeneous in tastes, their willingness to travel, and in their perceptions of utility. Or to put that differently, it is assumed that the average traveller in any region is an adequate indicator of the behaviour of the population of all travellers. This assumption may be relaxed by developing separate models for different types of travellers – such as different income strata. The model form, though, remains the same; you simply calculate a larger number of probabilities.

The model is also based on the assumption of equal (not necessarily perfect) knowledge. All destinations in a set are assumed to be equally familiar to the potential travellers. This, too, may be unrealistic and it can be relaxed if you are able to define weights that can be used to adjust probabilities to reflect knowledge levels. Before doing this, though, you may want to reread the previous chapter's discussion of the difficulty of developing a general model that can accommodate the varying levels of emphasis travellers place on familiarity with tourism destinations.

The importance of finding a valid measure of utility is obvious in this procedure. The challenge involves not only the identification of the relevant variables but also the proper specification of how they are to be combined. A common assumption is that variables are combined multiplicatively, with exponents of 1.0. Other structures or variable transformations could be used. Certainly there is empirical evidence to suggest that distance, when used as part of a gravity or probabilistic travel model, should carry an exponent somewhere between 1.00 and 2.00.

Finally, it will be helpful to describe a test of the explanatory power of this model. The accuracy of the calibrated model may be estimated using the formula:

$$r^2 = 1 - \frac{\Sigma(P_{ij} - \hat{P}_{ij})^2}{\Sigma(P_{ij} - \bar{P}_{ij})^2} \quad [5.23]$$

where: r^2 = the coefficient of determination;
P_{ij} = actual percentage of trips made by travellers from i to j;
$\bar{P}_{ij}$ = average percentage of trips made by travellers from i to all destinations;
$\hat{P}_{ij}$ = predicted percentage of trips made by travellers from i to j.

The interpretation of r^2 in equation [5.23] is the same as r^2 calculated for simple regression.

Procedures

1. Develop a quantitative measure of destination utility, incorporating both positive and negative qualities relevant to the travel system you are studying. The definition of utility must include not just the variables that affect utility, but also how these variables are to be combined. Wennergren and Nielsen (1968) suggested that their choices, size and distance, should be combined multiplicatively:

$$U_j = \frac{S_j}{D_{ij}} \qquad [5.24]$$

where: U_j = utility of reservoir j;
S_j = surface area of j in acres;
D_{ij} = distance from i to j in miles.

2. After deciding on an appropriate measure of utility, collect the data necessary to calculate utility for every destination. Record the data and calculate total utility by summing the individual utility measures: ΣU_j.

3. Determine the probability a traveller will choose any particular destination by dividing the utility of that destination by the total utility of all destinations:

$$P_{ij} = \frac{U_j}{\Sigma U_j} \qquad [5.25]$$

where: P_{ij} = probability a traveller will select j.

Example

Assume we are interested in predicting the probabilities that travellers from a particular city in a northern American state will choose each of three resorts along the coast of the Gulf of Mexico. In this example, let the distance from the origin to each destination be equal. Further assume that amenities and quality of service in the three resorts vary according to their price. Finally, assume that the major difference in the resorts is their capacity. The utility of each resort can be defined as:

$$U_j = \frac{C_j}{R_j} \qquad [5.26]$$

where: U_j = utility of resort j;
C_j = number of rooms at j;
R_j = average daily room charge at j.

The probability that the average traveller from i will choose any particular resort is

$$P_{ij} = \frac{C_j/R_j}{\Sigma(C_j/R_j)} \qquad [5.27]$$

Table 5.6 contains the capacity and room rates for three hypothetical resorts. The utility of the resort identified as '1' is equal to the capacity of the resort divided by the average room rate: 250/90 = 2.78. The same calculation is performed for the other resorts, and a total utility derived by summing the individual utilities: 8.36. The probability a traveller from i will select the first resort is: 2.78/8.36 = 33.2 per cent. The probabilities of selecting other resorts may be calculated the same way.

If desired, one can also develop a multiple regression model to predict the total number of trips that travellers from origin i are likely to generate to all three resorts, thus producing a two-component model that would be equivalent to a constrained gravity model.

Table 5.6 Hypothetical resort data for calibration of a probabilistic travel model

Resort	Daily room rate R_j (\$)	Number of rooms C_j	$U_j = C_j/R_j$
1	90	250	2.78
2	100	300	3.00
3	120	310	2.58
			$\Sigma(C_j/R_j)$ = 8.36

$$P_{i1} = \frac{2.78}{8.36} = 33.2\%$$

$$P_{i2} = \frac{3.00}{8.36} = 35.9\%$$

$$P_{i3} = \frac{2.58}{8.36} = 30.9\%$$

Delphi technique

Description

The Delphi technique is one of the best known and sometimes more controversial methods for making forecasts. The method was pioneered by the RAND Corporation in the USA back in the early 1950s (Dalkey and Helmer 1963) as a method for forecasting the development of events when historical or trend data are unavailable or when existing models require significant levels of subjective judgement.

The technique depends on a panel of experts, assembled by the analyst, that responds to several rounds of carefully constructed questionnaires. These questionnaires are designed to move the panel to a consensus on the identity, probability, and timing of future events. The panel may be assembled face to face or through a telephone or computer network, but the use of mail questionnaires is probably the most common and best format. A major advantage of the mail format is that it avoids the potential biasing effects of peer or committee pressure and other psychological influences on the respondents' answers. Most panels consist of 40 to 50 experts, although Brockhoff (1975) successfully used a panel of only 4 respondents in a computer technology application, while Shafer, Moeller, and Getty (1974) worked with a panel of 904 experts in their study of future leisure environments.

Delphi, like other forecasting models, begins with a question about the future. In the case of Delphi, this question often concerns qualitative trends or the emergence of new discoveries or other unprecedented events that cannot be studied using conventional trend extrapolation or structural models. Delphi is often selected, therefore, as the forecasting tool of last resort; it is available when no other model will work. This feature is perhaps Delphi's greatest recommendation, but it does have several other strengths.

The method brings together, in a controlled setting, experts with diverse abilities who can challenge one another's assumptions and arguments, and complement each other's strengths. Delphi is relatively simple to conduct, with no particular need for computer or statistical skill. This quality, though, is deceptive. Some researchers naïvely approach Delphi, thinking it to be 'quick and dirty'. In practice, it can take from nine months to two years to recruit a panel successfully, administer several rounds of questionnaires, and reach a consensus. The administrative costs and complexities of Delphi can be significant, and grow rapidly with the size of the panel and the length of the exercise.

Several other features of Delphi need to be highlighted. The success or failure of the exercise depends on the qualifications of the experts and on the skill of the researcher in designing and administering the questionnaires. Personal but unintentional biases on the part of the researcher can be incorporated into the wording of the questionnaire or the analysis of the results. The stability of the panel is also important. If the exercise lasts a year or more, some panel members may be expected to drop out. If too many leave, the validity of any consensus is suspect.

The predictions made by experts are typically expressed in percentage probabilities. Such probabilities, however, are actually subjective judgements and do not have any of the properties that true, quantitative probabilities exhibit. The use of numerical probabilities can impart an unwarranted air of precision and scientific rigour to what are ultimately personal opinions. The use of Delphi normally does not permit various events to be related to each other in any systematic fashion. In other words, if forecasts are made about ten different events that will influence the future development of tourism, Delphi treats these events as discrete and independent, with no interaction among them. This is not necessarily a valid assumption. Some panel members may attempt to incorporate such interactions, but there is no way to ensure that all do in a consistent fashion.

The most successful forecasts made with Delphi have been those concerned with technological or scientific developments. Experience with applications of Delphi to problems involving social interactions, human values, political priorities, economic growth, and the dynamics of the market-place have been sporadic and less successful.

Given these limitations, it should be apparent that the Delphi technique is not foolproof. It may be the method of last resort when it comes to forecasting, but under some circumstances even Delphi will not necessarily work. Nevertheless, Delphi may have value in helping tourism planners and policy analysts anticipate possible future developments when no other forecasting models are available.

Procedures

1. Define the forecasting problem and assemble the panel of experts. Problem definition is a crucial step in any forecasting problem, and especially so for the Delphi technique. A period of time devoted to reading background material and to identifying possible panel

members is an important part of this initial step. The ultimate selection of the panel of experts should involve the choice of individuals from a wide range of background to ensure representativeness and comprehensiveness of the predictions. For most tourism problems, panel members should come from both the public and private sectors, as well as from universities, consulting firms, and perhaps even from related areas such as recreation agencies, investment firms, conservation organizations, and advertising firms. The size of the panel is determined by the number of available experts and the complexity of the problem; a typical panel will often have 40 to 50 people.

2. Develop and distribute the first-round questionnaire. This first questionnaire is designed to introduce the general area of study and to invite the panel to identify possible future events, the probability they will occur, and the likely date of their occurrence. One method for framing questions is to ask respondents to identify those events that are likely to occur within some specified period of time, perhaps the next 20 years. They are then asked to indicate the date by which they believe the event has at least a 50 per cent chance of occurring.

3. Once the first-round questionnaires have been returned, the results are tabulated and summarized. The summary includes the median date – the date falling midway in the range of the panel's forecast. The two middle quartile ranges are also noted – the range around the median date that encompasses 50 per cent of the total forecasts.

4. Summary statistics from the first round are presented in the second-round questionnaire which is then mailed to the same panel of experts. Copies of their first-round questionnaire responses may also be provided for reference. Each panel member is asked to consider whether he wishes to change his forecast in light of the group's statistics. Those whose personal forecasts fell outside the two middle quartile ranges are also invited to explain why they made such a forecast, if they chose not to alter their original positions.

5. The results of the second-round questionnaire are tabulated and summarized. These results now include both new predictions as well as comments about why some experts do not agree with the emerging consensus.

6. Summary results and comments from the second-round questionnaire are incorporated into a third-round questionnaire. The instructions with the third-round questionnaire are similar to those of the second round. The major difference is the addition of arguments for dissenting forecasts.

7. Once the results of the third-round questionnaire are in, you will need to decide whether a fourth round is desirable further to refine

the consensus of your respondents. Some of the criteria you may wish to consider in taking this decision is whether there appears to be much chance of respondents making further alterations in their positions. The spread in the forecasts for any particular event can also indicate the need for further rounds. If most forecasts are already tightly clustered around the median date after two rounds, there is little point in prolonging the exercise. On the other hand, if the predictions show a high degree of variance, a third and maybe even a fourth round with accompanying written argument may help to establish a consensus.

Upon completion of the final round, the results are summarized. These results include median dates, inter-quartile ranges, and the identity of those events for which no consensus was reached.

Example

Shafer, Moeller, and Getty (1974) used the Delphi technique to identify those developments likely to occur in the USA by the year 2000 that would influence park and recreation management. A panel of 904 experts including recreation and park managers, biological and ecological scientists, demographers, and environmental technologists was formed (the panel eventually shrank to 405 as members dropped out). They were asked in the first-round questionnaire to list those events they believed had a 50 per cent probability of occurring by the year 2000 and to estimate the most probable date by which the event would occur.

After circulating the results of the first round in the second-round questionnaire, the authors discovered that the consensus of the panel regarding certain events was that they were likely to occur after the year 2000. As a result, they dropped the year 2000 as a cut-off and retained all events and dates. Two more rounds of questionnaires were distributed, using the basic procedure described above. The complete results are summarized in the authors' report, but a summary of some of the tourism-related predictions can illustrate the type of results produced. These are presented without comment, other than to note that they were made by an American panel in 1973–74.

By 1980

1. Computers will be used to advise recreationists where to go.
2. Interpretative material on flora and fauna as well as historic sites will be available at a majority of public sites.

By 1985

1. Tax credits will be established for private landowners to protect scenic resources.
2. Cable television will be available at a majority of campgrounds.
3. Use of the wilderness will be restricted.
4. Special fishing areas will be established in urban areas for disabled, elderly, and youth.

By 1990

1. Year-round skiing on artificial surfaces.
2. Salt-water fishermen required to have federal fishing licences.
3. National campground reservation system for public parks.
4. Public schools open year-round with staggered vacations.
5. Most homes have video-tape systems.

By 2000

1. Eight hundred kilometres (500 miles) is considered a reasonable one-way distance for weekend pleasure travel.
2. Average retirement age is 50.
3. Middle-class American families vacation on other continents as commonly as they vacation in the USA in the 1970s.
4. Electric power or other non-polluting engines replace internal combustion engines in recreational vehicles.
5. Travel in large parks limited to minimal-impact mass transit, e.g tramways, air transport, and underground rapid transit.

By 2020

1. Man-made islands are created solely for tourism and recreation.
2. Most metropolitan areas provide adequate outdoor recreation so that the majority of their residents do not feel the need to go to the country for pleasure.

By 2030

1. Most middle-income Americans own vacation homes.

After 2050

1. First park on the moon.

2. Fees at public recreation areas set to cover capital and maintenance costs.
3. Self-contained underwater resorts.
4. Average life-span is 100 years.

Summary

Forecasting demand is an important task in tourism analysis. The process of forecasting in tourism is a bit like a game of golf. A golfer must often approach the green along a path that may have a sharp dog-leg and several bunkers or other hazards. The approach is taken in a series of steps, with a different club used for different shots. In a similar fashion, a forecaster rarely has a clear and straight shot at the ultimate goal. He must approach his goal, an accurate prediction, in a series of steps, avoiding traps while attempting to improve the accuracy of his forecasts by using different tools at each step.

There are a range of tools available to the forecaster, including both qualitative and quantitative methods. We have examined some of the basic techniques in this chapter and noted both strengths and weaknesses of each. Two of these models, trend extrapolation and the gravity model, are based directly on statistical analysis of past behaviour. Forecasts are made by assuming that historical patterns will continue. Such an assumption is not unreasonable for short-term and middle-term forecasts, but it can become increasingly dubious for the longer term.

A third model, the probabilistic travel model, also utilizes empirical data. It is different from the first two in that the data do not directly relate to observed tourism demand but to measures of presumed utility. As a result, the predictions are not expressed in terms of demand *per se*, but rather in terms of probabilities or market shares.

The last model, the Delphi technique, relies heavily on expert opinion and the debatable assumption that a group consensus based on the exchange of those opinions will eventually produce reliable forecasts about the timing and likelihood of future developments.

Great progress has been made in the last 20 years in tourism and recreation forecasting. Although forecasting is still as much art as science, continued progress is likely in the next decade in both technical aspects of forecasting and in the application of forecasting methods to management and planning goals.

Further reading

Black W R 1973 An analysis of gravity model distance exponents. *Transportation* **2**: 299–312.

Boulogne R 1981 The concept of attraction: its meaning and measurement. *Tijdschrift voor Economie en Sociale Geografie* **72**: 362–7.

Brown T L and **Wilkens B T** 1975 Method of improving recreation projections. *Journal of Leisure Research* **7**: 225–34.

Clawson M and **Knetsch J L** 1966 *Economics of outdoor recreation*. Johns Hopkins Press, Baltimore, Md.

Ewing G O 1983 Forecasting recreation trip distribution behavior. In Lieber S R and Fesenmaier D R (eds) *Recreation planning and management*. Venture Publishing, State College, Pa., pp. 120–40.

Fujii E T and **Mak J** 1980 Forecasting travel demand when the explanatory variables are highly correlated. *Journal of Travel Research* **18**(4): 31–4.

Moeller G H and **Shafer E L** 1983 The use and misuse of forecasting. In Lieber S R and Fesenmaier D R (eds) *Recreation planning and management*. Venture Publishing, State College, Pa., pp. 96–104.

Salanick J R, Wenger W, and **Helfer E** 1971 The construction of Delphi event statements. *Technological Forecasting and Social Change* **3**: 65–73.

Smith V K and **Munley V G** 1978 The relative performance of various estimates of recreation participation equations. *Journal of Leisure Research* **10**: 165–76.

Smith S L J 1984 A method for estimating the distance equivalent of international boundaries. *Journal of Travel Research* **22**(3): 37–9.

Stynes D J 1983 Time series and structural models for forecasting recreation participation. In Lieber S R and Fesenmaier D R (eds) *Recreation planning and management*. Venture Publishing, State College, Pa., pp. 105–19.

Taylor P J 1975 *Distance decay in spatial interactions*, Concepts and Techniques in Modern Geography, No 2. GeoAbstracts, University of East Anglia, Norwich, UK.

Uysal M and **Crompton J L** 1985 An overview of approaches used to forecast tourism demand. *Journal of Travel Research* **23**(4): 7–15.

Wheelwright S C and **Makridakis S** 1980 *Forecasting methods for management*. John Wiley, New York.

CHAPTER 6

Selecting a site for business development

Introduction

An adage in business development states, 'The three most important factors to consider when starting a business are location, location, and location.' The emphasis on location is strong because changing a site once a business has been established is difficult and expensive, and because the process of site selection can significantly influence a business's profitability, perhaps even its survivability.

Despite the expressed importance of selecting the proper site, there is little published research on site-selection principles and procedures in tourism. Some of the larger hotel, resort, and restaurant franchises have sophisticated locational models, but these are proprietary to the franchisors. They are not made publicly available to the academic community because of the legitimate concern that competitors could benefit from knowledge of the site-location strategies of these firms.

The lack of published site-selection research in tourism, while unfortunate from a scholarly perspective, should not be surprising. As Grether (1983) has noted, academic researchers interested in studying marketing and entrepreneurship have generally ignored spatial and locational questions in their analyses. Since tourism research, even in universities, has been traditionally dominated by the marketing perspective, it is not unexpected that tourism research should have many of the same shortcomings of market research. To be fair, Grether also notes signs of a growing recognition of the need for research on locational issues. This growth is fed by the need to understand and manage all the forces that influence a business's operations and performance, including those forces such as site location that can directly influence a consumer's decision about which business to patronize.

Fortunately for marketing and tourism researchers, they do not need to start from scratch in developing locational research. There is already a large body of literature on the economics of location and the geography of business. This work may be found in the journals and books of applied geography, and to a degree in regional science and economic geography.

At the risk of over-simplifying a complex corpus of research, this work may be classified as being conducted from two perspectives: (1) locational theory; and (2) site-selection guidelines. The former tends to be nomothetic, formal, abstract, and mathematical. The latter tends to be idiographic, applied, empirical, and sometimes based on personal experiences and intuition as much as on objective procedures. As the title of this chapter suggests, our interest is in the second perspective. The reason for this, of course, is that the book is intended to emphasize practical research techniques rather than the development of theory. However, both perspectives are important for tourism research in the long run, and we will consider briefly the contributions of the locational theory perspective before turning to four specific site-selection procedures.

Location theory

Classical location theory is usually traced back to the work of von Thünen (1875). Beginning with a highly simplified model of an isolated market-place surrounded by a uniform plane, von Thünen developed a theory that predicted a concentric pattern of crops around the market-place. His model focused on the comparative value of various crops, the cost of transportation associated with each type of crop, their bulk, and perishability. Land close to the market-place would be used for highly perishable, valuable, and/or bulky items such as truck crops, milk from stall-fed cows, and eggs from laying hens. The next zone was devoted to forest because of the contemporary importance of wood for fuel. This was followed by more durable and less bulky crops such as potatoes and other root crops. Then would come fields for cereal grains, pasture-land (used for animals that could be driven to market), and finally wilderness tracts for hunting and trapping. Although modern agricultural economics, food production, storage technology, and transportation have created very different patterns, von Thünen's emphasis on the central role of transportation in determining land uses has been seminal. His model and the models of those researchers who have followed his lead (e.g. Weber 1928; 1911; Hoover 1948) are commonly recognized as the beginnings of the so-called 'transportation cost school' of location theory because of their emphasis on the importance of transportation in determining the optimal location of economic activity. Their work has also become the inspiration for several tourism development models such as those of Yokeno (1974) and Miossec (1977) as well as Vickerman's (1975) model of intra-urban recreation business location.

Work by some economists in the 1930s shifted the focus from rural land-use patterns to urban development and industrial lands. One of the most important of these early modifications of von Thünen's early work was the replacement of his central market-place with a localized resource used by some particular industry (Ohlin 1935). This line of enquiry grew in complexity and scope, leading ultimately to formal statements about the interrelationships of urban areas, industries, and economic regions developed by Christaller (1933) and Lösch (1944). Their work is known both as 'central place theory' and as the 'locational interdependence school'. The first name comes from Christaller's focus on urban areas as 'central places' or concentrations of economic activity and administration, while the second title derives from Lösch's attention to the interconnections between the development of economic regions and the nexus of urban areas and industrial locations.

Central place work continued to be a major force in both economic geography and regional science into the 1970s. Among the many contributions this work has made to the geography of economic activity has been formalizations of the concepts of:

- *Threshold populations* – the minimum number of people necessary to support a given type of industry or retail activity.
- *Hinterlands* – the geographic area containing the threshold population; the actual size varies with the type of good and the surrounding population density.
- *Hierarchies* – the pattern of a few large cities offering many goods and services and more, smaller cities and towns offering fewer goods and services.

Despite its importance to regional science, central place theory has had little to contribute to tourism research. In fact, when Christaller (1964) turned his attention to tourism, he observed that the pattern of tourism on the landscape seemed to be the result of processes that were in direct opposition to those that formed central places. However, his argument that resorts and other tourism developments were actually 'peripheral places' was unfortunately marred by an overly narrow and selective definition of tourism.

Despite the prestige and success of central place theory, some regional scientists eventually grew dissatisfied with it. Their major concern was that central place theory permitted a large number of different, independent, and conflicting models to develop. Each appeared to work under certain circumstances, but failed under others. The dissatisfaction with this growing number of contradictory *ad hoc* models led to the emergence of the 'generalized market school'. This school explicitly attempted to build on the strong points of earlier models while avoiding their weaknesses.

Two major approaches have been employed to develop a more general and powerful synthesis of economic concepts desired by the generalized market school. One of these was pioneered by Isard (1956). He examined all available models to identify common themes or components, assuming that each model had a bit of truth in it. By identifying common features and unique strengths, he attempted to combine them into one comprehensive model, without making any new detailed structural analyses or major structural innovations.

A contemporary, Greenhut (1956), argued that one could not overcome the weaknesses in existing models simply by combining parts of them. He believed it was necessary to adopt a new perspective on the problem of locational theory and site selection. One of the major contributions Greenhut made to the development of this new perspective was his emphasis on the role of risk and uncertainty in locational decision-making. Greenhut further rejected the common assumption that firms would act as would-be spatial monopolists (an assumption previous location theorists made) and assumed, instead, that they would behave as spatial oligopolists. In other words, Greenhut's model was based on a hypothetical world in which each firm looks at several other firms in the immediate vicinity, but with a conscious recognition that no single firm's owners can know for certain what the other owners are planning. Greenhut's model is still abstract, but it is more realistic than the models proposed by other location theorists. His emphasis on risk and uncertainty also helped prepare the way for the more recent application of simulation and game theory to problems of modelling locational development (e.g. Baligh and Richartz 1967; Barcun and Jeming 1973; Rao 1981).

Location theory has developed a useful base of concepts that support the scientific analysis of industrial, settlement, and urban development patterns. In practice, however, such theories are of limited utility to site-selection problems because too many variables and issues are assumed away. Often those that remain are modelled with mathematical tools that are beyond the experience of most planners and business people. None the less, location theorists have developed several concepts that are useful for site-selection work in tourism and other business sectors:

1. Location is both theoretically and practically important in determining the size and success of a firm.
2. The choice of a good location for a firm involves trade-offs among transportation costs, production costs, resource availability, labour availability, market accessibility, and land costs.
3. Certain types of businesses do well if they avoid locating close to competitors; others benefit from such closeness; still others are indifferent.
4. Population size and the number and location of competing firms can limit the potential for new business growth in predictable ways.
5. Businesses that require the shipping of heavy or bulky items required for production or that are closely tied to particular resources will tend to locate close to those resources. Businesses that produce heavy or bulky products will tend to locate close to their market.

These general observations provide some of the conceptual foundation for the more practical site-selection guidelines we will examine later in this chapter.

Checklist method

Description

The checklist method for site selection is a simple, systematic consideration of the key characteristics of a number of pre-selected sites. The list of pre-selected sites may be developed in the base of intuition, expert opinion, or from an inventory of available real eatate. This particular method then allows the developer to select either an optimal site or to rank order available sites in terms of their desirability for development. The use of a checklist is arguably the most common locational tool used by business planners. Its advantages include inexpensiveness, simplicity, flexibility, and general objectivity. It can be applied equally well to a range of different types of businesses and to virtually any scale of development, from the selection of a new foreign national market for a tourism promotional campaign to the choice of the best corner for an ice-cream vendor's wagon.

The ease with which the checklist method can be employed, however, does introduce potential risks. Although the specific site characteristics to be evaluated are identified objectively, the evaluation of each site on these characteristics depends heavily on the skill, experience, and insight of the evaluator. Further, comparison of each site on each individual criterion is relatively simple, but the method does not provide any form of calculation to permit sites to be compared against each other on the entire set of characteristics, as a whole. Consider, for example, a business planner comparing two sites on the basis of three characteristics, one of which is important and two that are less important. If one site is ranked high on the two less important characteristics and poorly on the important feature, while the other is ranked high on the important characteristic but poorly on the other two, how does the planner choose? The checklist method does not provide a solution, forcing the planner to use his own judgement. This method can ensure that the planner has all the necessary information arrayed in a consistent format, but the informed mind must still be called upon to analyse the data.

Finally, the checklist method does not provide any quantitative estimates of market share, return on investment, or net profitability. Such estimates might be derived as part of the site-selection process, but they involve modelling efforts not normally a part of the checklist approach.

Procedures

1. Identify the important locational characteristics for the type of business being considered. These characteristics should be divided into 'critical' and 'desirable' attributes. Critical attributes are those whose absence (or possibly presence) would eliminate a location from further consideration regardless of other qualities. For example, a local ordinance against serving alcoholic beverages would immediately eliminate a location from any further consideration as a place to open a restaurant where wine was to be served. Critical attributes act as filters to screen out clearly undesirable locations, reducing the total number of alternatives that have to be considered in detailed study.

Desirable attributes are those whose presence, in some varying degree, enhance the suitability of a location. As with critical attributes, these vary from business to business. Desirable attributes (like critical attributes) may be expressed either negatively or positively. With respect to adjacent land uses, for instance, the particular issue may be a concern for either the presence of other businesses that would enhance the potential success of a business or the desire to avoid selecting a site near certain incompatible land uses.

2. Once the list of critical and desirable attributes has been devel-

oped, each attribute must be operationally defined. This definition should be expressed in such a way that a planner or consultant can clearly understand what is meant by the attribute and what levels or features are associated with different degrees of desirability. For example, if the availability of labour is an issue, how is such availability to be measured? What types of skills are sought? What size employee force is desired? How far could one expect employees to travel? Is there potential for hiring unemployed workers and retraining them (especially with government assistance)?

If desired, an operational definition can be expressed as an ordinal scale. 'Neighbourhood cleanliness', for example, could be ranked on a scale ranging from '1', very clean, to '5', very dirty. Other types of qualitative attributes, however, could not be meaningfully summarized on a simple ordinal scale, such as summaries of zoning or deed restrictions. These would have to be described in some detail for the purposes of comparison.

3. Draw up a list of potential locations and identify appropriate data sources. This list may be based on informed judgement, a systematic consideration of all possible locations (clearly not feasible if the number of locations runs into the dozens or hundreds), or locations on which the business developer may hold options.

4. Prepare a worksheet listing all attributes. Each location might be evaluated on one or more sheets if lengthy verbal descriptions are necessary for some of the attributes. The critical attributes should be placed at the top of the list.

5. Begin completing the worksheets for each location by examining the critical attributes. Complete the worksheets only for those locations that meet the critical requirements.

6. Compare each location with all others. Resist the temptation to reduce all evaluations to a standard ordinal scale so that the scores could apparently be added up to obtain an overall ranking. The problem with this approach is that it requires all attributes to be measured on comparable, valid, interval-level scales. This assumption is met only in the rarest locational consideration problems. The evaluation of the checklists is best done in consultation with experts who can assist in the evaluation of criteria associated with engineering, real estate, and legal matters.

Example

A detailed example of the use of this procedure is not really needed because the method is quite straightforward, largely qualitative, and depends on field inspection and judgement. A typical list, however, would be informative as an example. The following checklist illustrates the type of information that might be collected for selecting a site for a hotel in an urban area.

Critical characteristics

1. Would a hotel be in conformance with existing zoning regulations and deed restrictions? If not, can a variance be obtained?
2. Is it possible to obtain a liquor licence for this location?
3. Can adequate parking be provided on-site?

Desirable characteristics

1. Is there a suitable structure on site or will new construction be required? What is the approximate cost of renovations or construction on this site?
2. What is the purchase price or the terms of a long-term lease?
3. What are the surrounding land uses? Is the neighbourhood attractive and safe? What are the likely trends in land use and social environment? Are neighbouring businesses or residential tenants likely to resist hotel development in city council?
4. Are other hotels near by? What is their quality, size, and clientele?
5. What is the distance to the airport serving the city?
6. How accessible is the site from major highways serving the city?
7. How far is the site from major visitor-generating institutions such as business complexes, government offices, tourist attractions, sport and cultural facilities, and military bases?
8. What is the pattern of traffic flow around the site: one-way streets, congestion, patterns of entrance and egress from the parking lot?

Analogue method

Description

The analogue method was pioneered by William Applebaum, a site-selection expert for the Kroger Company, in the early 1930s. It has found extensive application in other companies (Rogers and Green 1978; Thompson 1982) and has been adopted by the US Army Corps of Engineers as a model for predicting reservoir use at Corps projects (US Army Corps of Engineers 1974). The model lacks any theoretical base and, like many other site-selection tools, is highly dependent on the skill of the individual analyst. In the hands of an experienced and competent researcher, the method can be quite useful. The analogue method permits the development of a forecast of visits or sales by comparing a proposed site(s) with an existing site(s) that is similar in relevant characteristics. Central to the use of the analogue method is the analogue data base – a series of profiles of existing sites to be used for comparison and forecasting. Because of the importance of this data base, application of the analogue method is usually limited to those situations in which a prior investment in data collection has been made. With sufficient lead time, however, one can develop a series of profiles which can then be used to assess a known set of alternative sites. Each analogue site profile describes a successful site. The basic logic of the method is that if a proposed site closely resembles an existing successful site, then the proposed site has a good chance of success as well. Further, the level of success (measured in terms of revenues or visitors) is also likely to be similar.

Since the analogue method compares potential sites on the basis of how well they compare to known sites with various records of success or profitability, the method depends on: (1) the development of precise and valid profiles of existing sites or businesses; (2) the potential for finding close matches between the proposed site and existing sites; and (3) the ability of the analyst to 'correct' for discrepancies between the analogues and the proposed sites to make more accurate forecasts of potential sales or attendance at the proposed sites.

Procedures

1. The first and often the major task in the application of the analogue method is the development of the data base – the file of existing site inventory profiles. Each profile should contain site characteristics relevant to the particular business being studied. Although some variation will be necessary for different types of businesses, the following list is a general guideline:

(a) Location, size, and other basic information about the firm.
(b) A graph relating per capita sales or attendance by some geographical unit such as census tract, neighbourhood, or county versus distance between that unit and the firm. This graph may be a simple plot showing the tendency for sales to decline over distance, or it may be a plot combined with a regression

equation summarizing the relationship between business volumes and distance statistically.

(c) Population of the geographical units.

(d) A socio-economic profile of the population in the market area of the firm (typically that area surrounding the firm that encompasses 65 to 80 per cent of all business). This profile, however, may be irrelevant if the market area extends hundreds or thousands of kilometres, as in the case of major resorts.

(e) Descriptions of other relevant site characteristics such as the surrounding transportation pattern, local land uses, available parking, and significant deed restrictions or zoning regulations.

To use the profiles for comparing alternative sites for proposed developments, follow the next series of steps.

2. Identify a series of potential sites for the proposed development. This list of sites may be developed from a list of available real estate or from informed opinion combined with a review of actual properties.

3. Select the analogue site that most closely resembles the proposed site.

4. Estimate the probable market area of the proposed site.

5. Obtain estimates of the population in the census tracts, neighbourhoods, counties, or other geographical units surrounding the proposed site, within the limits of the defined market area.

6. Using the per capita sales (or use) curve from the analogue site and the associated population figures from the proposed site, develop estimates for expected sales for each geographical unit within the market area.

7. Sum the estimated sales figures to arrive at an expected total. Select the preferred site on the basis of the largest estimated total or other appropriate criterion.

Example

The following illustration demonstrates the basic logic used in the analogue method. This particular example considers only one analogue; actual applications will consider two or more. The steps in the calculation for each analogue would be identical, however; only the values would vary. This particular example concerns the selection of a site for a restaurant offering table service, entrées averaging from \$7.00 to \$12.00 for the evening meal, some finger foods, bar service in an attached lounge, a nostalgia theme in the décor and menu, and catering primarily to a university clientele. This particular restaurant

Table 6.1 Demographic profile for six areas in Waterloo, Ontario

Forward sortation area	Population	% married	% by age				% with income greater than:					Distance to site (km)
			<25	25–44	45–64	<64	$15k	$25k	$35k	$50k	$75k	
N2J	10 250	51	21	34	32	13	51	26	12	4	2	1.7
N2K	4 950	71	19	52	24	5	56	33	18	6	3	3.9
N2L	16 900	64	21	46	24	9	52	30	17	7	3	0.6
N2T	1 475	82	13	68	17	2	68	47	27	11	4	2.1
N2V	1 325	80	18	68	12	2	62	33	11	0	0	4.1

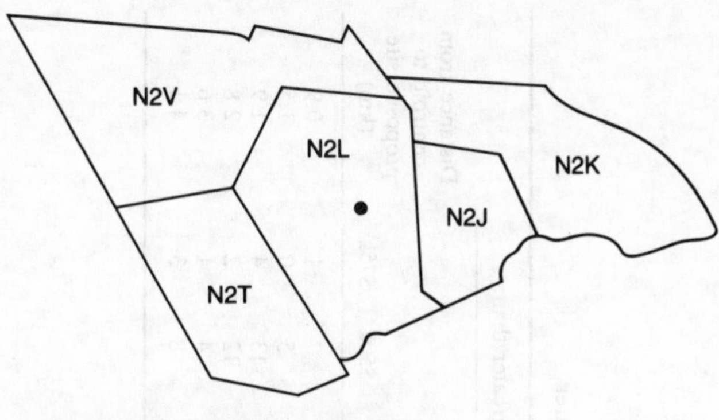

Fig. 6.1 Location of analogue restaurant and surrounding market area: Waterloo, Ontario

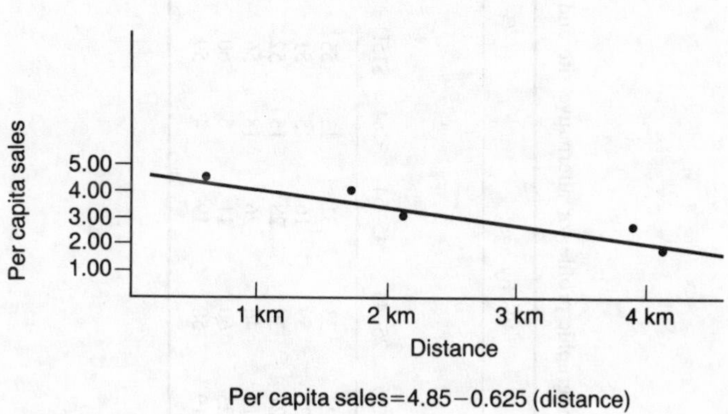

Fig. 6.2 Plot of distance versus per capita sales for analogue restaurant

(for the analogue) is located in Waterloo, Ontario. A customer survey revealed that over 80 per cent of the customers come from five 'forward sortation areas' (FSAs), which are postal code regions defined by the first three digits of Canada's six-digit postal codes. These FSAs were all within 5 km (3 miles) of the restaurant (see Fig. 6.1). Census files for the FSAs provided the demographic profile summarized in Table 6.1. A plot of per capita sales (estimated from survey data and the population of each FSA) against the distance between the population centroid of the FSA and the restaurant is given in Fig. 6.2. A regression line was estimated using least-squares regression, as described in Chapter 5.

Table 6.2 Demographic profile for alternative site and surrounding area

Forward sortation area	Population	% married	% by age:				% with income greater than:						Distance from centroid to proposed site (km)
			<25	25–44	45–64	<64	$15k	$25k	$35k	$50k	$75k		
1	12 300	46	23	33	31	13	55	30	19	7	1		0.9
2	15 125	52	20	59	16	5	51	29	12	5	0		1.5
3	7 050	63	21	36	28	15	52	26	23	13	4		1.9
4	1 200	85	10	46	26	18	56	40	17	12	2		2.8
5	6 550	55	23	60	11	6	60	41	12	4	1		3.6
6	10 000	71	19	58	19	4	59	28	14	8	3		4.1

Table 6.3 Calculation of expected sales figures for proposed restaurant location

Forward sortation area	Population	Distance	Estimated per capita sales ($)	Estimated total sales ($)
1	12 300	0.9	4.3	52 890
2	15 125	1.5	3.9	58 987
3	7 050	1.9	3.7	26 085
4	1 200	2.8	3.1	3 720
5	6 550	3.6	2.6	17 030
6	10 000	4.1	2.3	23 000
			Total	181 712

One of the key features associated with the analogue operation in Waterloo was the proximity of the restaurant to two universities, the University of Waterloo and Wilfrid Laurier University. This allowed the analyst to narrow the search to other Ontario communities that had universities as likely locations for expansion of the restaurant firm. A review of the census profiles of FSAs in the vicinity of universities in these communities led to the identification of one especially likely community. The profile of the FSAs from that community are provided in Table 6.2. Although the profiles do not match exactly, the analogue and the proposed site are similar in having a relatively high proportion of younger residents, singles, and mid- to upper-income households. Use of the plot and the regression equation in combination with data from the proposed community resulted in estimated per capita sales and total sales figures summarized in Table 6.3. The estimated annual sales for the probable market are $181 712. This figure, combined with a review of the existing competition in the city, led the developer to decide to begin negotiations for a tentative site in the selected community.

Analysis of residuals

Description

The analysis of residuals method is a quantitative technique for estimating the relative potential of several locations to support business growth. Like the checklist method, it permits examination of several locations simultaneously on the basis of previously specified attributes. Unlike the checklist method, analysis of residuals is applicable only to regional locational choice. It cannot be used to select specific sites. It is helpful in narrowing down the alternatives to be considered in greater detail, perhaps through application of the checklist or analogue methods in a second stage of analysis.

The analysis of residuals method is based, in part, on the notion of economic equilibrium – the idea that the number of businesses a region can support is influenced by a range of social and economic conditions and that the number of businesses slowly changes until an equilibrium is reached. The slowness of the change is due to the uncertainty that business people must cope with as they try to decide whether to start a new business (or to cut their losses and close an existing business) and to the fact that the conditions that dictate what the equilibrium number will be also change over time. The study of equilibrium conditions might ideally be conducted through longitudinal research whereby the changing numbers of firms are examined over time as they adjust to changing economic conditions. However, the time and budget requirements for a longitudinal design are usually too great for most business decisions. What is needed is some practical, efficient method for providing a rough estimate of the probable number of firms a region could support that would represent at least a short-term equilibrium. Such an alternative is a latitudinal or cross-sectional study. Within limits, one can argue that the economic development patterns in a large number of economically and politically linked regions (such as counties in a state or province) measured at the same time reflect different stages of economic development. In other words, one assumes that regions with different levels of development represent different stages in the economic evolution of the average region.

If you use a latitudinal design to estimate the expected number of some type of tourism business, a comparison of the actual number with the expected number (the calculation of residuals) will indicate the degree to which a region is overdeveloped or underdeveloped with respect to that type of business. Clearly, then, another basic assumption of the analysis of residuals is that the existence of residuals is due primarily to economic disequilibrium. In practice, of course, residuals may be due to other forces as well. One of the potential sources of a mismatch between the observed number and predicted number of businesses is the misspecification of the predictive model. Whether this is a likely explanation in any particular case can be assessed by examining the level of explained variance, R^2, in the model. A relatively high R^2 would indicate model misspecification is not likely to be a serious problem.

Omission of important variables could also produce residuals. Again, a review of the explained variance and the level of error associated with a model can give an indication of the potential seriousness of this source of residuals. Independent review of the model by other researchers may also provide a check against the omission of important causal variables. This type of peer review can be useful to determine if there is a source of systematic error in your analysis. A more difficult situation would be the omission of one or two variables that could play an important role in explaining the observed level of development in only a few counties, but which might be of negligible importance for the majority of the set. For example, particular zoning restrictions or local variations in the availability of venture capital might significantly affect some local patterns. It should be recalled, though, that analysis of residuals is intended to be used only as the first step in a more lengthy site-selection process. The omission of one or more variables at this early stage of research does not necessarily mean that these variables would never be considered at a subsequent stage of evaluation. In the case of zoning restrictions or the availability of investment capital, for example, these matters would clearly come to the fore before a final development decision could be made.

The dependent variable normally used in the analysis of residuals is the number of businesses because of the ease of data collection. Such a measure, however, ignores the variations in the size and profitability of firms. It also implies that the characteristics of the typical firm in each county are the same – only the number of firms and the market size of the county vary. Of equal or greater relevance is the fact that the model makes no allowances for clever and aggressive (or incompetent and bungled) management and marketing. A good location is no guarantee of success; a bad location is not an economic kiss of death.

Lastly, this site-selection model assumes that the critical social and economic environment and the primary source of customers is the local region. For some types of tourism businesses, this will not be true. To the degree that the number of businesses in a region is influenced by conditions in distant regions, the analyst must reflect those conditions in his model or risk producing misleading results.

Procedures

1. Define a set of regions relevant to the locational problem you are interested in. Regions that conform to existing political boundaries

such as counties are usually the most practical because most data sources are organized along political units.

2. Define a set of independent economic and social variables related to the success of the tourist business being studied. Collect data for each of these variables in each of the regions identified. Also determine the number of firms located in the region.

3. If data for a large number of variables have been collected and if some of these variables appear to be correlated with each other, you can reduce the data set through factor analysis. This will produce a small set of statistically independent variables.

4. Using standard multiple regression, regress the dependent variable (the actual number of businesses) against the independent variables. Obtain estimates of the number of firms expected in each region.

5. Compare the estimated and actual numbers of firms to obtain residuals (observed – estimated).

6. Some small residuals in the model are to be expected (no social science model is perfect). A tolerance interval needs to be defined to indicate whether any particular residual is 'small' and not worth comment or is 'large' and potentially meaningful. A convenient confidence interval is plus or minus one standard deviation. Any region with a residual within one standard deviation of the mean residual (which will be zero for a least-squares estimation) might safely be ignored; i.e. it can be interpreted as indicating a region near equilibrium.

7. Identify any regions that have unusually large residuals, perhaps greater than plus or minus three standard deviations. These extreme values are outliers that can significantly distort the results of the regression analysis (remember the effect of the very large values of intraprovincial travel in Ontario and the unusually high r^2 as described on page 119). Temporarily remove these from your data set.

8. Once any outliers have been removed, rerun the regression analysis and calculate new residuals. Also calculate the expected number of firms and the residuals for those regions that were removed in the last step because they were identified as outliers. This may be done by using your new regression model and substituting the appropriate values of the independent variables, and then solving for the dependent variable. Note any regions that now have residuals greater than plus or minus one standard deviation. Any region that has significantly fewer businesses than predicted, indicated by a negative residual greater than −1.0, may be interpreted as having the potential for an expansion of that business type. A region with significantly more businesses than predicted will have a positive residual in excess of 1.0,

and may be interpreted as having more businesses than local economic conditions can support – possibly leading to a 'shake-out'. All other regions are near equilibrium and are unlikely to experience significant growth or decline in the number of firms in the near future.

Example

An example of this type of analysis can be found in Smith and Thomas (1983). In a study of the potential for expansion in the number of golf-courses in southern Ontario, they began by identifying 34 demographic

Table 6.4 Independent variables selected for analysis

Variable label		Age (years)
001	Total number of males:	0–14
002		15–24
003		25–34
004		35–49
005		50–64
006		65+
007	Total number of females:	0–14
008		15–24
009		25–34
010		35–49
011		50–64
012		65+
013	Percentage of males between:	0–14
014		15–24
015		25–34
016		35–49
017		50–64
018		65+
019	Percentage of females between:	0–14
020		15–24
021		25–34
022		35–49
023		50–64
024		65+
025	Total number of tax returns showing taxable incomes over $30 000	
026	Urban/rural population ratio	
027	Total personal disposable income	
028	Number of licensed restaurants	
029	Number of licensed private clubs	
030	Population density	
031	Population	
032	Number of households	
033	Percentage of labour force employed in: management/administration	
034	Percentage of labour force employed in: farming/forestry/mining	

Source: Smith and Thomas 1983.

Table 6.5 Principal factor analysis loadings (highest loadings only)

Variable label[†]	Factor 1	Factor 2	Factor 3	Factor 4	Factor 5
001	0.974				
002	0.981				
003	0.983				
004	0.983				
005	0.989				
006	0.986				
007	−0.974				
008	−0.983				
009	−0.972				
010	0.986				
011	−0.988				
012	−0.909				
013			−0.848		
014					0.891
015			−0.760		
016			−0.766		
017			−0.900		
018			−0.727		
019			0.802		
020					−0.809
021			0.815		
022			0.888		
023			0.948		
024			0.779		
025		0.902			
026		0.954			
027		0.969			
028		0.973			
029		0.889			
030		0.937			
031		0.973			
032		0.974			
033				0.750	
034				−0.817	

Source: Smith and Thomas 1983.
[†] See Table 6.4 for interpretation of label numbers.

and social variables they believed were related to the demand for golf-courses (Table 6.4). Several of these variables were highly correlated with each other, so the authors used factor analysis to reduce the list of 34 variables to 5 independent factors (Table 6.5). The factor scores for each county were regressed against the number of golf-courses in each county. The first regression resulted in the identification of 7 counties out of 43 that were outliers. These were removed from the

Table 6.6 Number of golf-courses (observed and predicted) for southern Ontario counties, 1977)

County	Observed	Predicted	Residual	Status†
Dundas	1	2.3	− 1.3	
Frontenac	5	6.2	− 1.2	
Glengarry	0	2.7	− 2.7	Under
Grenville	1	3.7	− 2.7	Under
Hastings	6	4.5	1.5	
Lanark	4	4.9	− 0.9	
Leeds	6	3.3	2.7	Over
Lennox/Addington	1	2.2	− 1.2	
Ottawa	21	16.7	4.3	Over
Prescott	2	2.9	− 0.9	
Renfrew	1	4.2	− 3.2	Under
Russell	1	1.2	− 0.2	
Stormont	2	3.9	− 1.9	
Brant	6	5.2	0.8	
Dufferin	1	1.1	− 0.1	
Haldimand/Norfolk	5	3.5	1.5	
Hamilton/Wentworth	13	12.8	0.2	
Muskoka	8	4.5	3.5	Over
Northumberland	4	4.6	− 0.6	
Peel	11	11.8	− 0.8	
Peterborough	7	5.7	1.3	
Victoria	3	4.9	− 1.9	
Waterloo	13	9.4	3.6	Over
Wellington	5	5.1	− 0.1	
York	34	36.2	− 2.2	Under
Bruce	5	4.1	0.9	
Elgin	3	4.8	− 1.8	
Essex	10	10.4	− 0.4	
Grey	5	3.6	1.4	
Huron	5	3.3	1.7	
Kent	6	5.0	1.0	
Middlesex	11	10.6	0.4	
Oxford	4	3.6	0.4	
Perth	3	4.8	− 1.8	
Parry Sound	1	2.4	− 1.4	
Durham‡	17	4.7	12.3	Over
Haliburton‡	1	5.0	− 4.0	Under
Halton‡	16	6.7	9.3	Over
Niagara‡	21	11.4	8.6	Over
Simcoe‡	19	7.8	11.2	Over
Ontario‡	9	25.1	−16.1	Under
Lambton‡	11	5.4	5.6	Over

Source: Smith and Thomas 1983.

† Indicates probable over- or underdevelopment.

‡ Indicates outliers removed during second stage of regression.

data set and the regression repeated. The second multiple regression analysis produced the following equation:

$$Y = 6.573 + 1.443(X_1) + 1.223(X_2) + 0.513(X_3) + 0.727(X_4) - 0.175(X_5) \quad [6.1]$$

where: Y = number of golf-courses;
X_n = factor scores for the five factors.

The R^2 for this equation was 91.6 per cent, which suggests that the model structure is adequate and that the most important causal variables were included by the researchers.

Residuals were calculated using the actual and predicted number of golf-courses. Table 6.6 is a summary of the residual patterns.

Inductive reasoning

Description

Inductive reasoning, in the context of location choice, is more a research strategy than a specific technique. It is, in fact, the 'textbook' approach to empirical scientific investigation, including tourism analysis. As such, it deserves an entire book to itself. Given the relatively poor state of theoretical development in tourism and in locational modelling, however, there is still value in introducing the topic here.

Simply put, inductive reasoning is generalization. One observes systematically a number of occurrences of some phenomenon and works towards a generalized explanation of the process behind that pattern. Induction is not proof; it can never produce irrefutable laws. It is only the collection of evidence and the making of inferences from that evidence in support of a conclusion. Induction cannot exclude the possibility that any conclusion, however plausible, is false.

Induction is a slow and uncertain way of developing a locational model because it depends ultimately on the intuitive ability of the analyst to recognize a potentially meaningful pattern and to sense the possible cause of that pattern. That intuition may be wrong; even if the intuition is right, the interpretation of the cause of the pattern could be wrong. There is no 'cookbook' method of enquiry or set of inferential statistics that can be easily and directly applied to the inductive search for meaning. This type of enquiry is sometimes described as basic research. In basic research, positive results are not guaranteed. If successful, though, the discoveries of such enquiry can become an important part of social science understanding and knowledge.

Much of the potential for success in this research design depends on the researcher acquiring as much background knowledge about the phenomenon as possible. You must immerse yourself in the problem, exploring and reading widely on the subject-matter to collect ideas, references, and insights. Work on inductive model-building will tend to go on for a relatively long period of time, easily a year and perhaps a decade. This time will be characterized by periods of intense activity of data collection and analysis followed by periods of quiet reflection when the project is put on 'the back burner'.

If a researcher has the curiosity, time, and necessary skill to undertake this type of research. it can be an absorbing, rewarding, long-term project. If, on the other hand, the motivation for a site-selection project is to solve an immediate problem, some other procedure should be seriously considered.

Procedures

1. Begin with a question. This is not as trivial as it sounds. Induction can lead to an hypothesis only when you have a sense that there may be some meaningful pattern hidden in what, at first glance, appears to be an incoherent set of data. The way that belief is operationalized is by formulating a research question that defines some sort of goal to direct the research. For locational choice research the question will often be couched in terms relevant to regularities in pattern and process behind existing business locations.

2. Carefully define the units of observation. What types of businesses are you interested in? Are there several categories of the same type of business that should be treated separately? On what scale – neighbourhood, community, regional, provincial, national – should data be collected? Should data be collected from many regions at one point in time or should you concentrate on one region over time?

3. Systematically observe and record the observations defined in step 2. One or more maps will be useful as a supplement to tabulations of addresses and other locational characteristics. Some of the descriptive measures in Chapter 8, such as nearest-neighbour analysis or Lorenz curves, may also be useful.

4. Compare the observed locational patterns with the patterns of other phenomena. The location of ski resorts might be compared with patterns of snowfall, topography, access roads, population, and other types of resorts. Urban hotels might be examined in comparison with

traffic volumes on major urban arterials, visitor attractions, and airports.

5. Using any spatial correlations observed in step 4, other models of locational development, analogies, and any other potential source of ideas or inspiration, develop tentative hypotheses about the processes that give rise to the patterns observed. An important talent in this task is to be able to abstract the patterns enough to get a generalized or 'ideal' pattern without getting caught up in trying to explain every minor detail.

6. Use the hypotheses developed in step 5 to make predictions about the locational patterns to be expected in similar regions. Collect data from those regions and compare the observed pattern with the predicted. Verify the degree of accuracy of your hypotheses and make any modifications in them to account for significant discrepancies. Again, an ability is needed for recognizing the difference between insignificant and significant anomalies.

7. After the revised hypotheses have been tested in several different circumstances, and have been found to be valid, formulate a tentative theory formalizing the processes. This can then be scrutinized and tested by other researchers, which will ultimately lead to a better understanding of some important aspects of tourism development.

Example

An example of inductive reasoning may be found in Smith (1983). In this study the author was interested in identifying some of the forces that influenced restaurant location. More precisely, the author was curious about whether certain types of locations were 'better' for certain types of restaurants in the sense that restaurants located in such places were more likely to succeed than those located elsewhere. Smith began by mapping every restaurant and related dining establishments (e.g. bars and coffee-shops) in a study city. The initial pattern was hard to interpret. There was some clustering, some dispersal, but no consistent pattern. Figure 6.3 is an illustration of the type of pattern observed. When the restaurants were divided into specific types, and each type mapped separately, some meaningful patterns began to emerge.

These patterns were compared with land uses, street networks, and other aspects of the urban environment. Several spatial correlations appeared that seemed plausible. For example, pizza parlours tended to locate on moderately busy streets (annual average daily traffic counts of 10 000 to 15 000 vehicles) that delineated major residential areas.

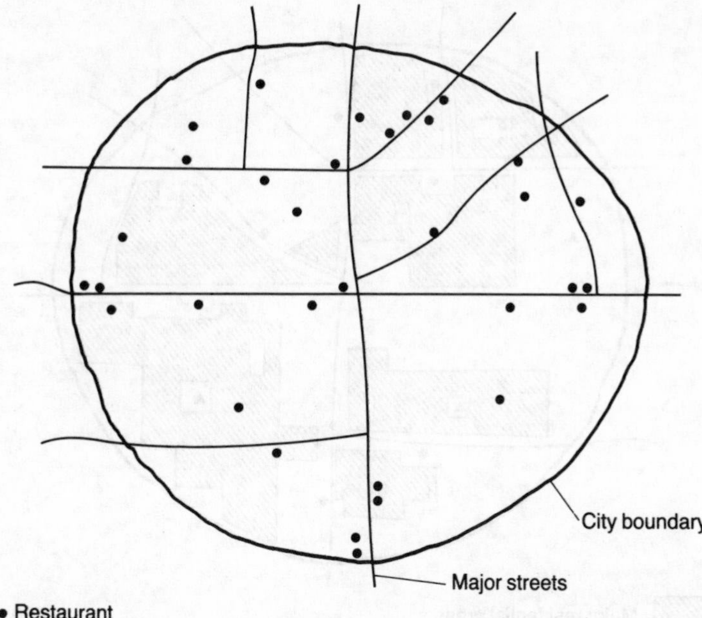

Fig. 6.3 Hypothetical locational patterns for several restaurant types

Pizza parlours also showed a tendency to disperse from each other, forming a 'necklace' around neighbourhoods (Fig. 6.4). Certainly this description does not perfectly describe pizza parlour locations, but the general pattern – reflecting an interaction of spatial competition and the need for high visibility, high traffic counts, and easy accessibility – appears valid.

Similar types of analyses were conducted for all other types of dining establishments, including ice-cream parlours (which tend to locate inside residential areas in locations with high levels of pedestrian traffic and near major shopping centres), fast-food outlets (which agglomerate on heavily travelled streets), and doughnut stores (which locate near fast-food outlets and avoid locating near other doughnut stores). These patterns are summarized in Figs 6.4 and 6.5. They were also formally expressed as a series of testable hypotheses that were examined in the light of data drawn from eight different cities. The results of that testing showed that several of the hypotheses appeared to be fairly accurate while several others needed rewording. This work eventually led to a preliminary articulation of locational principles for restaurants.

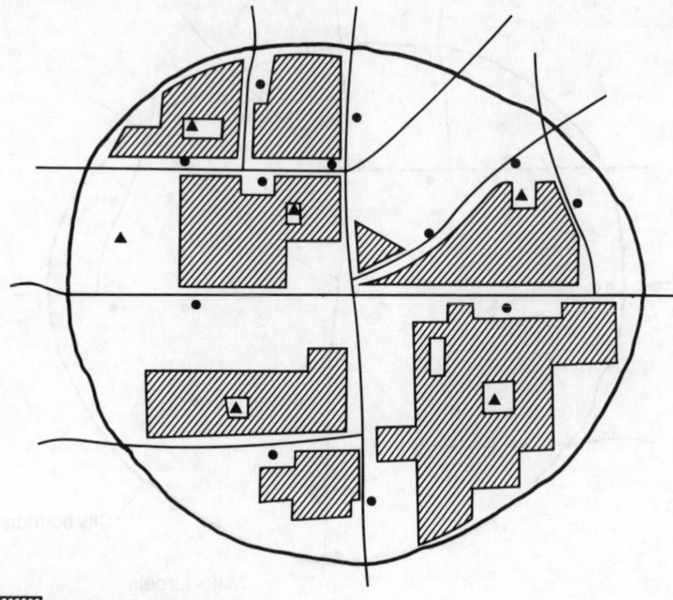

Fig. 6.4 Hypothetical locational patterns for pizza parlours and ice-cream stores

Summary

The adage that the three most important factors to consider in the establishment of a business are location, location, and location oversimplifies the complex problem of understanding the forces that influence business success. Location is certainly not the only decision a business planner must make; it is doubtful whether it is even among the more important. But it is far from being negligible.

The question of location in business may be expressed two ways. You can start with some particular business and then seek a good location, or you can begin with a location and then decide which type of business is most suitable for that location. We have concentrated on the first perspective in this chapter. It is probably the more common of the two, and it is the most relevant here because we are looking only at tourism businesses. With the general type of business already specified, the task is to find the best type of location.

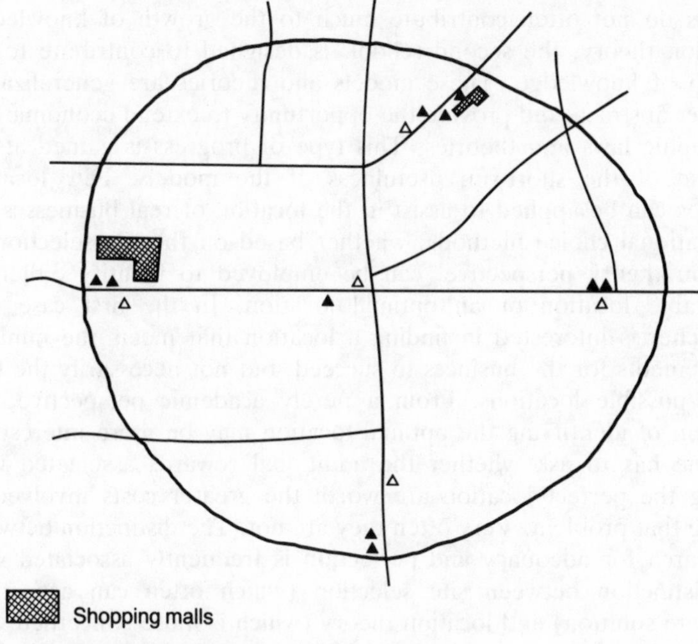

Fig. 6.5 Hypothetical locational patterns for fast-food restaurants and doughnut shops

Our methods and examples in this chapter concern the location of a single business operation. This is arguably the most common context for location decisions. One should note, however, that many location decisions in tourism involve the location of multiple units of a large franchise operation. The criteria used for selecting the site can be very different depending on whether the decision-maker is working for a single independent business, is a franchise holder with one or more operations, or is a franchisor concerned with maximizing the profitability of the entire chain. Zeller, Achabal, and Brown (1980) discuss some of the potential conflicts in site selection arising from these different viewpoints.

Location models designed to identify which location is best for a particular type of business belong to two different schools. One is the site-selection school. Site-selection methods are designed to provide quick, reliable, useful results for specific questions about specific businesses. The orientation is decidedly practical, and as a result, the models do not often contribute much to the growth of knowledge. Location theory, the second school, is designed to contribute to the growth of knowledge. These models and theories are generalizable, flexible, abstract, and provide the opportunity to extend economic and geographic laws and theories. This type of progress is gained at the expense of the short-run usefulness of the models. Few location theories can be applied to assist in the location of real businesses.

Locational choice methods, whether based on the site-selection or location theory perspective, can be employed to identify either an acceptable location or an optimal location. In the first case, the researcher is interested in finding a location that meets the minimal requirements for the business to succeed, but not necessarily the best of all possible locations. From a purely academic perspective, the problem of identifying the optimal location may be more interesting, but one has to ask whether the additional rewards associated with finding the perfect location are worth the greater costs involved in solving that problem. Very often they are not. The distinction between the search for adequacy and perfection is frequently associated with the distinction between site selection (which often can accept an adequate solution) and location theory (which is more concerned with finding the perfect location). You will need to decide yourself which is more appropriate for your project.

Finally, the locational methods described here do not normally include variables such as purchase price, terms of a lease, deed restrictions, and various financial aspects of site selection. These considerations can be introduced in the checklist method, as they were in our example, but they are not always present. This omission should not be taken to imply that researchers are hopelessly naive about the financial facts of life. The explanation for the omission, when it occurs, is usually a practical one. Much site-selection research demands that the researcher concentrate on selected aspects of potential sites and make assumptions about other aspects. For example, a planner working for a proposed ski resort might be concerned about soil stability and slope, but will probably ignore soil fertility and water content. He assumes that when it comes time to landscape the resort, someone else can resolve any problems about the suitability of the soil for plants by careful selection of ornamentals or by importing topsoil or soil conditioners. In the case of business location and development, most social scientists are more interested in social and economic variables, assuming (usually correctly) that when it is time to get down to the business decision itself, financial concerns will be worked out in a thoroughly business-like manner.

So although the ideals of rational comprehensive planning and research might lead one to wish that a site-selection researcher would also be able to make recommendations regarding purchase or lease negotiations of the sites he identifies, a realistic assessment of the business skills of most social scientists would lead the business decision-maker to rely on financial advisers for contract negotiations. In turn, one can also remember that very few financial and real estate experts have the scientific ability to undertake and successfully complete the original research needed before one should even consider making an offer on a site.

Further reading

Applebaum W 1968 Store characteristics and operating performance. In Kornlau C (ed.) *Guide to store location research*. Addison-Wesley, Reading, Mass.

Arbel A and **Pizam A** 1977 Some determinants of urban hotel location: the tourists' inclinations. *Journal of Travel Research* **15**(3): 18–22.

Collins C O 1979 Site and situation strategy in tourism planning: a Mexican case study. *Annals of Tourism Research* **6**: 351–66.

Epstein B J 1971 Geography and the business of retail site evaluation and selection. *Economic Geography* **47**: 191–9.

Gearing C E and **Var T** 1977 The site selection problem in touristic feasibility reports. *Tourist Review* **32**(2): 9–16.

Ghosh A and **Craigh C S** 1983 Formulating retail location strategy in a changing environment. *Journal of Marketing* **47**(Summer): 56–68.

Gruen C and **Gruen N J** 1966 *Store location and customer behavior*. Technical Bulletin 56. Urban Land Institute, Washington, DC.

Hodgson J N 1973 The feasibility study: determining the investment potential of a new Hotel. *The Cornell Hotel and Restaurant Quarterly* Nov: 13–31.

Mason J B and **Mayer M L** 1981 *Modern retailing theory and practice*. Business Publications, Plano, Tex.

CHAPTER 7

Defining the geographic structure of the industry

Introduction

Tourism is an industry with substantial geographic content. Its very nature involves travel and a sense of place. Tourists leave 'here' and visit 'there'. That may sound trivial, but the ability to describe precisely the difference between 'here' and 'there' is not trivial or always easy. This task of defining places is a prerequisite for much data collection, planning, and marketing effort in tourism. We examine in this chapter some of the tools used for describing the geographic structure of tourism. These tools are generically labelled as regionalization methods because a common product of their application is the definition of tourism regions. We will begin our review by defining regionalization more fully. We then turn to some of the basic uses of regionalization, different types of regions, regionalization logic, basic principles of regionalization, and some applications of regionalization work in tourism. Finally, we examine five methods in detail.

Definitions and goals of regionalization

Regionalization is areal classification. It is the defining of one or more areas on the face of the earth in order to identify them as separate entities. The process of definition involves both 'integration' and 'differentiation'. Integration here refers to the identification of some internal integrity (or homogeneity) in the region on the basis of selected features, while differentiation refers to the process of distinguishing between regions on the basis of those same features. If the features chosen for defining a system of regions are related to some aspect of tourism development, then each region may be referred to as a 'tourism region'. A few authors, though, have suggested that the phrase, 'tourism region', should be used more restrictively. Gunn

(1976), for example, has argued that the only regions that should be considered as true tourism regions are those: (1) located at some distance away from potential visitors; (2) seen as potential destination areas; (3) having a reasonable accessibility to a potential market; (4) having some minimum level of economic and social infrastructure that can support tourism development; and (5) large enough to contain more than just one community. Gunn's concept of a region is useful for certain purposes; indeed, it is discussed later in this chapter as the basis for destination zone identification. His concept, however, may be too narrow to be a useful, general definition of tourism regions. The basic problem is that Gunn's requirements would often eliminate many locations that tourism planners will want to study – locations that are important for tourism planning and development even though they do not meet all of the definitional criteria proposed by Gunn. For our purposes, therefore, a tourism region is simply a contiguous area on the face of the earth that has been explicitly delineated by a researcher, planner, or public official as having relevance for some aspect of tourism planning, development, or analysis.

The specific purposes for delimiting tourism regions are numerous, but they can be grouped into three broad goals:

1. *Regionalization assists in naming part of the world*. When an analyst or planner wants to talk about some part of the world, whether as an origin, a popular destination, or perhaps as a region that has no potential ever to attract tourists (if any exist), it helps to be able to attach a label to that area. Marketing experts also know the value of labels. Names not only help them organize their work and to improve communication, names can be used to promote destinations. For example, the Ministry of Tourism and Recreation of the province of Ontario, Canada, has labelled a group of counties in midwestern Ontario as 'Festival Country' because of the relatively large number of local and national festivals and special events held there year-round. 'Midwestern Ontario' would be an accurate label for the same group of counties, but it lacks that certain appeal that would draw the attention of a tourist browsing through a brochure on Ontario vacations. The points to be made here are two: (1) a person with a job to do usually finds it necessary to name the things he works with, including things like regions; and (2) the choice of names, if done carefully and imaginatively, can sometimes make the job of marketing much easier.

2. *Regionalization helps to simplify and order knowledge*. No individual can ever hope to know all relevant tourism facts and relationships about every place on earth. Regionalization provides a type of intellectual shorthand that simplifies and orders knowledge about

diverse places. Instead of trying to remember all the details about hundreds of Caribbean islands, many of which are similar, it is of help to be able to talk about them as examples of one category – the Caribbean region. Using the same logic, tourism planning and development in the European Alps, for instance, is simplified by our being able to discuss the Alps as a region composed of many locales that share essential characteristics. If we could not do this, we would have to treat every place on earth independently; this would greatly increase the cost and lower the efficiency of planning.

This use of regionalization does not imply that there are no differences among Alpine locales or Caribbean islands. Rather it merely indicates that for some purposes the benefits of grouping places together outweigh the disadvantages of ignoring their differences. The relative size of the region and the degree to which internal differences among specific places within a region can be ignored will depend on the purposes of the regionalization.

3. *Regions permit inductive generalization and predictions to be made*. Regions can be compared with each other to learn more about what relationships and characteristics are important for tourism development. Gunn (1979), for example, has identified certain structural relationships in tourism regions that he believed were important factors contributing to the success of those regions. If his hypotheses are correct, then one can make predictions about the potential success of other regions as possible tourism destinations on the basis of whether they possess those characteristics.

Before examining types of regions, it may be worth while to consider one use that is not an appropriate objective of regionalization: the development of regions, *per se*. The identification of regions is a means, not an end. There is no point in assigning a label to a region if nothing more is implied than a regional name. This does not contradict the first use of regionalization – the assigning of names. It means only that the names themselves must be needed to accomplish some larger task. Looking at this from another perspective, this caveat against regionalizing for its own sake implies that regions do not really exist as separate entities in the real world. If they did, then a perfectly acceptable scholarly objective for tourism analysts would be to identify and name as many tourism regions as possible, just as chemists search for new elements and compounds or taxonomic biologists discover and label new species. Unlike chemicals or species, tourism regions do not exist in themselves; they are created for, and only for, some larger purpose.

Types of regions

Three fundamental types of regions are generally recognized: (1) *a priori*; (2) homogeneous; and (3) functional. The first type is perhaps the most common and is, in many ways, the simplest to develop. An *a priori* region is essentially an area on the face of the earth around which someone arbitrarily draws a line and assigns a name. Its existence can be thought of almost as a 'given'. It is not the result of a methodical regionalization; rather it is the intuitive beginning of other tasks. The best-known example of *a priori* regionalization is political division. Most political units are defined on the basis of political advantage, tradition, history, conquest, or convenient natural boundaries such as rivers or coastlines. They are rarely based on a scientific analysis of internal structure. Many tourism regions defined by provincial or state governments or by the tourism industry are also the result of *a priori* regionalization. As with political divisions, many tourism regions are not based on objective analysis, but the intuition or political preferences of a single individual or a committee charged with defining the regions. This makes such regions unreliable for planning, marketing, and research purposes because they lack a reliable foundation.

A homogeneous region is a region defined by a set of objective, internal similarities. The important issues associated with defining a homogeneous region include the selection of the relevant characteristics and specification of the degree of similarity that would cause a locale to be included in a region. Homogeneous regions are the type of region most planners and researchers think of when they hear the term, 'region'; they may also be viewed as the model for *a priori* regionalization – but there is a major difference. The difference is that homogeneous regions are defined on the basis of the objective determination of regional characteristics; *a priori* regions are not.

The third type of region is the functional region. This is an area that has a high degree of internal interaction. For example, people who live in proximity to each other often tend to subscribe to the same newspaper. A map of the subscribers to a particular paper will define a region based solely on the circulation of that paper. The location and extent of this region might be of interest to competing newspapers or to retailers interested in advertising in certain neighbourhoods. Nothing is implied about the internal homogeneity of the people in that region beyond their subscriptions to a particular newspaper. Other functional regions can be defined on the basis of banking flows, spatial patterns of wholesale trade, vacation travel patterns, or of support for a particular athletic team.

Types of regionalization logic

We have identified three reasons for regionalization and three types of regions. Coincidentally there are also three basic types of logic used in regionalization. Each logic can be applied to define any of the three types of regions and for any of the three reasons. The basic logics are: (1) synthetic; (2) analytic; and (3) dichotomous regionalization. Actual regionalization methods will use one or a combination of these logics. Synthetic regionalization (also known as agglomerative or ascending regionalization) begins with small spatial units, perhaps townships or counties, and proceeds by combining contiguous and similar units. The extent of the synthesis depends on both the inherent similarity of relevant characteristics and on the degree of regional homogeneity desired by the analyst. If a province were composed of 10 000 spatial units, the logic of synthetic regionalization would begin with 10 000 regions of one unit each. The process would continue through successive combinations of increasingly different units until one region of 10 000 units was produced. The initial pattern is one of many regions with a high degree of homogeneity in each while the final pattern is one region with minimal homogeneity. The optimal solution is usually somewhere between these extremes. This form of synthetic regionalization might be more precisely described as areal-based synthetic regionalization.

A second form of this general logic is point-based regionalization. In this case data for discrete points located across a broad area of the earth's surface are obtained and then generalized to represent the entire area, perhaps by the production of a contour map. Regions are defined by delineating all parts of the map where data fall into specified ranges (see, e.g. Dorney 1976).

Figure 7.1 is an illustration of the basic process of synthetic regionalization. Note how a large number of small units are gradually incorporated into a smaller number of increasingly general regions. In the case represented by Fig. 7.1, ten individual spatial units (called the 'first-order regions' because they are the lowest level of regionalization) are grouped into four second-order regions. These are grouped, in turn, into two third-order regions. Finally, the third-order regions are agglomerated into one fourth-order region. The number of orders will vary with the regional system being developed, but in all cases a hierarchy of regions will be developed. The analyst may be interested

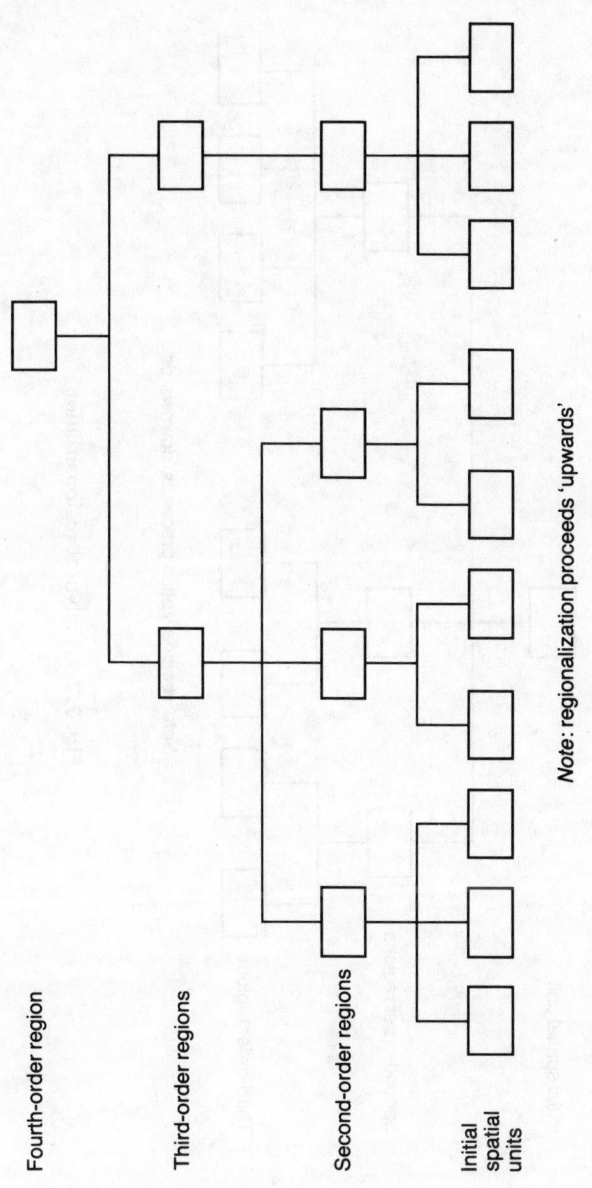

Note: regionalization proceeds 'upwards'

Fig. 7.1 Synthetic regionalization

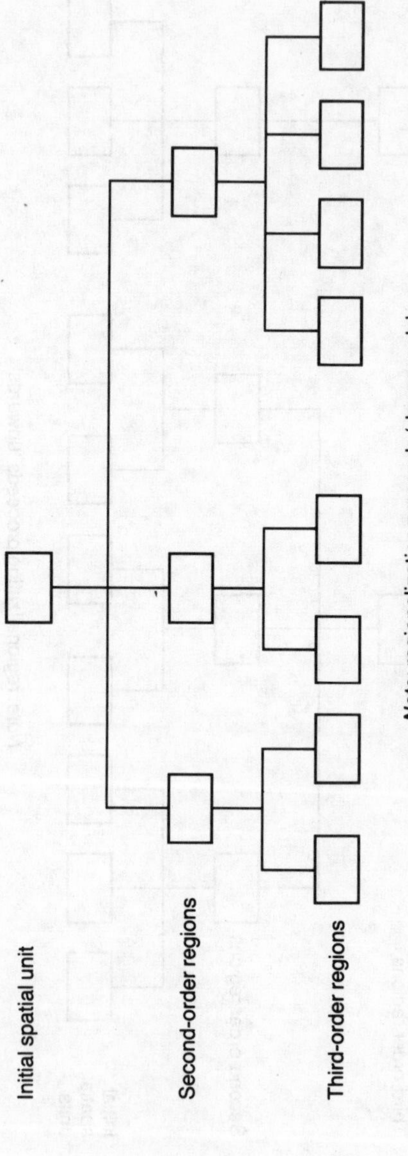

Note: regionalization proceeds 'downwards'

Fig. 7.2 Analytical regionalization

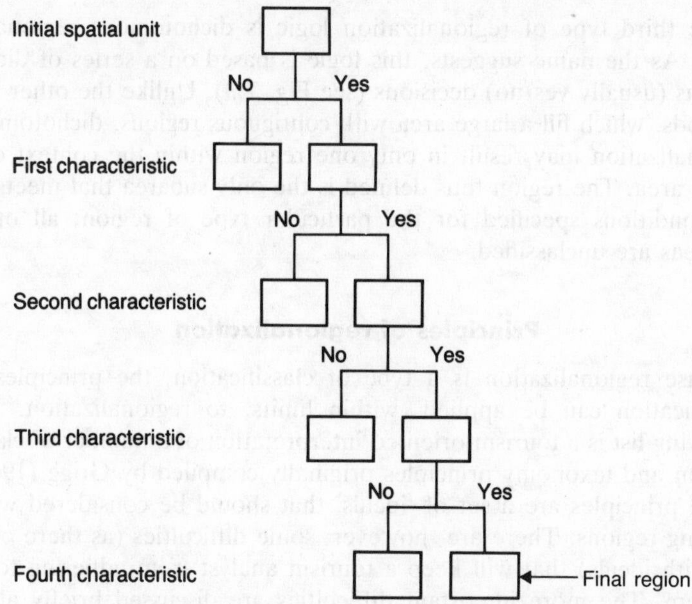

Fig. 7.3 Dichotomous regionalization

either in the entire hierarchy or in the pattern at only one level of the hierarchy.

Analytic regionalization begins with a relatively large area that is divided into smaller and smaller regions. This procedure is also known as deglomerative or descending regionalization. It is, in effect, the opposite of synthetic regionalization (see Fig. 7.2). The results of either procedure are the same: a hierarchy of spatial units defined in terms of greater or lesser homogeneity. Tourism analysts have thus far generally limited their use of analytic regionalization logic to examining natural resource distributions. For example, analytic regions are found in geomorphological or vegetative hierarchical systems used to describe the natural resources systems that can support the outdoor recreation industry in certain areas of the world. One such example is the Canada Land Inventory System (Coombs and Thie 1979). The main reason for the limited use of analytic logic in tourism is that the procedure requires a theoretical base upon which to base the structure of the agglomerative hierarchy. Such theoretical knowledge has yet to be broadly developed in tourism.

The third type of regionalization logic is dichotomous regionalization. As the name suggests, this logic is based on a series of dichotomous (usually yes/no) decisions (see Fig. 7.3). Unlike the other two methods, which fill a large area with contiguous regions, dichotomous regionalization may result in only one region within the context of a larger area. The region thus defined is the only subarea that meets all the conditions specified for the particular type of region; all other subareas are unclassified.

Principles of regionalization

Because regionalization is a type of classification, the principles of classification can be applied, within limits, to regionalization. The following list is a tourism-oriented interpretation of a number of classification and taxonomy principles originally compiled by Grigg (1965). These principles are a set of 'ideals' that should be considered when defining regions. There are, however, some difficulties (as there often are with ideals) that will keep a tourism analyst from adhering to all of them. The more important difficulties are discussed briefly along with the specific principles.

1. *Regional systems should be specific to the problem at hand*. The system developed should be based on a set of criteria and methods appropriate to the task before the analyst. A regional system developed for one tourism problem will rarely work well for another problem.

2. *Areas on earth that differ fundamentally in kind should not be subjected to the same regionalization procedure*. Many areas differ from each other in the degree to which they possess certain attributes – they will belong to different regions, but they still possess the same general set of characteristics. Other areas, however, will be so different they simply cannot be accommodated in one regional system: land versus water areas, for example. An oceanic regional system would make no sense applied to land areas. The point is to be sure of the appropriateness of whatever system you develop for all the areas to which you intend to apply it.

3. *Regionalizations should be changed as one gains a better understanding of the areas classified*. This principle may sound like common sense, but there are two difficulties that must be recognized. Although most analysts would like to keep their regional systems up to date, there is also a need to maintain some degree of stability within those systems. Regionalizations form a basis for subsequent work, so chaos

would ensue if the basis for a large body of planning of research work were changed too frequently.

The other problem is that the very nature of tourism regions changes over time. Not only do we learn more about regions, the regions themselves change. The effect of this is to add pressure to alter fundamentally the regional system, not just update the system. Some trade-off is needed between ensuring that a regional system reflects current conditions and constant tinkering that would prevent longitudinal studies.

4. *Regionaltzations of places should be based on properties of those places*. This principle, too, may sound self-evident, yet Grigg observes that it is one of the most frequently violated principles in areal classification. The problem occurs when the analyst tries to base a regional system on a model of the genesis of the phenomenon being studied. For example, many soil and agricultural regions are based on climatic conditions that are believed to affect soil and agriculture, and not on the actual characteristics of soil or crops. The results have been a large number of regional systems that have failed to serve their intended purpose. We will see later an example of this problem in tourism where a research team defined tourism regions on the basis of tourist behaviour but intended the system to be used as a regional organization strategy by the tourism industry. Even if there is some strong underlying force that influences the characteristics of the places you are studying, it is better to base your regions on the characteristics themselves rather than on the underlying forces.

5. *Regional divisions should be exhaustive*. Although this is a widely held principle in general classification, its relevance to tourism can be challenged. The issue here is whether there are places that a tourism analyst would consider non-regions. If the regional characteristics used for classification are a series of climatic variables, the regional system would presumably divide the entire earth's surface into regions, because all areas have climate. On the other hand, if the regions are defined as those places that are capable of supporting tourism development, many places would conceivably not be classified at all as development regions.

6. *Regional divisions should be exclusive*. The same place cannot be logically assigned to two separate regions. The characteristics used to define regions must be chosen carefully to make sure no inconsistency would violate this principle. In practice, such a violation will usually be obvious and can be corrected by a careful restatement of the relevant criteria.

7. *Regionalizations based on the analytic or synthetic procedures should use only one differentiating characteristic at each level of division, and each differentiating characteristic must be related logically to the characteristics at the next higher and the next lower level.* The first part of this principle indicates that, in hierarchical classification, the divisions made at any level of the hierarchy must be based on the same characteristics across the level. For example, one might begin to define tourism regions in a country on the basis of the predominant type of tourist attractions: wilderness, big cities, wine-producing areas, beaches and coastal recreation. One might then observe that each of these divisions implied other divisions or correlates. Wilderness areas might be found in interior, mountainous places; big cities may be found on the lowlands and near international boundaries; wine-producing regions may be located in a hilly, fertile agricultural region; and beaches and coastal recreation areas may be located primarily in the southern part of the country. There may be a temptation in the next level of the hierarchy to include geomorphology (mountains versus lowlands versus hills), land use (agriculture versus urban development), and relative positions (southern versus northern or interior versus coastal) all in the same level of the hierarchy. It should be apparent that a usable and logical regionalization could not be achieved by trying to incorporate all these features at the same level.

The second part of this principle indicates that one must be careful in the choice of criteria used at subsequent levels. To continue our example, if the first level of regionalization were based on the predominant type of attraction, the next level should be based on some characteristic that makes logical subdivisions of the four original classes. The level of existing development would be one possible characteristic. In contrast, dividing the four attraction classes into geomorphological subunits would not be a logical choice.

8. *The characteristics used for regionalization should be relevant to the purposes of regionalization*. Application of this apparently obvious principle requires ultimately assessment of the importance of potential regional features. This depends, in turn, on your having a sound understanding of the ultimate purpose of doing the regionalization. A system of tourism regions based on geomorphological landforms might be relevant for a project to identify potential areas for ski resorts, but it would not be especially helpful or meaningful if the problem were to plan for urban conventions.

9. *Characteristics that are used to define regions at the more general levels should be more important than the characteristics used to define regions at more specific levels*. This principle is related to the preceding one. When two or more characteristics are to be used to define

regions, the divisions should be made initially on the most important regional characteristic. It is not possible to give a fixed ranking of the relative importance of different criteria. This decision has to be made for each separate classification exercise. But the basic point is that you should begin the regional classification with the most important features and then further refine the regional divisions with successively less important features.

With regard to the question of selecting and ordering characteristics, you should be aware of the tendency of the number of regions to grow exponentially with the number of characteristics and the number of classes of each characteristic. If you had a regional system based on five characteristics with five classes each, analytic regionalization would produce $5^{(5-1)} = 625$ regions. The need to be conservative in the choice of the number of characteristics and classes should be evident.

10. *The use of more than one differentiating characteristic in either analytic or synthetic regionalization produces a hierarchy*. The existence of hierarchies in regionalization has been mentioned many times already; what is at stake here is whether or not the hierarchy is valid. Any regional hierarchy is valid if and only if the preceding principles have been observed. Failure to do so may result in an ambiguous or meaningless hierarchy. Logical validity, though, is not enough. Hierarchical classifications are representative of reality in the case of biological taxonomy, but one can raise doubts as to whether any tourism regional hierarchy is truly representative of anything. They may be no more than an artefact of a researcher's statistical procedures.

These ten principles could be supplemented by an eleventh: 'The first ten principles will be subject to pragmatic needs.' As we have suggested in our opening comments, there are some practical difficulties in adhering strictly to all these ideals. When regionalization is only an early step in a much larger planning process, it is unlikely the analyst will have the inclination to spend much time or money on regionalization alone. At best, these guidelines should alert you to potential dangers in the development of a regional system. With these in mind, you can make acceptable trade-offs between the demands of practical regionalization in tourism and the ideals of regionalization logic.

Regionalization in tourism research

Before moving to a discussion of some specific regionalization procedures, it may be helpful to examine some practical uses of regionalization in tourism to add some degree of 'reality' to the preceding general discussion of regionalization principles. Analysts define and use regions for many purposes in tourism: marketing, administration, promotion, planning, and research. One subject in which regionalization plays a significant but often unrecognized role is the evaluation of tourism impacts. Good or ill, the effects of tourism development are limited in space. Further, the nature and degree of those effects varies greatly from place to place as a function of regional conditions such as the size and complexity of the local economy, the number of tourists, the size of the host population, and the cultural context of development. Redefine or change the scale of a region wherein impacts are being studied and you change the conclusions drawn from those impacts. Some studies that have recognized the importance of regional differences or regional definitions include Pizam's (1978) study on social costs of development in tourism regions, Becker's (1979) analysis of regional conflicts between tourists on the Upper Mississippi, Ellerbrock and Hite's (1980) study of regional employment levels in tourism, Jud and Krause's (1976) paper on concepts and methods for evaluating tourism in developing areas, and Cooke's (1982) look at social capacity in different parts of British Columbia.

In the above studies, regionalization is a variable used to explain how one group of people perceive what is happening to them and their part of the world. This perspective can be turned around, allowing regionalization to be used as one variable explaining how different groups of people perceive other parts of the world. Woodside and Sherrell (1977) and Ehemann (1977) provide illustrations of this approach. Each author developed a model explaining variations in perceptions of potential tourist destinations by focusing on one or more groups of potential tourists in their origin regions.

A similar use of regional perceptions extends the academic interests in these papers to the marketing of destinations. By identifying what people look for in a vacation destination and comparing this with what they see in a given destination region, tourism planners can help to improve the competitive position of their own study region. For examples, see Hunt (1975), Goodrich (1978), Crompton (1979), and Woodside (1980).

Another twist on regional images is the *a priori* recognition that some origin regions will tend to have more favourable images of a destination than other regions. If these images are known, tourism marketing managers can work to reallocate promotional budgets so that those areas with the greatest likelihood of generating future trips receive the greatest share of the promotional budget. Such a study can be found in *Advertising Age* (1980).

Regionalization also provides the basis for identifying spatial variations in the potential for future tourism development. In one such study, Smith (1977) identified regions in Michigan capable of supporting growth in the accommodation industry. Var, Beck, and Loftus (1977) and Ferrario (1979a, b) have developed models for assessing regional potentials for even broader-based tourism growth.

The oldest use of regionalization in tourism is the definition of regions to provide a basis for regional planning and to guide tourism development. Notable among the early planners who developed the very concept of a tourism region is Gunn (1965, 1979; Blank and Gunn 1966). He has been a strong proponent of the value of a regional approach in tourism research and we will examine some of his work later in this chapter.

Finally, there is the most common and least sophisticated form of regionalization: the delineation of tourism regions in a political area such as a state by a tourism ministry or industry association. These regions are based on locally held perceptions and sometimes even personal intuition. They serve a useful purpose by helping to define tourism regions and attractions in what would otherwise be a large and amorphous destination area to potential visitors. These divisions, though, are rarely objective or verifiable – often bordering on the romantic or the silly. As long as these types of regions serve no more complex purpose than providing a convenient way of presenting attractions and accommodation in a brochure, they may be acceptable. Very often, though, these regions may become the basis for forming industry associations, for organizing cooperative advertising efforts, and even serve as a framework for collecting and summarizing tourism statistics. When regions are employed in the service of such serious and sophisticated matters, their definition should be more scientific than subjective. We now turn to an examination of several regionalization methods that will help us to meet this goal.

Cartographic regionalization

Description

Cartographic regionalization is a method of defining regions by drafting and then superimposing a series of maps showing the spatial distribution of important areal characteristics. The procedure may be used to divide a large area into a number of smaller regions or to delimit a single region located within a much larger area.

The procedures required for this method are relatively straightforward, but their successful application requires thought and careful work. The most difficult step of all can be the combination of the series of maps. The problem is not just the physical overlaying of two or more maps; rather the challenge is to develop a valid system for measuring and combining variables (which may be very different in kind) in a common metric that will allow them to be meaningfully combined into a single map. One possible solution is described in the example below.

Another step that may be valuable in this procedure is to identify and assess any 'critical' features. This step is quite similar to the identification of 'critical' locational variables described in Chapter 6 in the section on the use of the checklist method for site selection. In this case, critical regional features are those characteristics that might cause a place to be excluded from any further consideration for tourism planning. Environmentally sensitive areas of national significance are one example. The spatial distribution of any critical features should be mapped before any other features so that any place failing to meet the criteria for inclusion for further study can be eliminated at the outset.

As we will see, cartographic regionalization in practice has elements of the three basic forms of regionalization described previously. The task of collecting data for individual places and then generalizing it to larger areas is similar to the logic of synthetic regionalization. Once a combined map has been prepared and the pattern on this map divided into a series of new regions, the analyst is engaged in analytic regionalization. Finally, the use of any critical features to identify places to be excluded from consideration is an example of the logic of dichotomous regionalization.

Procedures

1. Define the basic study area. This is usually some political unit such as a county, province, or an entire nation. The advantage of using political units is that data sources will often be available for them.
2. Identify and operationally define appropriate regional characteristics.
3. Define a measurement scale for each characteristic. The number of classes on the scale is arbitrary; it may range upward from a minimum of two (such as present/absent). Most analysts find that four or five classes are the most practical number. Weights may be used to adjust individual characteristic scores to reflect the relative importance of each characteristic.
4. Collect the data for each characteristic and map separately.

Table 7.1 Index scales for 'touring' tourism

Factor	Weighted index	Scale				
		Very weak	Weak	Moderate	Strong	Very strong
1. Water, wildlife	8	0	1–2	3–4	5–6	7–8
2. Topography, soils, geology	10	0–1	2–3	4–6	7–8	9–10
3. Vegetative cover, pests	7	0	1-2	3–4	5–6	7
4. Climate, atmosphere	3	0	1	1	2	3
5. Aesthetics	13	0–1	2–4	5–7	8–10	11–13
6. Existing attractions, industries, institutions	10	0–1	2–3	4–6	7–8	9–10
7. History, ethnicity, archaeology, legend, lore	9	0–1	2–3	4–5	6–7	8–9
8. Service centres	15	0–2	3–5	6–9	10–12	13–15
9. Transportation, access	25	0–4	5–9	10–15	16–20	21–25
	100					

Source: Gunn 1979.

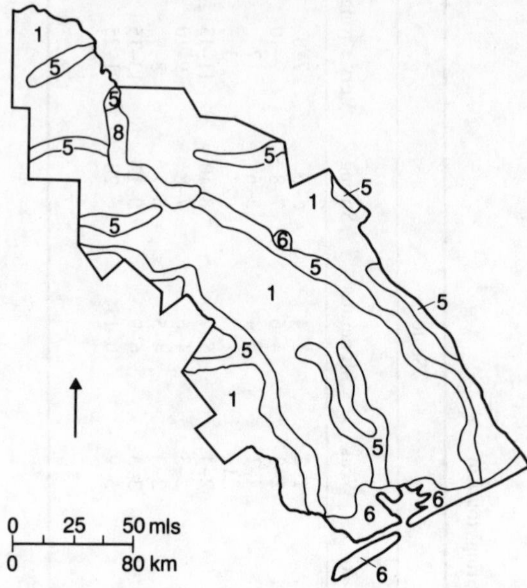

Fig. 7.4 Importance of water-wildlife for 'touring-tourism' potential (From Gunn 1979) Texas example

5. Combine the individual maps. This may be done by using transparencies of the individual maps or through a computer graphics program that mathematically superimposes the maps.
6. Define regions on the basis of the combined patterns.

Example

Gunn (1979) provides an illustration of the cartographic approach in some of his work in Texas. A research team was asked to identify tourism regions in central Texas that would have potential for automobile touring. The team began by identifying nine variables they believed were important for automobile touring potential: (1) water and wildlife; (2) topography, soils, and geology; (3) vegetative cover; (4) climate and atmosphere; (5) aesthetics; (6) existing attractions, industries, and institutions; (7) history, ethnicity, archaeology, legend, and lore; (8) service centres; and (9) transportation and access. Weights reflecting the relative importance of each feature were estimated by dividing a total of 100 points among the nine features. The resulting weights were assumed to represent a ratio scale.

The weights of each type of feature were translated into a five-part

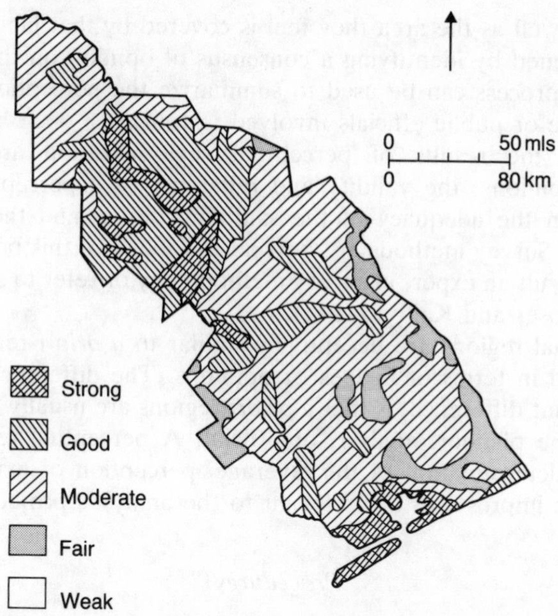

Fig. 7.5 Sum of natural and cultural resource factors – destination potential (Texas example) (Gunn 1979)

scale, ranging from 'very weak' to 'very strong'. Table 7.1 illustrates the results of this exercise. Note, for example, that 'water and wildlife' have a weight of 8; these eight points were divided into five classes to make up the five-part scale.

The team then collected data for the study area and prepared nine maps showing the distribution of value for each feature. Figure 7.4 is a draft of the map prepared for the 'water–wildlife' feature. The nine maps were combined by summing the scores for each part of the study area (the research team used a computer mapping routine called SYMAP, but the procedure can be done by hand by overlaying transparencies) to produce a map of regions of varying touring potential (see Fig. 7.5).

Perceptual regionalization

Description

Perceptual regionalization is basically the mapping of opinion. A survey is conducted to identify how tourists label the area they are visiting as well as the area they feel is covered by that label; a region is then defined by identifying a consensus of opinion on these points. The same process can be used to summarize the perceptions of business people or public officials involved in tourism.

Because the results of perceptual regionalization are basically mapped opinions, the validity and reliability of a perceptual region depends on the adequacy of the sampling design and the interview technique. Survey methods are beyond the scope of this book, so you should consult an expert in survey methodology or refer to survey texts such as Moser and Kalton (1974).

Perceptual regions are deceptively similar to *a priori* regions. Both are defined in terms of images or opinions. The difference, and it is an important difference, is that *a priori* regions are usually the perceptions of one planner, analyst, or official. A perceptual region is the objective determination of the 'average' perception of many individuals whose impressions are relevant to the analyst's project.

Procedures

1. If the opinions of tourists are of interest, begin by defining an appropriate sampling frame. This involves the selection of a number of places where a representative sample of tourists could be obtained: major attractions, accommodation, restaurants, visitor information centres. These places should be spread widely enough to cover more than the probable extent of the region you hope to identify so that a valid assessment of the full extent of the region can be obtained.
2. Select a random sample from each sampling locale. Ask each respondent (through a personal interview or in a mailback questionnaire) a series of questions similar to the following:
   (a) Do you have the impression you are in a vacation area?
   Yes ____ No ____
   (b) If 'yes', what do you call it? ________
   (c) Name the place where you entered the region. ________
3. Map the distribution of responses by sampling locale. Map the distribution of responses by entry point into the region.
4. Delineate the regional boundaries by inspection and determine whether there is a common name.

If your task is to identify the regional boundaries as perceived by local tourism planners and operators, you can also conduct a survey of them. Because you will typically be working with fewer respondents in this case than you would if you were interviewing tourists (because there are fewer operators and planners and because their opinions are likely to be more homogeneous than those of tourists), it may be feasible to ask each respondent to draw a boundary of the tourist region on a base map you provide. An average boundary can then be estimated by inspection of the individual maps.

Example

Gunn and Worms (1973) defined a perceptual region centred on Corpus Christi, Texas, using a process similar to the above procedure. They began by drawing up a list of possible subjects to interview. This

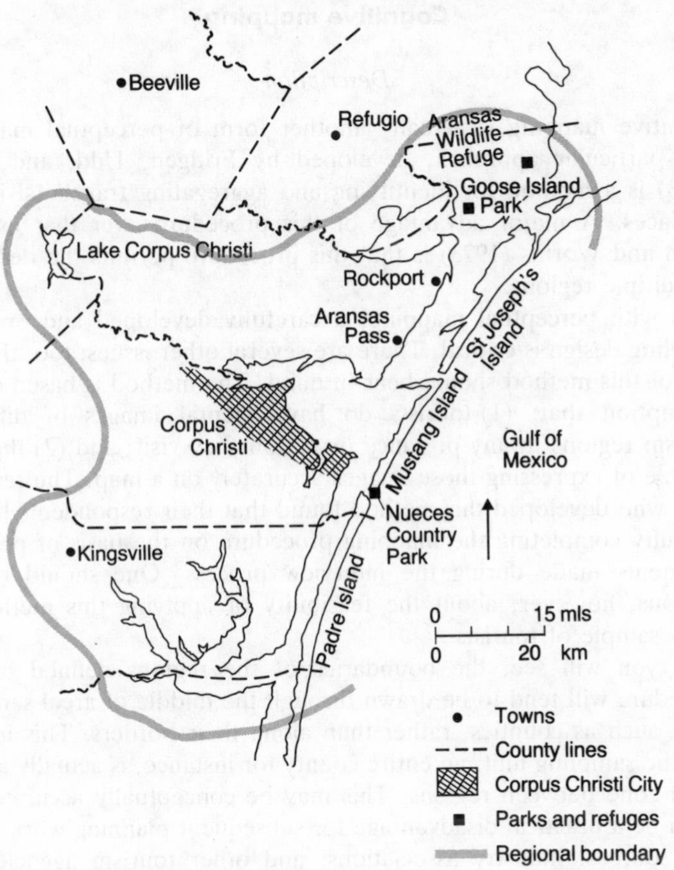

Fig. 7.6 The perceptual tourism region around Corpus Christi, Texas (Gunn & Worms 1973)

list was shown to planners, government officials, and other authoritative individuals in the Corpus Christi area for comment. All names that received a positive recommendation from at least three independent sources were selected for interview. The final sample size was 41 local tourism operators. Each was asked the question, 'We are trying to determine how broad a geographic area should be included in the Corpus Christi region from the viewpoint of tourist use. What area would you include in the region?' The respondents were then given a map and were asked to sketch their boundary on it. The researchers then combined all maps to produce the average perceived regional boundary as shown in Fig. 7.6.

Cognitive mapping

Description

Cognitive mapping is actually another form of perceptual mapping. This particular approach, developed by Fridgen, Udd, and Deale (1983) is a method for identifying and aggregating travellers' images of places. A major advantage of this procedure over that used by Gunn and Worms (1973) is that this procedure permits the definition of multiple regions.

As with perceptual mapping, a carefully developed and executed sampling design is critical. There are several other issues, too, that the user of this method should bear in mind. The method is based on the assumption that; (1) tourists do have mental images of different tourism regions in any province or nation they visit; and (2) they are capable of expressing those images accurately on a map. The research team who developed this method found that their respondents had no difficulty completing the mapping procedure on the basis of personal comments made during the interview process. One should remain cautious, however, about the feasibility of applying this method to every sample of tourists.

As you will see, the boundaries of the regions defined by this procedure will tend to be drawn through the middle of areal sampling units, such as counties, rather than along their borders. This implies that the sampling unit, an entire county for instance, is actually a transition zone between regions. This may be conceptually accurate, but it can be a practical disadvantage for subsequent planning work. Most data sources, industry associations, and other tourism agencies are organized along precise political boundaries. Consequently, if you use this procedure you may find yourself forced to use some judgement about placing the regional boundary along an existing political boundary.

Procedures

1. Choose a sampling methodology that will allow you to obtain a representative random sample of tourists or potential tourists.
2. Provide each respondent with an outline map of the area to be divided into regions. A typical map might be a province or state outline with county boundaries shown. Major cities could also be noted. Ask each respondent to circle three to five multi-county regions they perceive to be tourism regions. Each respondent should also be instructed to place an 'X' in the county they see as the 'heart' of the region.
3. Define a tourism location score for each county:

$$TLS = [(A + B)/(1 + C)][A + B + C] \qquad [7.1]$$

where: TLS = tourism location score;
A = number of times a county received an 'X';
B = number of times a county was fully circled;
C = number of times a county was partially circled.

4. Determine county scores by summing the *TLS*s calculated from each respondent's map. Plot these total scores on a new map.
5. The map produced in step 4 can be interpreted as a topographic map of hilly terrain. Unlike a regular topographic map, where points of equal height are joined by contour lines, the *TLS* regional map is produced by drawing lines along the 'valleys' to delimit areas of high *TLS* scores from each other.

Example

Fridgen, Udd, and Deale followed the procedure outlined above for a sample of motorists who stopped at visitor information centres as they crossed the state line into Michigan (USA). The maps from the respondents were analysed using equation [7.1], and a state regionalization map was compiled from the *TLS*s (Fig. 7.7).

It was the intent of the researchers to use these regions to make recommendations about a reorganization of the regional tourism associations in the state of Michigan. The problem with this intention was that it was based on the assumption that tourists' perceptions are relevant to the industry's regional organization. This assumption is a violation of the first principle of regionalization – the definition of

Fig. 7.7 The cognitive tourism regions in Michigan (Fridgen, Udd & Deale 1983)

regions should be based on variables that are specific to the problem at hand. If the researchers' basic interest was the spatial organization of the state tourism industry (as they suggest), a more useful set of regions could have been based on the perceptions of tourism operators. One example of the type of problem the violation of this principle causes is the fact that several regions appear to be too small to support independent regional associations. The location of regional boundaries in the middle of counties is another difficulty confronting the application of their regions to the needs of the tourism industry.

This example also illustrates that the magnitudes of the *TLS*s make sense only in comparison with each other. The absolute size of any county's score is a function not only of the number of Xs it received and the number of times it was circled, but also of the total number of respondents. Tourism location scores from one project or survey cannot be meaningfully compared to scores from other projects. Within the context of a single survey, however, and with recognition of the need to ensure that the selection of the sample is appropriate for the purpose of the regionalization, this method can produce useful results.

Functional regionalization

Description

The concept of functional regionalization is based on the notion that one can identify a set of tourism regions by examining patterns of personal travel. The basis of functional regionalization stems from Philbrick's (1957) exposition of his principle of 'areal functional organization'. At the risk of over-simplifying the complexities of Philbrick's ideas, one of his points is that there is a close, interdependent relationship between spatial structure and movement patterns within a spatial system. If you can identify the movement of commodities or people for a particular activity within a spatial system, such as an urban area, you can deduce (in theory, at least) some understanding of the structure of that system. Berry (1966) has applied this concept to national-level commodity flows, while Goddard (1970) and Stutz (1973a, and b; 1974) have explored its application in intra-urban structures. Functional regionalization can be applied to any scale ranging from international systems to neighbourhoods. Tourism analysts are likely to find that functional regionalization is most useful at the state/provincial or national levels.

From the perspective of tourism travel, functional regions may be interpreted as the result of trade-offs travellers make between the desire to have access to a variety of desirable vacation destinations (which tends to pull people further away from home and to disperse them across the landscape) and the desire to minimize travel costs (which tends to keep people closer to home and to minimize wandering about on the landscape). Unlike cartographic, perceptual, and cognitive regions, functional regions are not necessarily characterized by internal homogeneity. In fact, many physical and social characteristics of functional regions will vary as much within regions as between regions. The regions are distinguished from each other on the basis of a closely linked set of internally consistent travel patterns.

In other words, a functional region is defined by a portion of the landscape that contains a set of common origin–destination pairs and the transportation routes between them.

Calculation of functional regions requires a familiarity with factor analysis (or principal components analysis). Any potential user of this procedure must be sure to have an adequate understanding of factor analysis before attempting to define a set of functional regions. One particular aspect of factor analysis when used for functional regionalization should be noted since it is a phenomenon not always observed in other applications of factor analysis. Each factor produced by the analysis is associated with a separate region – except for the final factor. Goddard (1970) explains that factor analysis tends to produce one factor more than the number of meaningful regions. This final factor is a mathematical artefact describing 'residual' travel patterns in a study area that are not associated with any particular region. As a result, the pattern implicit in the final factor is usually ignored when developing a system of functional regions. The steps for extracting regions from the other factors are described more fully in the following section.

Procedures

1. Obtain data describing the number of vacation trips made between each of a number of areas, such as states or provinces. These data will form an asymmetrical square matrix where the rows represent origins and the columns represent destinations. The matrix is asymmetrical because the number of people leaving origin i to travel to vacation destination j is not necessarily the same as the number of people leaving j to travel to i. Vacations taken by people within their home area are also recorded. The data should be expressed in per capita trip rates to adjust for population variations among origins.
2. Reduce the data matrix through factor analysis. The conventions of an eigenvalue cut-off of 1.00 and varimax rotation are usually appropriate. Record the factor loadings for all variables on each factor.
3. Obtain factor scores for each origin from the factor analysis.
4. Identify regions by one of two methods:
   (a) For each factor, list all areas with high loadings (these represent important destinations for that component). List all the areas with high scores (which represent important origins). The definition of 'high' is arbitrary; but for

Table 7.2 Partial linkages for region 1

State/province	Loading (destination)	Score (origin)
New Brunswick	0.87	23.13
Newfoundland	—	9.65
Nova Scotia	0.71	22.16
Ontario	0.52	9.77
Prince Edward Island	0.82	16.42
Quebec	0.81	12.80
Connecticut	—	2.07
Maine	0.68	7.72
Maryland	0.75	2.25
Massachusetts	0.89	2.21
New Hampshire	—	5.17
Vermont	—	3.40

Source: Smith 1983.

loadings you might use those loadings with values greater than 0.70 and scores greater than 1.00 (either positive or negative values). Locate these origins and destinations on a map and link with straight lines. The pattern of these lines defines a functional region.

(b) Alternatively, group areas on the basis of their factor scores to define regions of destinations with common origins. This grouping is usually done with a hierarchical grouping algorithm such as that defined in Chapter 3 in the section on factor-cluster segmentation.

Example

Functional regionalization was used by Smith (1983) to define a set of tourism regions for Canada and the USA. The number of vacation trips between each of the 50 states, the District of Columbia, and the 10 provinces were obtained from government sources and summarized in a 61 × 61 matrix. Factor analysis reduced this matrix to a set of 18 factors explaining about 77 per cent of the original variance. Table 7.2 lists the high loadings (greater than ± 0.50) and high scores (greater than ± 1.00). These were then plotted and connected as described in step 3(a) to produce the map in Fig. 7.8. A strong regional pattern emerges, but mapping of the other factors produced some overlap. To identify exclusive regions, step 4(b) was followed. This led to the identification of the seven-region solution shown in Fig. 7.9. The names

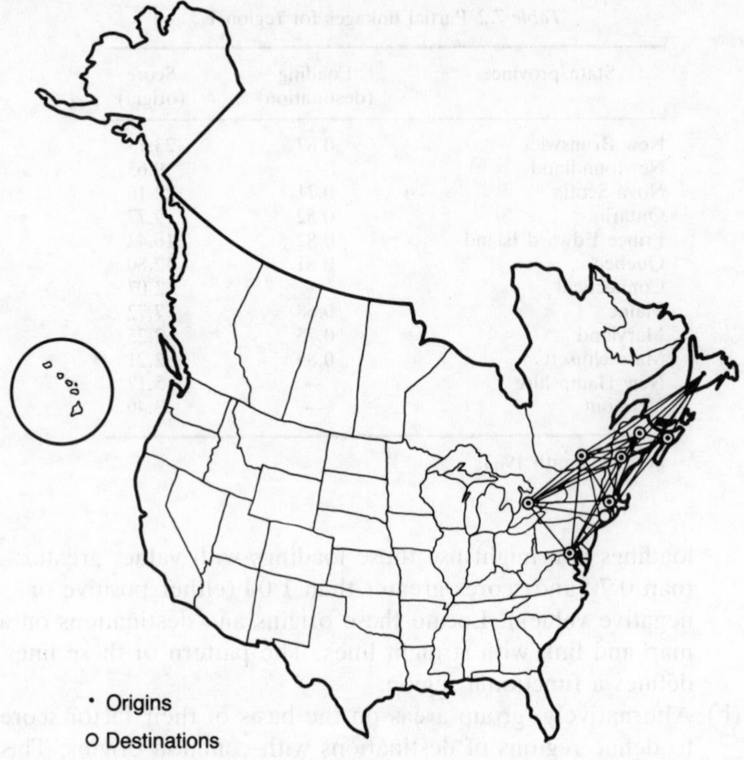

Fig. 7.8 Origin–destination linkages for one North American functional tourism region (Smith 1983a)

given to each region were somewhat arbitrary, chosen to reflect either traditional regional identities or the presence of a geographical feature that seemed to be closely associated with the location and orientation of each region.

Destination zone identification

Description

Destination zone identification is a type of regionalization based on an inventory of qualitative characteristics of a region relevant to a given tourism planning problem. Although it does not have the formal objectivity usually associated with statistical regionalization methods,

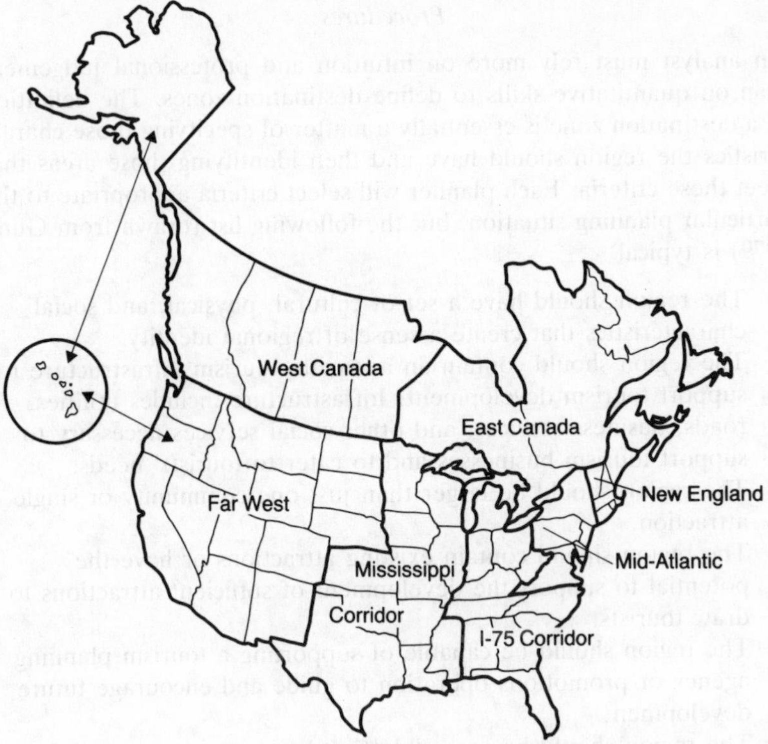

Fig. 7.9 Seven-region solution for North American vacation patterns (Smith 1983a)

this procedure does permit a planner or analyst to include many different types of variables and regional qualities in the regionalization system that the more quantitative approaches cannot handle.

The definition of a destination zone involves the type of logic used for dichotomous regionalization. You begin with a large area and systematically identify those subsections that have certain features and those that do not. Working through a list of criteria, you slowly narrow the study area into one or more regions that meet all the criteria established for a destination zone.

The concept of a destination zone is useful, but rather imprecise. A number of misperceptions are sometimes associated with their identification and use. We will look at these misperceptions after the presentation of the procedures and an example of the application of destination zone identification in Saskatchewan, Canada.

Procedures

An analyst must rely more on intuition and professional judgement than on quantitative skills to define destination zones. The definition of a destination zone is essentially a matter of specifying those characteristics the region should have and then identifying those areas that meet these criteria. Each planner will select criteria appropriate to the particular planning situation, but the following list (drawn from Gunn 1979) is typical.

1. The region should have a set of cultural, physical, and social characteristics that create a sense of regional identity.
2. The region should contain an adequate tourism infrastructure to support tourism development. Infrastructure includes utilities, roads, business services, and other social services necessary to support tourism businesses and to cater to tourists' needs.
3. The region should be larger than just one community or single attraction.
4. The region should contain existing attractions or have the potential to support the development of sufficient attractions to draw tourists.
5. The region should be capable of supporting a tourism planning agency or promotions operation to guide and encourage future development.
6. The region should be accessible to a large population base. Accessibility may be by road, scheduled passenger air service, or cruise ships.

Example

An example of the establishment of destination zones may be found in the tourism plan for the Canadian province of Saskatchewan, developed for the Department of Tourism and Renewable Resources by a consulting firm, Balmer, Crapo, and Associates. The consultants were provided with the following criteria for the definition of tourism zones:

1. Regions should have common features upon which to develop an identity, such as important historical, cultural, or physical resources. Regions may attract pleasure, business, or personal travellers or some combination of these.
2. The region must be large enough to have access to the financial and human resources necessary adequately to develop and promote tourism on a regional basis, but must not be so large that it is impractical to plan for or manage.

3. Each part of the zone must have the strength of the whole zone. That is, one city or town must not dominate the zone.
4. Zones should follow present municipal or county boundaries.
5. Each zone should possess a sufficient quantity of tourism plant facilities.

The intent of each of these criteria in the context of Saskatchewan tourism was discussed by the consultant with the Ministry of Tourism and Small Business. The firm then collected information relating to each criterion from existing data sources, maps, and regional development reports as well as from a series of discussions with public and private agencies.

The consultants came to the conclusion that the regions should not be centred on major urban areas because travellers might tend to visit only those cities and ignore the rest of the province. This would violate the third criterion listed above. Destination zones and the accompanying promotional material should be designed to encourage side-trips off the main highways, which would be likely to lead to longer tourist visits and greater expenditures throughout the province. This approach had the result of making the major cities serve as 'hubs' for several zones at the same time. Each zone could then draw visitors and residents alike from the 'hub' cities for day, weekend, or week-long trips.

The zones defined this way also had highways serve as their borders (a violation of criterion 4 that was agreed to by the province). A couple of exceptions to this new rule were made when the areas immediately adjacent to the proposed highway borders were too similar on either side of the highway to warrant separation into separate themes or zones or when side-road development was too sparse to permit side-trips. In general, though, development zones were delimited by highways, with major cities at their corners. Figure 7.10 is a map of the resulting pattern.

The destination zones in Saskatchewan were intended originally to serve both as promotional regions and for a series of industry associations. It was discovered after defining the zones that, while they did form plausible regions for promotion, the level of tourism development in most was insufficient to form a workable industry association. The number of tourism operators who could be counted on to join an association was too small to form a viable organization. This was the same difficulty experienced in some of the Fridgen–Udd–Deale regions in Michigan. In the Saskatchewan example, the problem was resolved by aggregating individual destination zones into a smaller number of large industry regions.

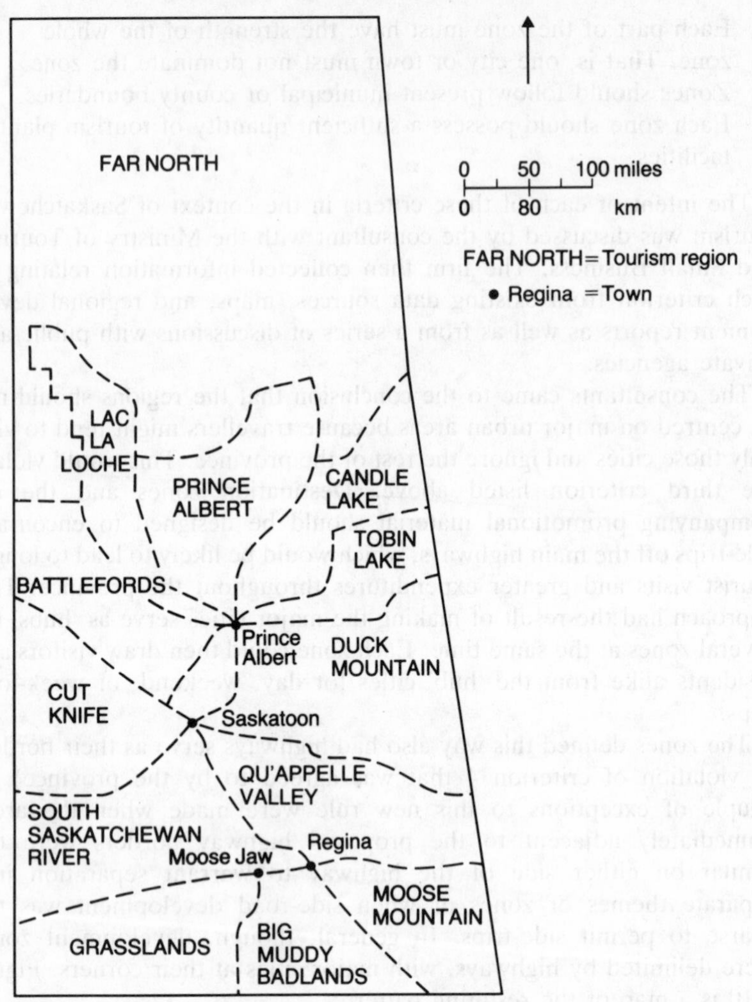

Fig. 7.10 Tourism destination zones for Saskatchewan (Redrawn from Balmer, Crapo and Associates)

The concept of destination zones is useful for many purposes: marketing, promotion, industry organization, physical planning, and the formation of national policy. Gunn (1982) has attempted to clarify some of the confusion and ambiguity surrounding the phrase 'destination zone' as it is used in these diverse contexts. This list of 'corrected misconceptions' is based on his work for Tourism Canada.

Misconception 1: Destination zones have precise boundaries. In fact, the boundaries of destination zones are wide transitional belts. There may be practical cartographic or administrative reasons for drawing narrow and precisely located lines delimiting adjacent zones on a map, but it is naïve to really believe that two plots of land separated by a 6 m ($6\frac{1}{2}$ yd) stretch of macadam pavement belong to distinct tourism regions.

Misconception 2: Destination zones exist for ever. Zones not only have fuzzy boundaries, they have fuzzy life expectancies. They do not exist in perpetuity; they may be created through human intervention and they can be dissolved through the same process. Natural landscape evolution may also change the boundaries of zones or terminate their very existence.

Misconception 3: Developers and local communities may simply define themselves to be a destination zone. Local initiative can go a long way towards creating the conditions needed for tourism growth, but enthusiasm and boosterism are not enough. These must be coupled with physical development and actual success in drawing tourists. Promotion is useful, but there has to be more to encourage tourists to come to a destination for repeat visits or extended stays than just a marketing agency with a wild imagination.

Misconception 4: Destination zones are exclusively tourist areas. Destination zones may be created to aid in tourism development, but they require more than tourism attractions. They must also contain utilities, hospitals, fire and police protection, travel agents, transportation linkages, and a variety of other business and personal services. There are still some isolated resorts that do not depend on local community structures for many utilities and services, but these are the exception in modern tourism.

Misconception 5: Identification of destination zones is the same as doing a feasibility study. The identification of destination zones can be a useful part of a feasibility study, but zone identification is not always necessary and it is never a substitute for a full feasibility study. Locating a tourism business in an area designated as a destination zone is no guarantee of success. Planning, design, financing, promotion, and management are all more important in determining the success or failure of a business than just its location in an identified tourism region.

Summary

Tourism analysts often find it useful to be able to define regions as part of a research or planning project. There are a number of different methods available; each has its own particular strengths and best applications. Destination zones, for example, are helpful for the development of a state-wide or province-wide tourism strategy; functional regions are valuable research tools for studying the linkages created by vacation flows; perceptual and cognitive regions tell us important information about how other people, especially tourists, view our regions.

These methods have been developed through application and evaluation; each is designed to assist you in the completion of a larger task that includes, but is not limited to, regional definition. As a result, tourism analysts have not always paid sufficient attention to some of the more abstract or scholarly principles of logic required for effective regionalization. We have examined both the logic of regionalization in this chapter and its application to defining the geographic structure or the industry. As a result, you will be better able to achieve a workable balance between scientific rigour and logic, on the one hand, and the demand for being able to produce quickly and efficiently a workable regional system, on the other. You will also be in a better position to evaluate the reliability of regional systems proposed by other analysts.

Further reading

Carvajal B and **Patri J** 1979 Principio basicos para la obtencion de un indice de jeraquizacion turistica, aplicado a la provincia Antartica Chilena. *Information geographia de Chile* **26**: 65–80.

Davis K R and **Taylor III B W** 1980 A goal programming model for allocating state promotional effort to regional markets in accordance with tourism potential. *Journal of Travel Research* **18**(4): 24–30.

Goodrich J N 1977 Differences in perceived similarity of tourism regions: a spatial analysis. *Journal of Travel Research* **15**(1): 10–13.

Lawson F and **Baud-Bovy M** 1977 *Tourism and recreation development*. Architectural Press, London.

Pearce D 1981 *Tourist development*. Longman, London.

Piperoglou J 1967 Identification and definition of regions in Greek tourist planning. *Papers of the Regional Science Association* **18**: 169–76.

Ries A and **Trout J** 1980 *Positioning: the battle for your mind*. McGraw-Hill, New York.

Schewe C D, Scott D R and **Frederick D G** 1978 A multi-brand/multi-attribute model of tourism state choices. *Journal of Travel Research* **16**(1): 23–9.

TDC-SGV (Netherlands Institute of Tourism Development Consultants and Na Thalang and Company) 1976 *National plan for tourism development, final report*. Tourist Organization of Thailand, Bangkok.

Vedenin Y A and **Miroshnichenko N N** 1970 Evaluation of the natural environment for recreation purposes. *Soviet Geography: Review and Translation* **11**(3): 198–208.

CHAPTER 8

Describing tourism regions

Introduction

Good research depends on good description. Description is so much a part of everyday life, though, that it is easy to overlook its importance to the development of new knowledge. Progress in the scientific understanding of tourism begins with descriptive procedures such as naming, classifying, measuring, comparing, and summarizing. Without accurate description we miss much of what the world has to teach us.

Consider for a minute a stroll through a forest. Almost everyone will have some sort of emotional response to the solitude, grandeur, mystery, and fragrances of the deep woods. Now, add a companion who is also a scientist who understands some aspect of the forest. In addition to the sensory impact of the forest, your appreciation will be changed and heightened as your companion identifies the parts of the forest environment and speaks of their relationships. That appreciation will be different depending on your companion's expertise: botany, ornithology, entomology, forestry, or some other natural science. Certain parts of the forest will acquire vivid new meaning while others fade into the background. Description has changed your world by changing your perception of it. The actual change depends on the methods you use to observe and on the things you choose to describe. Ideally you will not have lost your ability to respond emotionally as your view becomes more 'scientific', and you will have gained a new and keener appreciation of some part of reality.

The history of science over the last 400 years can be viewed as a history of improvement in description. In fact, the genius of the Newtonian synthesis, which marks the birth of modern physical science, was the recognition that the central challenge to scientists was to *describe* the physical forces of the universe accurately and quantitatively and not to attempt to answer philosophical questions about why those forces existed.

The challenge for a tourism analyst is similar: to provide the most accurate description possible. It is common to hear some research criticized because 'it is merely descriptive'. This type of criticism misses the point. The problem is often not that the research is descriptive, but rather that the description is not informative or detailed enough to be useful. Description works best when it is tied to another problem. Description for its own sake is rarely sufficient in any social science, and that includes tourism analysis. It must be undertaken with the spirit of trying to uncover some new, hidden relationships or patterns that will teach us new, useful things about the world. Thus the use of the mean centre, Defert's *Tf*, and any other method discussed in this chapter will not tell us much about tourism unless it is used to answer a question that extends beyond the calculation of the descriptive statistic. These methods are only means to an end; they are not ends in themselves. With that in mind, we can prepare to examine some of the more useful descriptive tools available to tourism analysts.

Mean centre

Description

A basic problem in tourism analysis is how to summarize the spatial distribution of facilities, resources, or tourists. One of the simplest methods to do this is the mean centre – the spatial equivalent of the arithmetic mean. The mean centre is located by a pair of coordinates that provide that point which is most typical or representative of the distribution of a large number of points representing some tourism phenomenon.

The mean centre may be determined for one particular set of data or it may be determined for several different sets of data and then compared. For example, determining the mean centre of the distribution of tourists at an attraction for each hour a facility is open during a representative day may reveal valuable information about the behaviour of those visitors. The mean centre might also be mapped for different sets of facilities – perhaps hotels, motels, restaurants, travel agencies – to compare the relative location of each. From this summary information you may be able to achieve a better understanding of some of the forces affecting the location and operations of each type of business.

It should be noted that any measure of central tendency, including the mean centre, necessarily loses much information. One cannot, for instance, work backwards from the mean centre to reproduce the original pattern of points. Further, different patterns can yield identical mean centres. A major implication of this weakness is that it is often wise to present the mean centre with additional information such as a map of the actual array of points and the standard distance or the standard deviational ellipse (described later in this chapter).

The mean centre is based on the abstraction of actual facilities or other observations to dimensionless points. Many times this presents no problem, but if the units being mapped occupy a significant portion of the base map or are long linear features, the use of points, and thus the use or the mean centre, may be inappropriate.

Another problem with the mean centre is its sensitivity to extreme values. Because the value of the mean centre is calculated from the sum of coordinates, the addition of one coordinate with a very large value will have much more effect on the location of the mean centre than the addition of several points with small coordinates. The existence of one or more extreme values can usually be detected by examining either a plot of the actual data points or by use of the standard distance. If such points exist, you may wish to consider whether there is any justification for excluding them from your analysis. You should, at least, note their potential biasing effect in your discussion of the mean centre.

It may have occurred to you that if you can calculate a mean centre, it should be possible to calculate a median centre. Such a measure does exist. It is defined as the intersection of two perpendicular lines, each of which divides the point pattern into halves (Cole and King 1968). An example may be seen in Fig. 8.1. (It should be noted that some geographers define the median centre as the point of minimum aggregate travel, such as Neft 1966, and King 1969. This is not the definition used here.) A basic problem with the median centre is that different median centres are defined depending on the orientation of the perpendicular lines. An example of the lack of stability in the location of the median centre may also be seen in Fig. 8.1. In this case, a second median centre is determined by turning the perpendicular lines by 45° from those used for the first median centre. The failure to be able to determine a reliable median centre obviously limits the usefulness of this measure in tourism analysis. A procedure developed by Seymour (1968) can be used to reduce the lack of reliability; his method is based on a converging algorithm that iteratively estimates the location of the optimal point that most closely matches the statistician's notion of a median. A brief and clear discussion of the median centre problem can also be found in Taylor (1977: 30–2).

Procedures

1. Prepare a map of the study area and plot the locations of the features as points.
2. Superimpose a square grid as a coordinate system. The grid may be oriented as desired.
3. Determine the coordinates for each point with reference to the grid. List these on a worksheet similar to that in Table 8.1. For some types of problems it may be appropriate to weight each point. Accommodation firms such as hotels, for instance, might be weighted by their room capacity.
4. Sum the *X*-coordinates and divide by the number of points to obtain the arithmetic mean:

$$\bar{X} = \frac{\Sigma X_i}{n} \qquad [8{\cdot}1]$$

where: $\bar{X}$ = *X*-coordinate of mean centre;
X_i = horizontal coordinate of point *i*;
n = number of points.

Repeat for the *Y*-coordinates.

If weighted points are used, multiply each point by its weight before calculating the mean coordinate:

$$\bar{X} = \frac{\Sigma(W_i X_i)}{\Sigma W_i} \qquad [8{\cdot}2]$$

where: W_i = weight of point *i*; other variables are as defined previously.

Example

Table 8.1 and Fig. 8.1 provide an illustration of this calculation. In this case the pattern is the location of hotels and motels in Kitchener-Waterloo, Ontario (Canada). Each establishment has been mapped on an outline map of the metropolitan region. An arbitrary coordinate system was overlaid and the coordinates of the points, designated by the letters A to T, noted in the table. Weights equal to the number of rooms are also given. Locations of both the unweighted and weighted mean centres were then calculated. This may be compared to the locations of two median centres, which are also plotted on the map.

Table 8.1 Calculation of unweighted and weighted mean centre

Location	Wtd	X	Y	Wtd X	Wtd Y
A	81	15.2	34.8	1 231.2	2 818.8
B	30	14.2	31.5	426.0	945.0
C	29	21.6	28.6	626.4	829.4
D	17	11.1	24.1	188.7	409.7
E	22	12.8	23.8	281.6	523.6
F	10	16.0	25.5	160.0	255.0
G	22	16.5	24.8	363.0	545.6
H	130	15.5	22.5	2 015.0	2 925.0
I	44	16.5	21.6	726.0	950.4
J	47	17.5	22.5	822.5	1 057.5
K	36	20.1	24.1	723.6	867.6
L	40	21.4	23.9	856.0	956.0
M	21	22.6	23.8	474.6	499.8
N	44	24.0	22.2	1 056.0	976.8
O	45	18.0	18.0	810.0	810.0
P	102	19.6	16.8	1 999.2	1 713.6
Q	25	20.0	15.8	500.0	395.0
R	122	20.0	13.8	2 440.0	1 683.6
S	40	19.9	8.4	796.0	336.0
T	20	21.5	5.8	430.0	116.0
Total	927	364.0	432.3	16 925.8	19 614.4

$\bar{X}: \frac{364.0}{20} = 18.2$ $\quad$ Wtd$\bar{X}: \frac{16\,925.8}{927} = 18.3$

$\bar{Y}: \frac{432.3}{20} = 21.6$ $\quad$ Wtd$\bar{Y}: \frac{19\,614.4}{927} = 21.1$

Coordinates of unweighted mean centre = 18.2, 21.6

Coordinates of weighted mean centre = 18.3, 21.1

Standard distance

Description

As noted previously, the mean centre loses information about the distribution of facilities or tourists in a region. A useful supplement to that statistic is the standard distance, the spatial equivalent of standard deviation. This is a measure of the variation in facility or tourist locations around their mean centre. The more widely spread the locations, the greater the value of the standard distance.

Standard distance is also a function of the size of a region. If the distribution of hotels and other accommodation in Greater London, UK, were compared to those in Kitchener-Waterloo, you would find

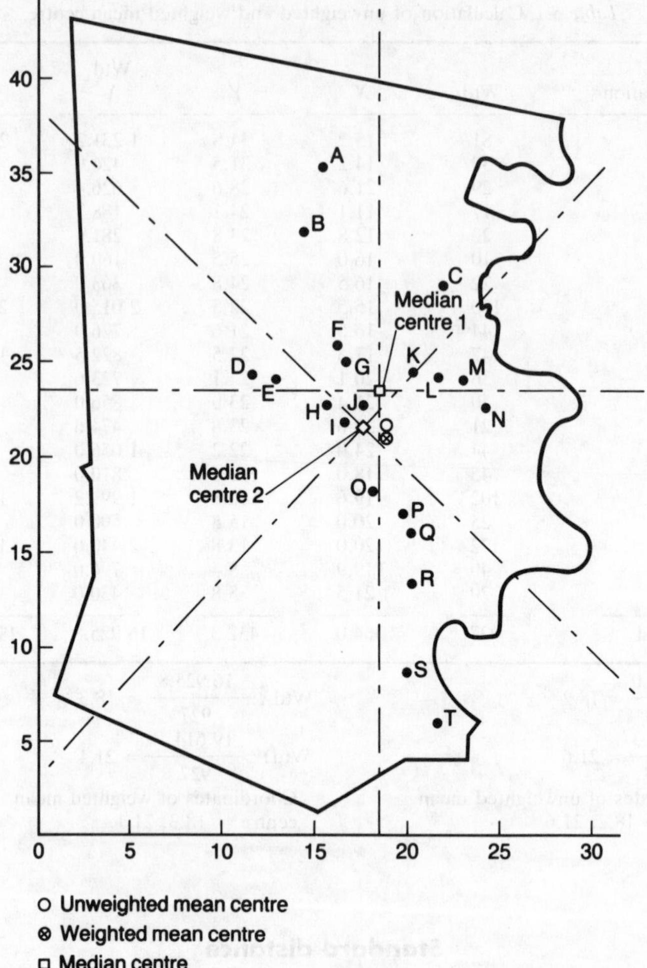

Fig. 8.1 Locational patterns of hotels and motels in Kitchener-Waterloo, Ontario: mean centre and median centre

a much greater standard distance for London. The difference in values does not necessarily indicate anything directly about the relative dispersal of accommodation in a large British city and a medium-sized Canadian urban area. Instead, the difference would probably reflect more directly the differences in the areas of the two cities. Hesitate, therefore, before comparing standard distances between regions. If their areal extent is the same, a direct comparison might be made. If their sizes are significantly different, you must convert the standard distances to a common scale. One way to do this is to calculate both the standard distance for the population of a city as well as the standard distance of the phenomenon you are studying. A simple method for estimating the standard distance of the population is to map the population of the city as an array of points located at the geographic centres of enumeration areas or other census subdivisions. These points are then weighted by the population they represent to provide a weighted standard distance for the population. The standard distance of the point pattern being studied is then divided by the weighted standard distance for the population:

$$RD = \frac{SD_x}{SD_{pop}} \qquad [8.3]$$

where: SD_x = standard distance of the point pattern as defined below in equation [8.4];
SD_{pop} = standard distance of the population;
RD = relative dispersal.

The relative dispersal of the two regions may then be compared. This approach requires, of course, that you have sufficient information to calculate the standard distance of the population. Lacking this information, you might try another technique.

This alternative method is to interpret the standard distance as the radius of a standard circle. The standard circle contains all points within one standard distance of the mean centre. Additional concentric circles can be drawn at intervals of one standard distance until the entire region is covered. You then calculate the percentage of points within each ring and then compare these frequencies between regions or with some other theoretical pattern.

Procedures

1. Prepare a map of the distribution of facilities or tourists as described in the procedures for the mean centre. Calculate the mean centre.
2. Set up a worksheet similar to that in Table 8.2.
3. Measure the distance between each point and the mean centre. Use either 'map distance' or real-world distance.
4. Calculate the standard distance:

Table 8.2 Calculation of standard distance

Point	Distance to mean centre	Distance squared
A	5.9	34.81
B	4.7	22.09
C	3.4	11.56
D	3.3	10.89
E	2.7	7.29
F	2.1	4.41
G	1.7	2.89
H	1.4	1.96
I	0.9	0.81
J	0.7	0.49
K	1.3	1.69
L	1.6	2.56
M	2.0	4.00
N	2.3	5.29
O	1.5	2.25
P	2.0	4.00
Q	2.5	6.25
R	3.4	11.56
S	5.5	30.25
T	6.7	44.89
		Σ = 209.94

209.94 ÷ 20 = 10.50
$\sqrt{}$10.50 = 3.24 units
3.24 units × 1.25 km/unit = 4.1 km

$$SD = \sqrt{(\Sigma D_i^2/n)} \qquad [8.4]$$

where: SD = standard distance;
D_i = distance between each point and the mean centre;
n = number of points, not including the mean centre.

Example

Figure 8.2 and Table 8.2 provide an illustration of the calculation of standard distance. As in the previous example, the data came from a study of the distribution of commercial accommodation firms in Kitchener-Waterloo. The above procedure was followed, using an arbitrary distance metric for measuring the distance between each point and the mean centre. The result was a standard distance of 3.24 map units. To convert this to real-world distance, 3.24 units was multiplied by the representative fraction, 1.25 km (0.77 mile) per unit, to obtain a standard distance of 4.05 km (2.51 miles).

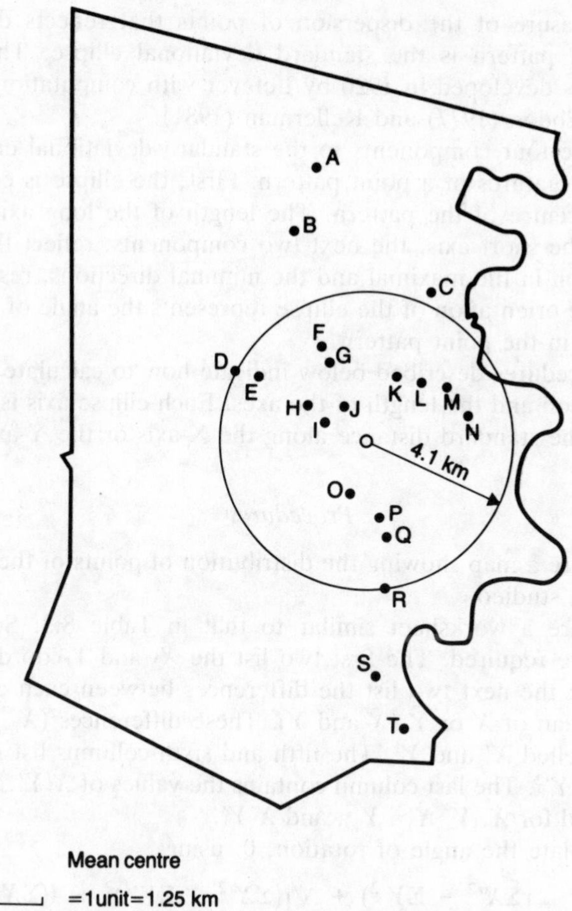

Fig. 8.2 Standard distance for hotel and motel pattern in Kitchener-Waterloo, Ontario

Standard deviational ellipse

Description

As you probably noted in the map of accommodation units in Kitchener-Waterloo, the dispersion of point patterns is often greater in one direction than another. In this case, the accommodation units are spread further north-south than east–west. The standard distance is unable to reflect this quality because it has a single value. A more precise measure of the dispersion of points that reflects directional biases in a pattern is the standard deviational ellipse. This spatial statistic was developed in 1926 by Lefever with computational refinements by Ebdon (1977) and Kellerman (1981).

There are four components to the standard deviational ellipse that reflect key features of a point pattern. First, the ellipse is centred on the mean centre of the pattern. The length of the long axis and the length of the short axis, the next two components, reflect the degree of dispersion in the maximal and the minimal directions, respectively. Finally, the orientation of the ellipse represents the angle of the directional bias in the point pattern.

The procedures described below indicate how to calculate the angle of orientation and the length of the axes. Each ellipse axis is twice the length of the standard distance along the X-axis or the Y-axis.

Procedures

1. Prepare a map showing the distribution of points of the phenomenon being studied.

2. Prepare a worksheet similar to that in Table 8:3. Seven data columns are required. The first two list the X- and Y-coordinates for each point; the next two list the differences between each coordinate and the mean of X or Y ($\bar{X}$ and $\bar{Y}$). These differences ($X - \bar{X}$; $Y - \bar{Y}$) are labelled X' and Y'. The fifth and sixth columns list the values of X'^2 and Y'^2. The last column contains the values of $X'Y'$. Totals are also needed for X, Y, X'^2, Y'^2, and $X'Y'$.

3. Calculate the angle of rotation, θ, using:

$$\tan \theta = \frac{(\Sigma X'^2 - \Sigma Y'^2) + \sqrt{[(\Sigma X'^2 - \Sigma Y'^2)^2 + 4(\Sigma X'Y')^2]}}{2(\Sigma X'Y')} \qquad [8.5]$$

where: $\tan \theta$ = tangent of the angle of rotation, θ; all other variables are as defined previously.

4. Calculate the standard deviation along the X-axis of the ellipse:

$$\sigma_X = \frac{\sqrt{[\Sigma(X'^2)\cos^2\theta - 2(\Sigma X'Y')\sin\theta\cos\theta + (\Sigma Y'^2)\sin^2\theta]}}{n} \qquad [8.6]$$

where: σ_X = standard deviation along the X-axis; all other variables are as defined previously.

5. Calculate the standard deviation along the Y-axis of the ellipse:

$$\sigma_Y = \frac{\sqrt{[(\Sigma X'^2)\sin^2\theta + 2(\Sigma X'Y')\sin\theta\cos\theta + (\Sigma Y'^2)\cos^2\theta]}}{n} \quad [8.7]$$

where all variables are as defined previously.

6. Plot the standard deviational ellipse by centring the ellipse on the mean centre. The lengths of each axis are obtained by multiplying the standard distances, σ_X and σ_Y, by two. Orient the ellipse according to the angle θ measured clockwise from 'north' (the Y-axis passing through the mean centre). If it is negative, measure the angle anticlockwise. It is often possible to verify the correct orientation by visual examination of the ellipse and the scatter of points.

Example

Tables 8.3 and 8.4 and Fig. 8.3 provide an illustration of the calculations involved using the data from our Kitchener-Waterloo example. Equation [8.5] yields a tangent value for θ of −0.23, which is associated with an angle of approximately 13° and 347°. Since the tangent is negative, the orientation of the ellipse is anticlockwise 13° from 'north' (or clockwise 347°).

Table 8.3 Data for calculating standard deviational ellipse

Location	X	Y	X'	Y'	X'^2	Y'^2	$X'Y'$
A	15.2	34.8	−3.0	13.2	9.0	174.2	−39.6
B	14.2	31.5	−4.0	9.9	16.0	98.0	−39.6
C	21.6	28.6	3.4	7.0	11.6	49.0	23.8
D	11.1	24.1	−7.1	2.5	50.4	6.3	−17.8
E	12.8	23.8	−5.4	2.2	29.2	4.8	−11.9
F	16.0	25.5	−2.2	3.9	4.8	15.2	−8.6
G	16.5	24.8	−1.7	3.2	2.9	10.2	−5.4
H	15.5	22.5	−2.7	0.9	7.3	0.8	−2.4
I	16.5	21.6	−1.7	0.0	2.9	0.0	0.0
J	17.5	22.5	−0.7	0.9	0.5	0.8	−0.6
K	20.1	24.1	1.9	2.5	3.6	6.3	4.8
L	21.4	23.9	3.2	2.3	10.2	5.3	7.4
M	22.6	23.8	4.4	2.2	19.4	4.8	9.7
N	24.0	22.2	5.8	0.6	33.6	0.4	3.5
O	18.0	18.0	−0.2	−3.6	0.4	13.0	0.7
P	19.6	16.8	1.4	−4.8	2.0	23.0	−6.7
Q	20.0	15.8	1.8	−5.8	3.2	33.6	−10.4
R	20.0	13.8	1.8	−7.8	3.2	60.8	−14.0
S	19.9	8.4	1.7	−13.2	2.9	174.2	−22.4
T	21.5	5.8	3.3	−15.8	10.9	249.6	−52.1
	$\bar{X}$ = 18.2	$\bar{Y}$ = 21.6		Σ =	192.0	930.3	−181.6

Table 8.4 Calculation of standard deviational ellipse

$$\tan\theta = \frac{(\Sigma X'^2 - \Sigma Y'^2) + \sqrt{[(\Sigma X'^2 - \Sigma Y'^2)^2 + 4(\Sigma X'Y')^2]}}{2(\Sigma X'Y')}$$

$$= \frac{(192.0 - 930.3) + \sqrt{[(192.0 - 930.3)^2 + 4(-181.6)^2]}}{2(-181.6)}$$

$$= -0.23$$

$$\theta \simeq -13°$$

$$\sin\theta = -0.22 \qquad \cos\theta = 0.97$$

$$\sigma_X = \frac{\sqrt{[(\Sigma X'^2)(\cos^2\theta) - 2(\Sigma X'Y')(\sin\theta)(\cos\theta) + (\Sigma Y'^2)(\sin^2\theta)]}}{n}$$

$$= \frac{\sqrt{[(192.0)(0.95) - 2(-181.6)(-0.22)(0.97) + (930.3)(0.05)]}}{20}$$

$$= 0.62$$

$$\sigma_Y = \frac{\sqrt{[(\Sigma X'^2)(\sin^2\theta) + 2(\Sigma X'Y')(\sin\theta)(\cos\theta) + (\Sigma Y'^2)(\cos^2\theta)]}}{n}$$

$$= \frac{\sqrt{[(192.0)(0.05) + 2(-181.6)(-0.22)(0.97) + (930.3)(0.95)]}}{20}$$

$$= 1.56$$

X-axis = 2(0.62) = 1.24 units
Y-axis = 2(1.56) = 3.12 units

Equations [8.6] and [8.7] provided values for σ_X and σ_Y which, when doubled, give the lengths of the greater and the minor axes of the ellipse. These values, combined with the angle of rotation and mean centre, produced the ellipse shown in Fig. 8.3. As previously the units of measurement are arbitrary; they can be selected to conform to any scale appropriate to the problem at hand.

Defert's Tf

Description

Defert's *Tf* ('tourist function') (Defert 1967) is a crude measure of the importance of tourism within a regional economy. Specifically, *Tf* is the ratio between the number of tourist beds and the resident population. Because it is only a surrogate for the actual importance of tourism in a region, it must be used with caution. If the following warnings are observed, however, *Tf* can provide a useful measure of tourism development in a region.

The first warning is that comparison of values of *Tf* between cities of greatly different sizes can lead to some logical but misleading conclusions. Very large cities such as London, Paris, or Tokyo will

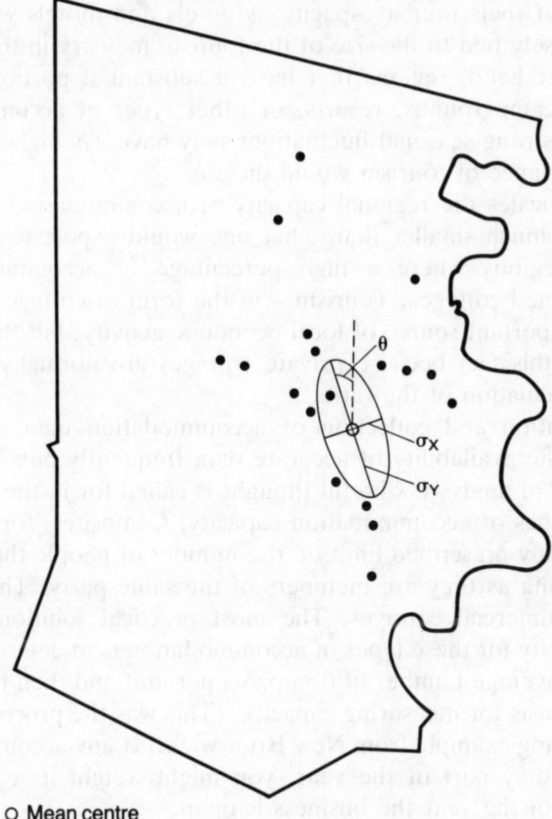

Fig. 8.3 Standard deviational ellipse for hotel and motel pattern in Kitchener-Waterloo, Ontario

usually have *Tf*s that are small to moderate, especially in comparison to *Tf*s of resort towns. This suggests, of course, that tourism is only a small to moderate sector of the economy of these large cities. This is true, but it should not be taken (as it easily could be) as evidence that tourism in large cities is of only small to moderate importance for the region or nation in which the city is located. Although the *Tf* for London, for example, will certainly not be the highest in the UK, London is responsible for more tourist-nights than any other single location in the UK. Care should be taken when making inferences from the size of a *Tf* about the importance of a city as a tourism generator in the context of a much larger region.

Also, *Tf* is vulnerable to a seasonal bias. Regions that have a large percentage of their tourist capacity as hotels and motels will usually have *Tf*s closely tied to the size of the tourism industry in that region. On the other hand, regions that have a substantial portion of their capacity in campgrounds, resorts, or other types of accommodation that exhibit strong seasonal fluctuations may have *Tf*s higher than the actual importance of tourism would dictate.

In some locales the regional capacity of accommodation may yield a *Tf* that is much smaller than what one would expect to find. This occurs in regions where a high percentage of accommodation is privately owned cottages. Tourism – in the form of cottage use – can be a very important source of local economic activity, but the *Tf* ratio would miss this fact because private cottages are normally excluded from the calculation of the ratio.

The definition and collection of accommodation data also poses problems. The availability of accurate data frequently puts a limit on the accuracy of analysis. Careful thought is called for in the definition of certain types of accommodation capacity. Campsites, for example, rarely have any prescribed limit on the number of people that can use them – as long as they are members of the same party. This is true, too, for commercial cottages. The most practical solution for estimating capacity for these types of accommodation is to determine from surveys the average number of occupants per unit and then to interpet that as the basis for measuring capacity. (This was the procedure used in the following example from New Brunswick.) If any accommodation is open for only part of the year, you might weight its capacity by the fraction of the year the business is open.

Procedures

1. Identify the range of tourist accommodation in a region: hotels, motels, cottages, resorts, campgrounds. Obtain reliable counts of the nightly capacity (in terms of 'beds' or 'person-nights') for each type of accommodation. Sum these and designate the total as *N*.
2. Obtain a reliable estimate of the local population, *P*.
3. Calculate *Tf*:

$$Tf = \frac{100(N)}{P} \qquad [8.8]$$

where the variables are as defined above.

Table 8.5 Calculation of *Tf* for selected counties in New Brunswick, Canada, 1980

	Hotels and motels (beds)	Cottages (beds)	Campsites (places)	Total capacity	Population	*Tf*
Albert	567	1 952	2709	5 228	21 946	23.8
King's	651	8 128	3651	12 430	43 137	28.8
Westmorland	5574	10 200	6321	22 095	102 617	21.5

Source: Keogh 1982.

Example

Table 8.5 is an example of the calculation of *Tf*. These data come from an unpublished study (Keogh 1982) of the New Brunswick (Canada) tourism industry. The number of hotel and motel rooms and campsites was collected for each county in the province (only three counties are shown in this example). The number of commercial cottages was also obtained from government sources. The number of rooms and campsites was multiplied by three, the average number of guests in a room or at a campsite; the number of cottages was multiplied by four, the average number of guests staying at a cottage. The number of beds in hotel and motel rooms was not weighted. These estimates were then totalled and transformed using Equation [8.8] to obtain county values of *Tf*.

Compactness index

Description

Much tourism research is concerned with describing the characteristics of destination regions: size, climate, attractiveness, level of development. One quality that is often overlooked but that can be of value is the shape of the region. Shape is a simple and valid measure of the overall internal accessibility of the region. The more compact a region, the easier it will be to ship commodities or to move tourists around the region, everything else being equal.

Many shape definitions, if given at all, tend to be qualitative. Brazil is triangular; Italy looks like a boot. These descriptions clearly have limited usefulness to planners or researchers, yet quantitative measures of shape have been slow to be developed. There are two major reasons for this slowness.

First, there are formidable technical problems to developing a usable measure of shape. Some of the indices that have been proposed involve the use of integral calculus, a level of mathematics not usually covered in most tourism programmes. Others require a lengthy list of every change in the direction of the boundary line. This latter procedure is commonly used on land deeds and in real-estate transactions, but it is not a practical, concise index of shape.

The other reason for the lack of interest traditionally in the shape of tourism regions may be that shape is determined by the boundary of the region – and the boundary is the edge of the irrelevant. Once a researcher gets to the boundary, he may not be interested in looking any further. This lack of interest in what lies beyond the boundary of a region can unintentionally be translated into a lack of interest in the shape of the boundary – and thus the shape of the region itself.

A number of shape indices have been developed by geographers. An overview of many of these is found in Coffey (1981: 101–4). One of the measures described by Coffey that shows some promise for tourism research is the compactness index, C. The use of C is appropriate because of the emphasis placed by planners on providing services to tourists in a region. The difficulty of service provision tends to vary inversely with the shape's compactness. The measure is also useful as an indicator of the relative degree of physical contact with surrounding regions (potential origins or destinations). The less compact the shape, the greater the relative boundary length and the greater the degree of contact with adjacent regions.

The compactness index has ratio scale properties. This makes it available for use in a wide variety of additional analyses. Like other measures of shape, though, it is incomplete. It indicates nothing about size, smoothness of the border, the presence of 'holes' within a region, or of separation of the region into two or more portions. The impossibility of developing a single measure of shape that contains all this information means that additional information, including maps, should be used to complement the compactness index.

Procedures

1. Obtain a base map of the region. Calculate the area of the region. A planimeter may be used if one is available, or you can use the simple but tedious process of overlaying a grid and counting squares. Designate the area as A.
2. Measure the greatest diagonal, D', of the region. This diagonal

Table 8.6 Calculation of index of compactness

Chile
Area measured from map: 56 square units
D' measured from map: 40 units
$D = 2\sqrt{[A/\pi]} = 2\sqrt{[56/3.1416]} = 8.44$
$C = \frac{D}{D'} = \frac{8.44}{40} = 0.21$

Zimbabwe
Area measured from map: 234 square units
D' measured from map: 21 units
$D = 2\sqrt{[A/\pi]} = 2\sqrt{[234/3.1416]} = 17.26$
$C = \frac{D}{D'} = \frac{17.26}{21} = 0.82$

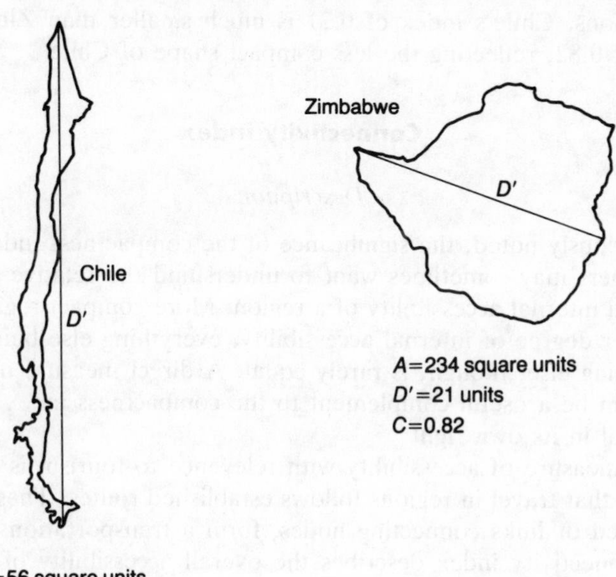

Fig. 8.4 Indices of compactness: Chile and Zimbabwe

is the longest straight line that can be drawn between any two points on the boundary of the region.

3. Calculate the diameter, D, of a circle with the same area as the region:

$$D = 2\sqrt{(A/\pi)} \qquad [8.9]$$

4. Calculate the compactness index, C:

$$C = \frac{D}{D'} \qquad [8.10]$$

The extreme values of C are 0.00, if the region were a line, and 1.00, if the region were a circle. The higher the value of C, the more compact the region.

Example

Equations [8.9] and [8.10] have been applied to two countries that illustrate the extremes of shape: a compact country, Zimbabwe, and an elongated country, Chile. Table 8.6 and Fig. 8.4 summarize these calculations. Chile's index of 0.21 is much smaller than Zimbabwe's index of 0.82, reflecting the less compact shape of Chile.

Connectivity index

Description

As previously noted, the significance of the compactness index is that researchers may sometimes want to understand the relative compactness and internal accessibility of a region. More compact regions have a greater degree of internal accessibility, everything else being equal. Everything else, though, is rarely equal. A direct measure of accessibility can be a useful complement to the compactness index and may be useful in its own right.

One measure of accessibility with relevance to tourism is based on the fact that travel in regions follows established routes. These routes, composed of links connecting nodes, form a transportation network. The connectivity index describes the overall accessibility of a region in terms of the level of interconnectivity among nodes in the network. In general, the higher the level of connectivity, the better for tourism.

The connectivity index comes from a branch of mathematics known as graph theory. Graph theory is concerned with the properties of networks. Taylor (1977: 58–65) identifies and discusses six basic measures used by graph theorists. Of these six, the gamma index, γ, also called the relative connectivity index, is the most appropriate for tourism. Gamma is independent of the absolute size of the network (a desirable quality when you want to compare different levels of network development), and it is relatively simple to calculate.

Gamma is based on the ratio of actual to possible linkages; it indicates nothing about the ease of travel, travel time, or the lengths of individual line segments. The higher the degree of connectivity within a network, the higher the value of γ. This simple statistic can produce deceptive results if you use it to draw conclusions about networks of greatly different physical size. Two networks might both have indices of 0.75, indicating a good degree of connectivity, but if one region has linkages averaging 10 km (6 miles) long and the other has linkages averaging 100 km (60 miles), the conclusion of equal accessibility must be properly interpreted. In this type of comparison, equal connectivity is not the same as equal travel cost or time.

Procedures

1. Obtain a map showing the major transportation corridors between towns, resorts, and other significant nodes or points. The definition of 'major corridors' and 'significant points' is a matter of professional judgement and will depend on the particular problem being studied. Because the index is based only on the topological properties of the network, the map need not be drawn to scale. In fact, a rough sketch or a stylized cartogram showing routes and notes is usable.
2. Count the number of direct links between pairs of points. Label this L.
3. Count the number of points, P.
4. Calculate γ:

$$\gamma = \frac{L}{3(P - 2)} \quad [8.11]$$

Equation [8.11] is basically the ratio between the actual number of links in a network and the total possible number given the existing points. Extreme values are 0.00 for a system of points totally unconnected with each other, and 1.00 for a system of points with all possible connections made. The index is meaningful for any network with three or more points.

Example

Figure 8.5 is an example of the calculation of γ for a portion of the highway network in Sweden. The value of 0.52 for γ indicates a system with only a moderate degree of connectivity. This can easily be seen by

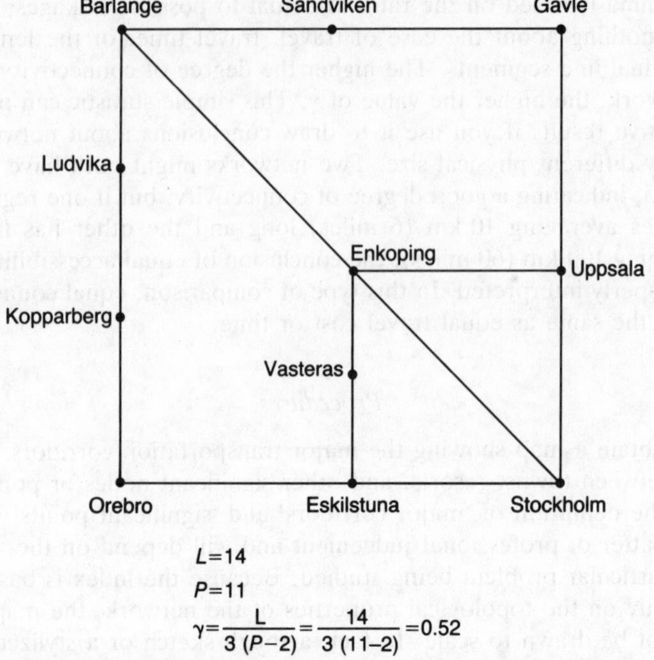

Fig. 8.5 Index of linkage connectivity: the example of a road network in Sweden

noting the relatively large number of towns that are linked to only two other towns.

You should note that equation [8.11] is appropriate only for networks that can be represented on a flat sheet of paper – so-called planar networks. This is normally no problem if we are studying road linkages for which every intersection is meaningful. Many times, though, in tourism networks linkages cross but do not form meaningful nodes. The flight paths of airlines are an example. These networks are non-planar and require a modification of equation [8.11]:

$$\gamma = \frac{L}{(0.5)P(P - 1)} \qquad [8.12]$$

If we apply equation [8.12] to our Swedish example, $\gamma = 0.25$. Note that this is much lower than the previous value of γ. The reason for the drop is that there are many more possible linkages if we are free to 'hop' over established lines to connect all points of the network.

Lorenz curves

Description

The Lorenz curve is an especially useful tool for answering a variety of questions about distributions. For example, tourism is sometimes identified by planners as a desirable industry for a region that wants to diversify its economic base. A fundamental question that should be answered when considering this suggestion is determining just how specialized is the current economy. The Lorenz curve can be used to describe this. Other analysts might be interested in examining the patterns of traffic on a road network in order to better understand the problem of tourist-generated traffic congestion. Again, the Lorenz curve can be employed to describe the degree of congestion.

More generally, one may define the Lorenz curve as a graphic comparison of the similarity between two patterns. It consists of a square with a diagonal and one or more curved lines connecting the ends of the diagonal, but falling some distance away from the diagonal over most of its length. The Lorenz curve can be interpreted visually, but it is best supplemented with the calculation of an index of dissimilarity.

In practice, there are two types of Lorenz curves: (1) a categorical curve; and (2) a bivariate curve. The first compares the concentration of some phenomenon over a range of categories to uniform distribution in those categories. The second compares the concentration of some phenomenon to a second or independent phenomenon. The two are closely related, but there are certain differences in the method of calculation of the index of dissimilarity, so they will be discussed separately.

Procedures for the categorical Lorenz curve

1. Data used for a Lorenz curve must meet certain requirements. The data must: (1) be expressible as percentages; (2) make sense when the percentages are added; (3) consist of positive values only; and (4) be capable of being assigned to discrete categories. Types of data that *cannot* be used include annual changes in the numbers of tourists, population or tourist density, attitude measures, and measures of regional attractiveness. In contrast, actual numbers of tourists, tourists' expenditures, business revenues, and numbers of trips can be described with a Lorenz curve. Once you have determined that your data meet

these requirements, arrange the data in a table similar to that in Table 8.6.

2. Set up a square graph similar to Fig. 8.6. The variable you wish to describe, *Y*, is plotted along the vertical axis; the categories are placed along the horizontal axis. Divide the vertical axis into equal intervals from 0 to 100 per cent. Divide the horizontal axis into an appropriate number of equal-sized units (the number being determined by the number of categories).
3. Sum the values of *Y*. Convert the individual values into percentages of this total. Order the percentages from high to low.
4. Plot the cumulative percentages of *Y* over all categories on the graph, beginning in the lower left-hand corner. The curve will begin steeply and become continuously less steep as it rises to the upper right-hand corner.

Example

Table 8.7 and Fig. 8.6 illustrate the construction of a categorical Lorenz curve. In this case the data describe the levels of employment in various sectors of a national and regional economy, represented by two separate curves. If employment in either the nation or the region were evenly distributed over all sectors, their curve would fall on the diagonal. On the other hand, if all employment were concentrated in one sector, the curve would form a right triangle covering the upper left-hand half of the square. In most cases the curve will fall between these extremes.

Note that in Fig. 8.6 the regional curve is further from the diagonal than the national curve. This indicates a higher degree of economic specialization in the region. A more precise measure of the relative degrees of specialization may be obtained in either of two ways. The simplest conceptually, but often the more tedious in practice, is to compare areas on the graph:

1. Calculate the area of the triangle formed by the diagonal, the lefthand border, and the top border.
2. Calculate the area between the curve and the diagonal.
3. Divide the area from step 2 by the area from step 1. The quotient is an index of dissimilarity that ranges from 0.00 (no concentration) to 1.00 (complete concentration in one category).

An alternative method requires a bit more arithmetic but allows for more flexibility and avoids the task of having to calculate areas:

Table 8.7 Hypothetical employment data for a 13-sector economy

Sector	Raw percentages: % in region	Raw percentages: % in nation	Ranked percentages: % in region	Cumulative region	% in nation	Cumulative nation	Cumulative percentages for diagonal (even distribution)
Fisheries	0.1	0.2	23.0	23.0	17.2	17.2	7.7
Forestry	0.2	0.5	18.5	41.5	14.6	31.8	15.4
Mining	0.7	0.1	13.4	54.9	11.3	43.1	23.1
Agriculture	2.8	3.5	12.0	66.9	11.1	54.2	30.8
Manufacturing	18.5	14.6	11.0	77.9	11.0	65.2	38.5
Construction	3.3	5.4	5.7	83.6	9.9	75.1	46.1
Transportation/communication	5.7	11.3	4.7	88.3	8.7	83.8	53.8
Trade	13.4	11.1	4.6	92.9	6.5	90.3	61.5
Finance, Insurance, Real Estate	4.7	6.5	3.3	96.2	5.4	95.7	69.2
Business/personal services	23.0	17.2	2.8	99.0	3.5	99.2	76.9
Commercial services	12.0	9.9	0.7	99.7	0.5	99.7	84.6
Other services	11.0	8.7	0.2	99.9	0.2	99.9	92.3
Public administration/defence	4.6	11.0	0.1	100.0	0.1	100.0	100.0
				$A = 1023.8$ $M = 13 \times 100 = 1300.0$		$R = 955.2$	$R = 699.9$ (100% ÷ 13 ≃ 7.7%)

Graphic method for regional curve:

$$\text{Index of dissimilarity} = \frac{\text{area between curve and diagonal}}{\text{area of upper left-hand triangle}} = \frac{2700 \text{ square units}}{5000 \text{ square units}} = 0.54$$

Arithmetic method for regional curve:
Using national curve as a reference:

$$I = \frac{A - R}{M - R} = \frac{1023.8 - 955.2}{1300.0 - 955.2} = 0.20$$

Using the diagonal as a reference:

$$I = \frac{1023.8 - 699.9}{1300.0 - 699.9} = 0.54$$

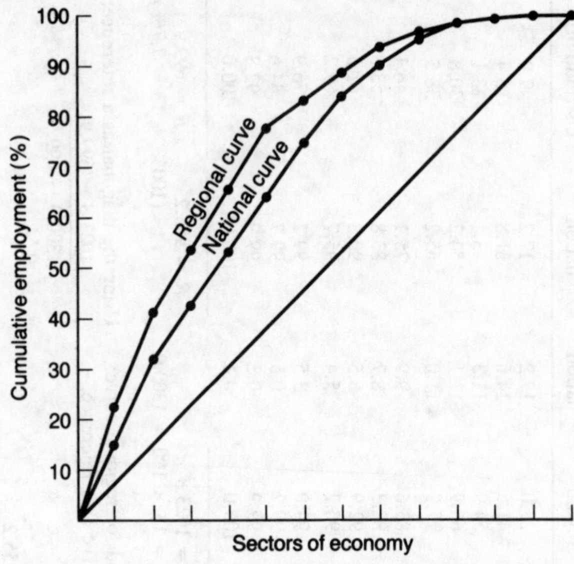

Fig. 8.6 Example of a categorical Lorenz curve using hypothetical employment data

1. Create a new column in the original data table showing the cumulative percentages. Sum the values of the cumulative percentages and designate the total as A.
2. Determine the maximum possible value of A – the value if the pattern were one of complete specialization. This would be represented by a value of 100 per cent in the first category; all subsequent categories would thus also show a value of 100 per cent. With 13 categories, the total would be $13 \times 100 = 1300$. Designate this value as M.
3. Compute the cumulative percentage total for a reference curve, usually (but not necessarily) the diagonal. Alternatives to the diagonal as a reference curve could include using the national curve as a reference for a regional curve. Designate the total cumulative percentage for the reference curve as R. With 13 categories, each category would have $100/13 = 7.7$ per cent. The cumulative percentages are shown in Table 8.6.
4. Calculate the index of dissimilarity, 1, with the following equation:

$$I = \frac{A - R}{M - R} \quad [8.13]$$

Note that the value of I depends on which curve is used as the reference curve. In any case, the lower the value of I, the greater the similarity between the two curves. A value of 0.00 indicates a perfect match; a value of 1.00 indicates no similarity between the two curves – complete specialization.

The index of dissimilarity has been calculated for our example with both methods. Indices using both the diagonal and the national curve as the references are determined for the regional curve as well. Notice that the index of dissimilarity should have the same value for the graphic and the arithmetic method when the diagonal is used as the reference curve.

This example illustrates a limitation in the Lorenz curve we have not yet mentioned. If we were to combine forestry, mining, and fisheries into a single category called 'primary industries', both the region and the nation would show a more balanced economy. The reason for this is not, of course, due to any structural change in the economy but only to statistical reasons: the new, aggregated sector has a larger percentage of the total employment than any of the three original sectors. Care must be taken, therefore, to make sure the scope of the categories used to report the data are the most appropriate for the problem at hand.

Procedures for the bivariate Lorenz curve

The major difference between the categorical and the bivariate curves is that the bivariate curve uses a second variable, X, in place of the categories. Both variables must meet the same data requirements described previously.

1. Begin with the construction of the Lorenz curve as described above, except mark both axes in percentages.
2. Before ranking the percentage values of Y in decreasing order, divide the value of Y for each observation by its corresponding X value. Use the resulting ratios to rank the observations from high to low. This step is necessary to ensure that the Lorenz curve will have the desired shape.
3. Plot the ranked percentages of Y against the corresponding percentages of X. Remember to use the ratio between Y and X to rank Y, but plot the cumulative percentages of X and Y, not the ratios.

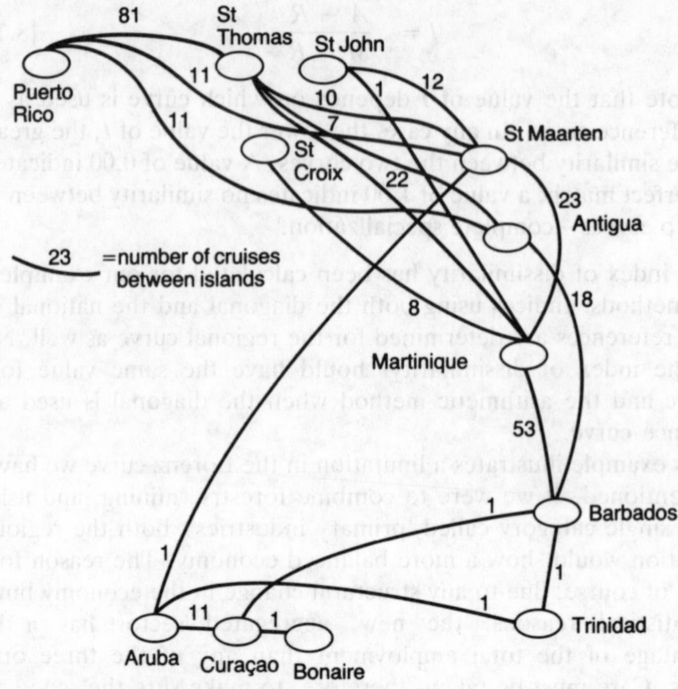

Fig. 8.7 Sample of cruise ship routes and voyages in the Lesser Antilles

4. If desired, calculate an index of dissimilarity using either method described previously.

Example

As an example of the calculation of the bivariate curve, consider the distribution of cruise ships and voyages in the Lesser Antilles. A quick glance at Fig. 8.7, a sketch-map of the relative locations of various islands and connecting ship routes reveals that there is a very uneven distribution in the number of voyages.

Table 8.8 contains a summary of the number and distribution of cruises. Distances between islands and the percentage distribution of distances is also shown. The ratios between the number of cruises and distances was then determined (Table 8.9) and used to rank the

Table 8.8 Distribution of a sample of cruise ship routes and voyages

Route	Routes between:	Cruises No.	Cruises % of total	Distances (km)	Distances % of total
1	Puerto Rico and St Thomas	81	29.7	100	1.2
2	St Maarten	11	4.0	300	3.6
3	Antigua	11	4.0	500	6.0
4	St Thomas and St Maarten	10	3.7	200	2.4
5	Antigua	7	2.6	400	4.8
6	Martinique	22	8.1	600	7.1
7	St John and St Maarten	12	4.4	200	2.4
8	Martinique	1	0.4	600	7.1
9	St Maarten and Martinque	23	8.4	600	7.1
10	Aruba	1	0.4	1000	11.9
11	St Croix and Martinique	8	2.9	500	6.0
12	Antigua and Barbados	18	6.6	500	6.0
13	Martinique and Barbados	53	19.4	200	2.4
14	Barbados and Trinidad	1	0.4	400	4.8
15	Curaçao	1	0.4	1100	13.1
16	Trinidad and Aruba	1	0.4	1000	11.8
17	Bonaire and Curaçao	1	0.4	100	1.2
18	Curaçao and Aruba	11	4.0	100	1.2
	Totals	273	100.0	8400	100.0

percentages of the number of cruises. Finally, a Lorenz curve was plotted (Fig. 8.8) and the index of dissimilarity calculated.

Nearest-neighbour analysis

Description

A researcher examining a map of the location of tourism facilities may sometimes wonder whether the pattern shows any semblance of order. Such a question is more than just idle interest. If you know that a pattern is clustered, for example, you may have a clue that will eventually lead to an insight about the forces that have given rise to that pattern.

Occasionally a simple visual inspection of a map is sufficient to indicate whether a pattern is clustered, uniform, or random. More often, though, simply looking at a map is not sufficient because

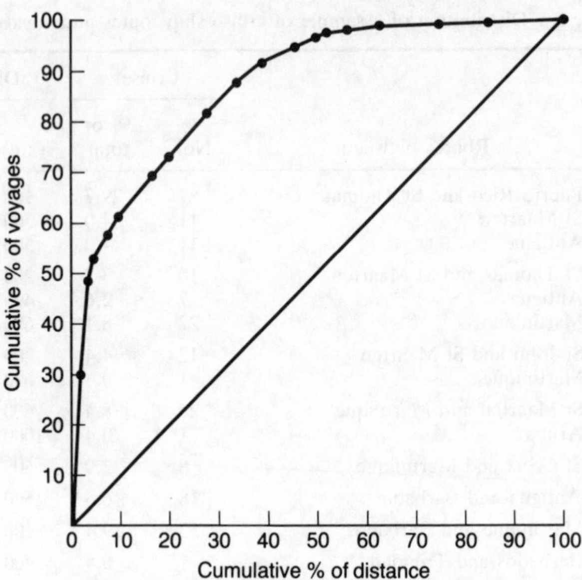

Fig. 8.8 Bivariate Lorenz curve for cruise ship concentration in the Lesser Antilles

elements of all three patterns may be present. A method to determine more precisely and objectively the nature of a point pattern is nearest-neighbour analysis. This procedure, originally developed by ecologists (Clark and Evans 1955, Grieg-Smith 1952) to study the distribution of vegetation, compares the average distance between each point and its nearest neighbour to a theoretical pattern based on the assumption of a random distribution. The decision whether a pattern is clustered, random, or uniform is based on the value of that ratio. More precisely, if the ratio between the observed average distance between nearest neighbours and the expected distance is less than 1.00, implying that the points are closer together than expected, one concludes the pattern is tending towards clustering. A value greater than 1.00 indicates a tendency towards uniform spacing. A value equal to 1.00 indicates a random pattern.

The concept of nearest-neighbour analysis is relatively simple, but there are several issues that need to be emphasized regarding its application. First, the ideal shape for delimiting an area to be studied is a square. It is not uncommon, though, to find that the use of a square to delimit a study area may include empty regions. We will look at an example of this issue later when we study the distribution of spas

Table 8.9 Rankings of percentages of cruise ship voyages and route lengths

Route	Ratio*
1	81.0
2	3.7
3	2.2
4	5.0
5	1.8
6	3.7
7	6.0
8	0.2
9	3.8
10	0.1
11	1.6
12	3.6
13	26.5
14	0.3
15	0.1
16	0.1
17	1.0
18	11.0

† Ratio = number of voyages/distance in 100 km units.

	Cruises		Distances	
Route	%Voyages	Cumulative %	% Distance	Cumulative %
1	29.7	29.7	1.2	1.2
13	19.4	49.1	2.4	3.6
18	4.0	53.1	1.2	4.8
7	4.4	57.5	2.4	7.2
4	3.7	61.2	2.4	9.6
9	8.3	69.5	7.1	16.7
2	4.0	73.5	3.6	20.3
6	8.1	81.6	7.1	27.4
12	6.6	88.2	6.0	33.4
3	4.0	92.2	6.0	39.4
5	2.6	94.8	4.8	44.2
11	2.9	97.7	6.0	50.2
17	0.4	98.1	1.2	51.4
14	0.4	98.5	4.8	56.2
8	0.4	98.9	7.1	63.3
16	0.4	99.3	11.8	75.1
10	0.4	99.7	11.8	86.9
15	0.4	110.0	13.1	100.0
		$A = 1441.9$		

$M = 18 \times 100 = 1800$

$R = 950.7$ (5.56% per route accumulated over 18 routes)

$$I = \frac{A - R}{M - R} = \frac{1441.9 - 950.7}{1800.0 - 950.7} = 0.58$$

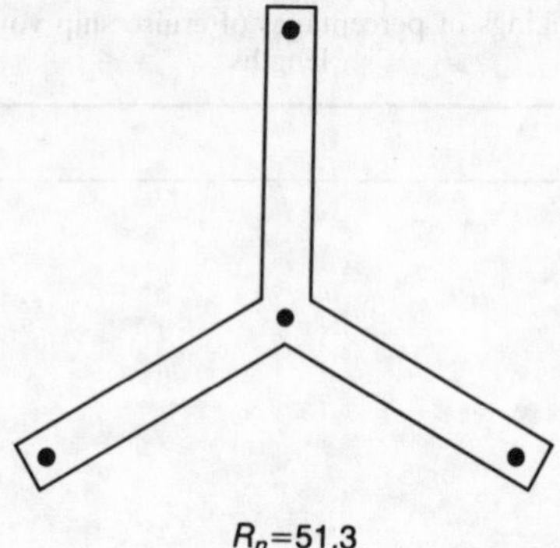

Fig. 8.9 Example of a figure capable of producing an extremely high R_n value

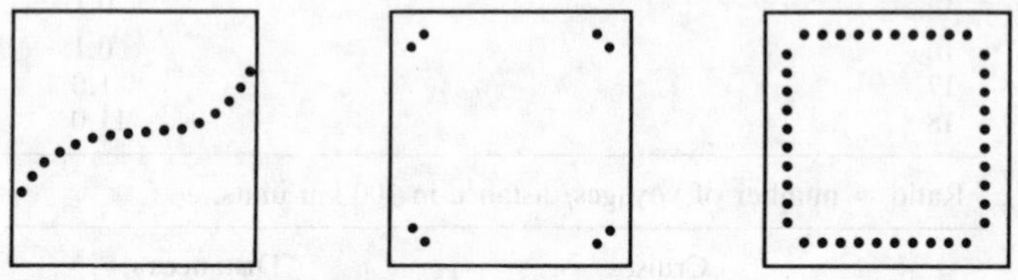

Fig. 8.10 Examples of patterns capable of producing small R_n values

in Europe. The square we will place over Europe includes portions of the Atlantic Ocean and the Mediterranean sea. The nearest-neighbour statistic applies to the entire area of the square, not just the land portion. Under such circumstances, geography can cause a bias towards clustering that may not necessarily reflect reality.

An alternative to the use of the square is to use the actual boundaries of the study area. While this is, in fact, a common practice, there is a potential danger because certain shapes can bias the empirical results of the analysis. An extreme example is given in Fig. 8.9. The theoretical maximum for the nearest-neighbour ratio is about 2.15; in this particular example the value of the ratio is 51.30.

Another difficulty that may be encountered in interpreting the value of the nearest-neighbour ratio is based on the fact that the ratio is calculated from averaged distances. Figure 8.10 is an illustration of three different patterns that have low ratios, indicating clustering. None of these, however, represent what most people would consider to be a clustered pattern.

One of the longest standing problems with nearest-neighbour analysis is known as the boundary effect. This effect arises when a boundary is drawn delineating, as a sample, a subregion causing the true nearest neighbours of some points to fall outside the boundary. If these points are ignored (which they should be), the nearest-neighbour ratio will be biased too high. The problem becomes greater with smaller numbers of points and smaller squares. The boundary problem had long been a serious obstacle to use of the method. A variety of procedures to correct it were ineffective, unreliable, or too complicated. The problem was ultimately resolved by Pinder (1978) who observed that the boundary effect is due to the procedure for estimating the theoretical distance. He developed a different method for estimating the distance by accounting for variable numbers of points and variable square sizes. His procedure has been incorporated into the method given below.

Finally, distances between nearest neighbours are measured as straight lines on a map. In reality, this ignores the effects of perceptions, borders, physical barriers, and transportation networks. For example, a spa on the northern coast of France may have its nearest neighbour in England, across the English Channel. The effects of a political boundary, language differences, and the physical barrier of open water may mean the two spas are functionally more distant than two spas, 100 km (60 miles) apart, but still in France. Little work has been done to develop the use of perceptual distance or accessibility as substitutes so it remains an area of needed research.

Procedures

1. Obtain a map of the region being studied. Plot the location of the features you are studying as points.

2. Draw a square to encompass the distribution of points. The size of the square is important. The larger the square the more likely that you will produce a low nearest-neighbour ratio, and thus conclude that the pattern is clustered. There is no firm rule to determine the size of the square to be used, but some guidelines are possible. If you are studying a sample space in a larger region, draw the square of such a size that it fits well within the total region. If, on the other hand, you are examining an entire population of points, choose between two strategies on the basis of project characteristics. A square may be drawn that is just large enough to encompass all the points, ignoring natural boundaries. This is appropriate if there is little chance the pattern will ever grow beyond its current range. Should you expect the

pattern to grow, however, then it is more appropriate to use a square just large enough to encompass the entire study region.

Although the size of the square is important, its orientation is not. The square may be rotated in any direction to make the closest fit to the point pattern.

3. Calculate the area of the square, a.
4. Count the number of points, n, within the square.
5. Measure the distance between each point and its nearest neighbour. Add these and divide by n to obtain the mean distance, d_o.
6. Determine the theoretical average distance if all points were randomly distributed:

$$d_r = C[\sqrt{(a/n)}] \quad [8.14]$$

where: d_r = theoretical mean distance;
$C = 0.487 + 0.127[\sqrt{(a/n)}]$

7. Calculate the nearest-neighbour ratio:

$$R_n = \frac{d_o}{d_r} \quad [8.15]$$

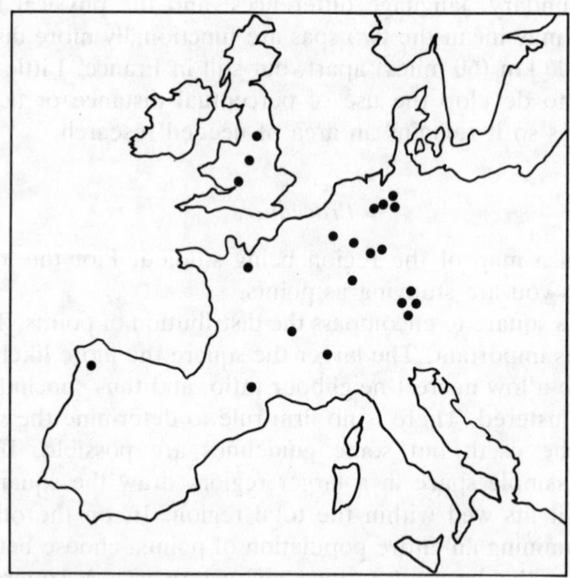

a=1936 square units
n=21 points

Fig. 8.11 Locational patterns of major spas in Europe

8. Interpret the value of R_n. Interpretation is based on the null hypothesis of a random distribution indicated by $R_n = 1.00$. Values significantly larger than 1.00 indicate a tendency towards regularity or uniform spacing. A perfectly uniform hexagonal pattern (the pattern with the maximum degree of dispersal) has an R_n value of 2.15. Values significantly less than 1.00 indicate a tendency towards clustering. Complete clustering (when all points occupy the space location) produces a value of 0.00.

When you study the distribution of an entire population of points, it is not necessary, strictly speaking, to use significance tests to make inferences about the patterns. However, because patterns that give values of precisely 0.00, 1.00, or 2.15 are quite rare, a significance test can help interpret whether an observed pattern reasonably approaches one of these values. A test for the significance of R_n has been developed by Pinder (1978) and may be found in the Appendix at the end of this book.

Example

An illustration of the use of nearest-neighbour analysis can be seen in reference to the map of European spas in Fig. 8.11. Each of the 21

Table 8.10 Nearest-neighbour analysis for pattern in Fig. 8.11

Nearest-neighbour distances (arbitrary units)	
5.5	$C = 0.497 + 0.127 \sqrt{(a/n)}$
3.0	$= 0.497 + 0.127 \sqrt{(1936/21)}$
3.0	$= 1.716$
1.0	
1.0	$d_r = C \sqrt{(a/n)}$
1.0	$= 1.716 \sqrt{(1936/21)}$
1.0	$= 16.48$
2.5	
1.0	
1.0	$R_n = \dfrac{d_o}{d_r}$
1.5	
1.5	$= 1.9/16.48$
0.5	$= 0.12$
0.5	
0.5	
0.5	
6.5	
2.0	
2.0	
2.0	
2.0	
39.5	$39.5/21 = 1.9 = d_o$

major spas has been located on a map and the entire region delineated by a square. For the purpose of this example, the square includes much of Western Europe and some of Eastern Europe. The map area was calculated in arbitrary units; it covers a total of 1936 square units. Distance to the nearest neighbour of each point was determined directly by measuring them on the map using the same scale applied to determining map area. The distance for each pair of points is listed in Table 8.10. Here R_n was calculated using the procedure described above. The value of 0.12 indicates a clustered pattern. This is due, in part, to the geological processes that create the hot springs on which the site selection of spas is based. It is also due to the fact that the spas are 'forced' into relatively close proximity within the context of the square by the limited land area of the European continent.

Linear nearest-neighbour analysis

Description

Linear nearest-neighbour analysis is a modification by Pinder and Witherick (1975) of regular nearest-neighbour analysis for use in linear situations such as patterns along highways, rivers, or coastlines. It is of special value when studying the spacing of tourism businesses such as hotels or restaurants along a highway or urban street.

The distances between tourism businesses or other landscape features are usually measured in physical units. Other measures, however, are possible. Travel time, travel cost, and even the number of intervening features might be adapted for use if they are pertinent to your problem and can be defined on an objective, ratio scale.

The same precautions about the use and interpretation of the nearest-neighbour ratio generally apply for the linear version, with the exception of the question of the shape of the study region. It also bears stressing that both versions should be used only when a good working hypothesis has been developed concerning the expected distribution of points. Calculation of these ratios with no particular purpose in mind is pointless.

Procedures

1. Begin with a dot map showing the distribution of facilities along a linear feature. Measure the length of the line, L. This line may be defined by reference to either natural end-points, such as the points where a highway crosses a political boundary, or

by reference to arbitrary end-points. The most common arbitrary end-points are the two extreme observations in the distribution. If these are used as the termini for the line, they must not be used in the subsequent analysis as observation points. To do so would bias the ratio value high, leading you to conclude a greater tendency towards regularity than is the correct case.

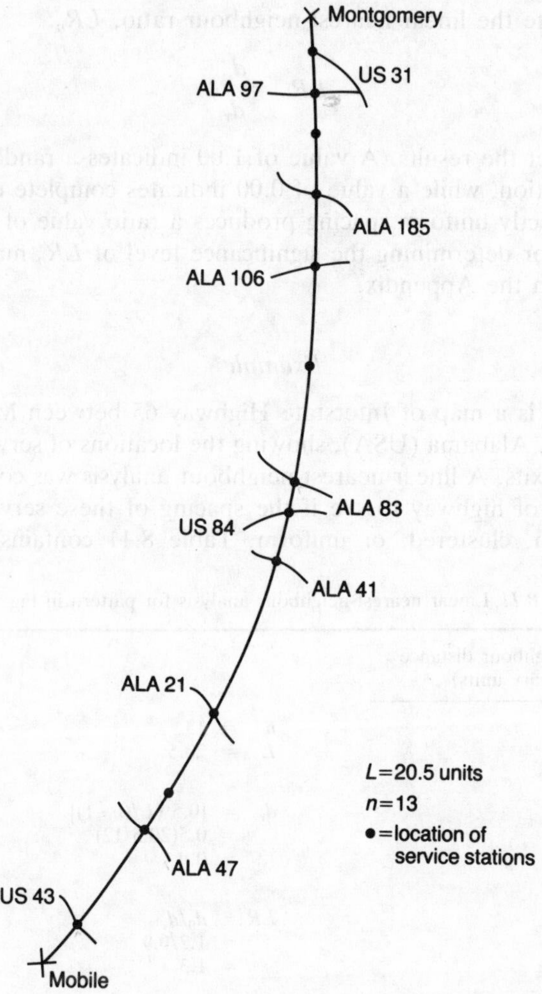

Fig. 8.12 Locational pattern of service stations along I-65 between Montgomery and Mobile, Alabama

2. Count the number of observation points, n.
3. Measure the distance between each point and its nearest neighbour along the length of the line. Determine the mean distance, d_o.
4. Estimate the theoretical distance between points under the condition of a random distribution:

$$d_r = 0.5[L/(n-1)] \quad [8.16]$$

5. Calculate the linear nearest-neighbour ratio, LR_n:

$$LR_n = \frac{d_o}{d_r} \quad [8.17]$$

6. Interpret the results. A value of 1.00 indicates a random distribution, while a value of 0.00 indicates complete clustering. A perfectly uniform spacing produces a ratio value of 2.00. A graph for determining the significance level of LR_n may be found in the Appendix.

Example

Figure 8.12 is a map of Interstate Highway 65 between Montgomery and Mobile, Alabama (USA), showing the locations of service stations at various exits. A linear nearest-neighbour analysis was conducted on this stretch of highway to see if the spacing of these service stations was random, clustered, or uniform. Table 8.11 contains the calcu-

Table 8.11 Linear nearest-neighbour analysis for pattern in Fig. 8.12

Nearest-neighbour distance (arbitrary units)		
2.3		$n = 13$
0.9		$L = 20.5$
0.9		
1.8		
1.0		$d_r = [0.5\ (L/(n-1))]$
0.6		$= 0.5(20.5/12)$
0.6		$= 0.9$
2.0		
1.4		$LR_n = d_0/d_r$
1.4		$= 1.2/0.9$
0.7		$= 1.3$
0.7		
0.7		
15.0	$15.0/13 = 1.2 = d_0$	

lations involved for the 13 observations. The ratio between the observed nearest-neighbour distance and that expected was 1.3. Referring to the significance graph in the Appendix, a value of 1.3 for 13 observations falls just within the area that indicates a randomness in spacing.

Spatial association index

Description

The spatial association index, developed by Lee (1979), is a method for comparing point pattern distributions. Like nearest-neighbour analysis, this index uses the logic of comparing an expected pattern to an observed pattern to reach a conclusion about the degree of clustering, dispersion, or randomness. It differs from nearest-neighbour analysis in one important way. The spatial association index compares the distribution of one set of points to the distribution of a second set; regular nearest-neighbour analysis merely compares the distribution of a single set to a theoretical pattern.

The usefulness of the spatial association index might be seen in a simple example. Assume you have the task of analysing the distribution of fast-food franchises in a large urban area. You suspect that the outlets of any one chain, say 'McSmith's Burgers', tend to avoid locating near other outlets of the same chain, but seek locations close to other franchise operations. Regular nearest-neighbour analysis can tell you whether McSmith's outlets tend to disperse with respect to each other, but it could not be used to indicate anything about the patterns of McSmith's in comparison to all other franchise fast-food operations. This is when you would use the spatial association index.

The values of the spatial association index range from 0.00 upwards. Its interpretation is similar to that of nearest-neighbour analysis: a value of 1.00 indicates a random distribution; values significantly less than 1.00 indicate clustering of one set of points with reference to the other set; values significantly greater than 1.00 indicate spatial avoidance. There is no upper limit to the value of the spatial association index. The reason for this is that the maximum value is a function of two separate point patterns and their respective densities.

Procedures

1. Follow steps 1 to 4 as described in the section on nearest-neighbour analysis. Be sure, however, to use separate symbols

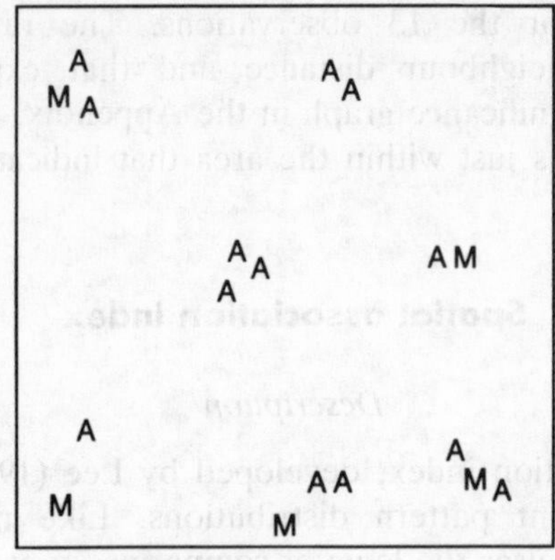

Fig. 8.13 Hypothetical location pattern of fast-food franchises

for the two sets of points you plot. Also be sure to obtain separate counts for the number of points in each set. Label these counts n_1 and n_2. Designate their total $(n_1 + n_2)$ as N.

2. Calculate the relative proportions of the two sets of points:

$$m_1 = \frac{n_1}{N} \quad [8.18]$$

$$m_2 = \frac{n_2}{N} \quad [8.19]$$

note that $m_1 + m_2 = 1.00$.

3. Measure the distance between each point in the set you are studying and its nearest neighbour in the reference set of points. Total these distances and divide by the number of points in the study set to obtain the mean distance, d_o.
4. Determine the theoretical average distance if all points were randomly distributed:

$$d_r = \frac{m_1}{2[\sqrt{(n_2/a)}]} + \frac{m_2}{2[\sqrt{(n_1/a)}]} \quad [8.20]$$

5. Calculate the spatial association index:

$$R^* = \frac{d_o}{d_r} \quad [8.21]$$

Table 8.12 Calculation of spatial association index for Fig. 8.13

Area = 59.29 square units

5 McSmith's restaurants = n_1

13 Other restaurants = n_2

18 = N

$$m_1 = \frac{5}{18} = 0.28$$

$$m_2 = \frac{13}{18} = 0.72$$

$$d = \frac{0.28}{2\sqrt{(13/59.29)}} + \frac{0.72}{2\sqrt{(5/59.29)}} = 0.30 + 1.24 = 1.54$$

Nearest-neighbour distances for McSmith's (arbitrary units)

0.4
0.3
1.2
0.5
0.7

$3.1 \div 5 = 0.62 = d_o$

$$R^* = \frac{d_o}{d} = \frac{0.62}{1.54} = 0.40$$

6. R^* may be interpreted the same way as R_n is interpreted described previously in this chapter. A significance test for R^* can be found in the Appendix.

Example

A comparison of the distribution of two sets of hypothetical restaurants will illustrate the application of the spatial association index. Figure 8.13 is a map of the locations of a hamburger franchise (McSmith's) and all other fast-food restaurants in an urban area. The procedure described above was followed, and the results summarized in Table 8.12. The result was a spatial association index of 0.40, indicating that McSmith's tends to be found close to other fast-food outlets.

Peaking index

Description

A characteristic of many tourism businesses is that the number of customers varies dramatically over time. Restaurants boom on weekends and holidays, but are quiet in the early part of the week. Resorts are booked solid for a few weeks or months and then operate at a much reduced level the rest of the year, It can be helpful for a business planner or recreation programmer to be able to measure quantitatively the tendency for people to use a facility or visit a region in one time period as opposed to other periods. Tabulation of frequencies for different time periods can be of use, but these do not provide a succinct index. A measure that summarizes a substantial amount of data on temporal use levels into a single value is the peaking index (Stynes 1978). This measure is an open-ended scale with a minimum value of 0.00. The greater the degree of concentration (peak use), the greater the value of the index. The index is derived from a graph called an exceedance curve – so called because the curve illustrates the number of times a particular use level was reached or exceeded.

By itself, the index, P_n, is not especially informative. The value depends not only on the degree of peaking but also on the total volume of business and on the choice of time periods used for analysis. The primary use of the index, therefore, is for comparison between businesses or for examination of trends in peaking over time in one facility.

As noted, P_n varies also with the size of the time period chosen for analysis. For example, if you are working with hotel occupancy data, you will be likely to work with monthly averages. If the busiest month had an occupancy rate of 90 per cent, while the slowest month had a rate of 40 per cent, some days in the busiest month will have exceeded 90 per cent while some days in the slowest month will have fallen short of 40 per cent. The use of daily data would lead to different conclusions from those reached with monthly data. There is insufficient information and experience to suggest the degree to which aggregation of time periods into larger units changes the results of P_n, but in general the value of the index indicates less peaking as longer time periods are chosen for analysis.

In the absence of objective guidelines for selecting the size of the time period to study, the choice must depend on the availability of data, the purposes of study, and common sense. It would not be wise, for example, to collect hotel occupancy data on an hourly basis if you are interested in annual patterns. Not only would the volume of data be unwieldy, rooms are let (in most reputable establishments) on a nightly basis, not hourly. On the other hand, an analysis of use levels in a theme park on a typical weekend might well be based on hourly periods.

Procedures

1. Obtain use figures for the business or facility in question. Group these by day, week, or other appropriate time period. The data must

cover a reasonably long period, often an entire year. Either actual numbers of users or occupancy rates may be used.

2. Place the individual use levels and their associated time periods in decreasing order.

3. Plot the data on a graph similar to that in Fig. 8.14. The graph itself provides a quick visual indication of the relative peaking of use at the business: the sharper the drop-off in the curve, the greater the concentration of visitors in a short period of time.

4. A more precise measure of peaking of use is obtained through the equation:

$$P_n = \frac{V_1 - V_n}{(n - 1)V_1} \times 100 \qquad [8.22]$$

where: P_n = peaking index;
V_1 = number of visitors during busiest period;
V_n = number of visitors during nth period;
n = reference period (1 = busiest period).

Here P_n equals 0.00 when the number of visitors is the same in all time periods. Its value increases as use levels concentrate in certain periods. As explained previously, the upper limit of P_n depends on the total level of use and the choice of n. The value of n, the time period used for comparison with the busiest period, is largely a matter of choice. You might choose the mid-point in the data (and exceedance curve) or else a value of n reflecting some natural division in the schedule of the facility. If a resort finds its year divided into four seasons of about three months each, with different visitor patterns, activities, and marketing issues in each season, you might select an n of 3 (the length of one season) as a useful basis for analysis.

Example

Table 8.13 and Fig. 8.14 provide an example of the calculation of P_n. In this case, the occupancy rates are for various tourist accommodations in Vancouver, British Columbia (Canada). The busiest month in Vancouver is traditionally August, with an average occupancy rate of 96 per cent. This drops off until a low is reached in December. A value of 6 for n, reflecting the mid-point in the number of months over a year, was arbitrarily chosen for the analysis. Application of equation [8.22] produced a value of 2.90 for P_n.

Table 8.13 Recent occupancy rates for hotels and motels in Vancouver, Canada

Month	Occupancy rate (%)
August	96
July	91
September	91
June	89
October	85
May	82
April	74
March	72
November	70
February	60
January	53
December	49

$$P_n = \frac{V_1 - V_6}{(n - 1)V_1} \times 100 = \frac{96 - 82}{(5)\ 96} \times 100 = 2.9$$

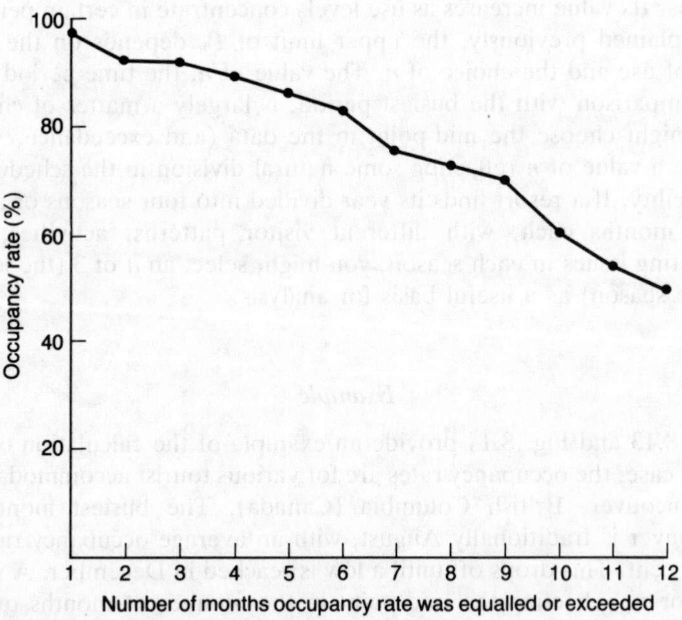

Fig. 8.14 Exceedance curve for tourist accommodation in Vancouver, British Columbia, 1979

Directional bias index

Description

Vacation travel, whether that of individuals, groups, or entire populations, often shows a predilection for one particular direction. The percentage of Canadians travelling south in the winter, for example, is much higher than the number of Canadians heading north. The directional bias index, developed by Wolfe (1966), is a simple measure of this tendency. It is an origin-specific index because it summarizes the travel patterns of an origin with respect to each of its destinations. The index can be used as one component of a large systematic description of the travel patterns of a region or population, or it can be used as an independent variable in modelling travel flows and in testing hypotheses about the forces affecting travel patterns.

The index is only a measure of the proportion or relative distribution of trips from one origin to each destination. It does not reflect the net balance of travel between two regions. For those situations in which you might wish to study the reverse flow, the index may be easily generalized to cover this need. All regions may be considered in turn as an origin and then as a destination. The index, though, still indicates nothing about net travel between two regions. If this is of interest, it must be calculated separately. It should be noted, though, that net flow by itself does not indicate a directional bias. Both statistics, net flow and directional bias, can be used together to obtain a fuller picture of travel flows than either would indicate by itself.

The directional bias index also ignores the actual route of the trip, and it does not indicate anything about travel time or costs. The index is not useful either for vacations that do not have a single destination, such as touring vacations.

On the positive side, the index does have ratio scale properties so it can be subjected to a wide range of statistical analyses. Although its applications are quite limited, it is a useful and reliable index of one particular tourism phenomenon.

Procedures

1. Construct an origin – destination matrix, similar to that in Table 8.11. Each origin is represented by a row; each destination by a column. The individual cells contain the number of trips (person-trips, person-nights, or other appropriate unit) for an

Table 8.14 Hypothetical travel data for calculation of directional bias index

Origins		Destinations j A	B	C	D	$\Sigma T_i =$
i	a	50	30	10	25	115
	b	60	90	15	5	170
	c	10	10	80	15	115
	d	25	5	30	75	135
	$\Sigma T_j =$	145	135	135	120	

For travel from a to A:

$$D_{aA} = \frac{10^5(T_{ij})}{\Sigma T_i \, \Sigma T_j} = \frac{10^5(50)}{(115)\,(145)} = 300$$

origin–destination pair. Designate each cell as T_{ij}, where i is the origin and j is the destination.

2. Calculate the totals for each row and column. Designate these as ΣT_i and ΣT_j respectively.
3. Obtain the directional bias index, D, for any origin from:

$$D = \frac{10^5(T_{ij})}{\Sigma T_i \Sigma T_j} \qquad [8.23]$$

where 10^5 is a scaling factor; any weight of appropriate size may be substituted as desired.

Example

Table 8.14 and Fig. 8.15 offer an illustration of the calculation of the directional bias index. Hypothetical data have been created for this system of four regions and four destinations. We can see in Table 8.14 that the number of trips from origin *a* to destination B is 30. Origin *a* generates a total of 115 trips distributed over all destinations, while destination B receives 135 trips from all origins. Using equation [8.23],

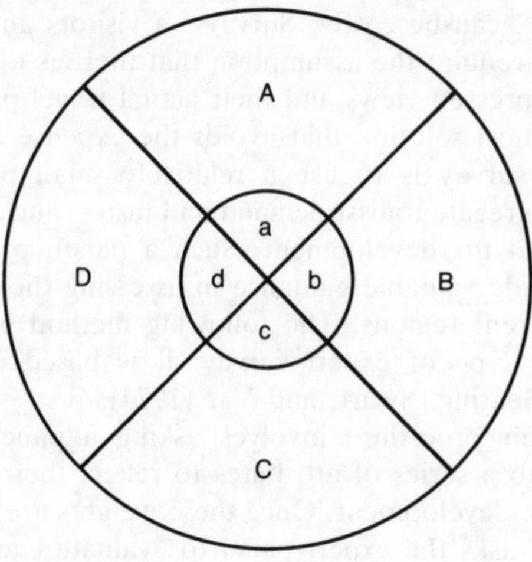

Fig. 8.15 Hypothetical tourism system with four origins and four destinations

we obtain index values for trips from *a* to A of 300, *a* to B of 193, and so forth.

Tourism attractiveness index

Description

An important problem in regional tourism planning is the assessment of the potential of candidate regions for attracting tourists. A region with few historic sites, little natural beauty, poor climate, no beach, limited recreational or shopping opportunities, and little potential to develop these will be a poor choice for public or private investment. A planner familiar with a number of different regions being considered for development may have an intuitive feel for the relative attractiveness of different regions, but personal impressions are not always reliable enough for business or policy decisions. A better method would be to use the evaluations of a number of informed individuals, objective data, and a systematic evaluation procedure. In the best of all possible worlds, such a method might also use the expressed preferences of actual and potential visitors to obtain insights into visitors' decision-making criteria. An adequate sample of the general travelling public, however, can be costly. Surveys of visitors and potential visitors would also require the assumption that there is a high correlation between the expressed views and their actual travel patterns.

A more practical solution that avoids the expense and difficulty of a large public survey is to use a relatively small panel of experts familiar with aggregate tourist demand and tastes, and with the regions being considered for development. Such a panel, properly administered, can provide valuable guidance in assessing the tourism attractiveness of different regions. The following method is an outline for conducting this type of expert survey; it is based on a procedure developed by Gearing, Swart, and Var (1974).

Basically, their procedure involves asking a panel of experts to assign weights to a series of attributes to reflect their overall importance for tourism development. Once these weights are established, the researcher then asks the expert panel to evaluate each of a series of tourism regions on these attributes. This evaluation is done with a numerical scale so that regional scores can be weighted by attribute weights. Relative attractiveness scores are then obtained by adding up the individual attribute scores for each region.

The potential user of this method should be aware of certain assumptions on which the validity of this procedure rests. Anyone employing the tourism attractiveness index should take care to verify the validity of these assumptions before placing too much faith in the results.

First, the method requires that all relevant attributes be identified. Failure to do so will bias the results to an unknown degree and in an unknown direction. A user of this method further assumes that all attributes identified can be adequately evaluated in terms of a ratio scale. The key word here is 'adequate'. No one would presume to suggest that the artistic and architectural features of the region including Rome (if these were one set of attributes) could be adequately described on a ten point scale. On the other hand, the relative overall attractiveness of the Rome region *vis-à-vis* other regions of Italy might well be capable of being summarized on such a scale.

The use of a simple scale can also be problematic when you are trying to summarize and compare complex criteria, such as climate, for regions whose characteristics run the entire spectrum of possible qualities. For example, if you were evaluating the states of the USA on the basis of climate, what type of meaningful comparison could be made between Florida with warm temperatures and sunshine and Colorado with an excellent winter sports climate? When this type of comparison causes problems, the solution is to make a more precise designation of the criteria and of the type of development to be used as a reference for evaluating the regions.

A user also assumes the scales are reliable and valid measures of the criteria. One test that can be used to check on the reliability of the experts' judgements is to examine the overall similarity of standardized criteria weights across all judges. Kendall's coefficient of concordance (described in many standard statistical texts) is often an appropriate measure to use for this. The question of validity of the experts' judgements is more difficult. Indeed, it is virtually untestable. Your best assurance here is to select the most reputable, able, and sincere judges available.

Finally, this entire procedure rests on the assumption that the total attractiveness of a region may be estimated by the addition of weighted attribute scores. This assumption means that there is no significant interaction effect between the various regional characteristics that would affect attractiveness. It further means that the failure of a region to provide any level of some quality (indicated by a score of 0.00 for that criterion) does not eliminate that region from consideration as a candidate for development.

This last assumption may be the most dubious, yet it is difficult to refute empirically. In the matter of critical attributes (those that must be present for a region to be considered), you could use these as filters in the same way that critical attributes were described in Chapter 6 in connection with the checklist method for site selection.

With respect to interaction effects, you could examine each attribute in relationship to every other attribute to identify any obvious problems such as two qualities that actually measure the same thing, one attribute that would negate the possibility of another, or two variables whose combination would produce a result greater than the simple sum of those two variables would otherwise imply. If any such problem pairings are found, you can identify new attributes that might avoid the problem.

Any user of this procedure needs to maintain a balance between the blind and uncritical belief in the potential for quantifying the attractiveness of a tourism region and a defeatist scepticism about the value of any quantitative tool for providing usable attractiveness information. If this sense of balance is achieved, and if the research design is followed carefully with attention paid to the need to identify and evaluate carefully all relevant regional characteristics, the tourism attractiveness index can be a valuable planning tool.

Procedures

1. Establish a list of attributes for judging the attractiveness of tourism regions. These attributes will be specific to the regions being considered; the list should be as comprehensive as possible. The attributes should be stated as precisely as is practical, and should be mutually independent, not implying the existence of each other and not contradicting the potential existence of each other. The list can be developed by yourself if you have adequate expertise or it may be developed with the aid of a series of experts.

2. Group the individual criteria into a small number of major categories. Gearing, Swart, and Var (1974) used the following attributes and categories: (1) *natural factors* – (a) natural beauty, and (b) climate; (2) *social factors* – (a) architecture, (b) festivals, (c) other folk cultural attractions; (3) *historical factors* – (a) ancient ruins, (b) religious shrines and practices, and (c) historical importance; (4) *shopping and recreational resources* – (a) sport opportunities, (b) museums, zoos, aquaria, gardens, (c) health and relaxation opportunities, (d) stores and shops; and (5) *tourism infrastructure* – (a) adequate roads, utilities, health services, and (b) adequate food and lodging facilities.

3. Select a panel of experts to assign weights to these criteria. There is no firm rule about the number and make-up of the panel, but aim for diversity in the background, competence, and ability to work in a group. A panel of 20 to 40 individuals is probably a number to work with. Gearing, Swart, and Var, for example, chose a panel of 26 experts from travel agencies, government tourism policy offices, airlines, hotels, and universities.

4. Present the panel with the criteria and instructions for assigning weights. Numerous weighting procedures are possible; a method developed by Churchman, Ackoff, and Arnoff (1957) has received widespread acceptance and is appropriate in this type of problem. Details of their procedure are provided in the Appendix. Basically, their method involves a systematic comparison of weights between pairs of attributes to produce a series of weights, W_i, ranging from 0.00 to 1.00.

5. Once the panel has assigned weights to each criterion, have them evaluate the degree to which each region meets that criterion. Each region should be rated on a 0.00 to 1.00 scale. Obtain the mean ranking across all panel members for each criterion in each region. Designate the mean criterion score for each criterion in each region as S_{ij}, where i refers to the criterion and j refers to the region. Multiply

Table 8.15 Calculation of a hypothetical touristic attraction index

Criteria	Weight ×	Hypothetical regional evaluation	= Weighted score
Natural beauty	0.132	0.80	0.106
Infrastructure	0.131	0.80	0.105
Food and lodging	0.125	0.70	0.087
Climate	0.099	0.50	0.050
History	0.065	0.60	0.039
Archaeological sites	0.057	0.90	0.051
Local attitudes	0.054	0.70	0.038
Religious significance	0.053	0.70	0.037
Art and architecture	0.051	0.50	0.026
Sports facilities	0.046	0.30	0.014
Nightlife	0.045	0.30	0.013
Shopping	0.036	0.30	0.011
Peace and quiet	0.032	0.80	0.026
Festivals	0.029	0.80	0.023
Local features	0.026	0.70	0.018
Educational facilities	0.015	0.50	0.007
Fairs and exhibits	0.011	0.60	0.007
		Touristic attractiveness score =	0.658

each score, S_{ij}, by the appropriate weight, W_i, to obtain a measure of the attractiveness of each region in terms of any criterion.

6. Finally, sum each region's A_{ij}s to derive a single measure of the relative tourism attractiveness of that region, A_j.

Example

Gearing, Swart, and Var's (1974) study was conducted for 65 tourism regions in Turkey. The procedure outlined above was followed for establishing weights for each of the 17 criteria noted in step 2, resulting in the weights shown in Table 8.15. Each of the tourism regions was then evaluated by a panel of experts to produce relative attractiveness scores. Scores for one region are also shown in Table 8.15, along with the weighted attractiveness score calculation.

Summary

Tourism analysts have a wide choice of descriptive procedures. The possibilities include simple tabulations and percentage summaries as well as the better-known univariate statistics such as mean and variance. Tourism analysts, however, are not limited to these methods;

more specialized and more informative descriptive tools are available. Many of the more important ones have been discussed in this chapter. A few of these – Defert's *Tf*, the peaking index, the directional bias index, and the tourism attractiveness index – were developed specifically for tourism and recreational travel applications. Still others have been borrowed from various social sciences, especially geography. The importance of the geographic perspective in tourism may be seen in the fact that 10 of the 15 measures are spatial or regional statistics.

This does not mean, of course, that only geographic problems may be studied with these tools or that the geographic perspective is the only relevant one in tourism description. These tools have the potential for being applied in a wide variety of tourism topics. One of the challenges to tourism analysts is not just to use the tools presented here, but to combine them, elaborate them, and build on them to provide more powerful and useful methods for solving the complex problems of tourism description.

Further reading

Gunn C A 1972 *Vacationscape*. University of Texas Press, Austin, Tex.
Gunn C A 1979 *Tourism planning*. Crane Russak, New York.
Lavery P (ed.) 1971 *Recreational geography*. David and Charles, London.
Pearce D 1981 *Tourist development*. Longman, London.
Smith S L J 1983 *Recreation geography*. Longman, London.

GeoAbstracts, East Anglia, Norwich, publishes a series of monographs on a variety of applied statistical methods, many of which have direct bearing on tourism description. The series is entitled Concepts and Techniques in Modern Geography.

CHAPTER 9

Determining the value of public resources used in tourism

Introduction

A common challenge facing many policy-makers and managers who are responsible for allocating resources is that there are usually more uses for a resource than the supply can support. Open space, for example, may be subject to competing claims from park planners, shopping centre developers, and residential subdivision developers. A historic building might be the object of competing demands from an architectural preservation group, a retail developer interested in potential boutique locations, and a municipal government that is being pressured to demolish old buildings to provide for additional parking space. The decision about which use a particular resource should ultimately serve can be complicated and contentious, involving arguments from economists, special interest groups, and the general public, as well as restrictions imposed by legislation, zoning, and master plans. One of the most basic items of information a policy-maker or manager needs to help sort through all these issues and eventually be able to make a decision about the use of resources is the value of the resource in competing applications.

The question of the value of a resource can be difficult. First of all, the word 'value' (as we saw with the word 'demand', in Ch. 5) has different meanings for different people. If you were to ask someone, 'What's the value of that trip that Professor X took to that conference last week?', you will get a variety of answers depending on whether you ask Professor X, his chairman, or the owner of the hotel that hosted the conference. Professor X would describe the value of the trip in terms of the personal benefits of exchanging information on research or curriculum matters with his peers. The chairman may emphasize benefits such as professional development for Professor X and the greater visibility of the department. The hotel owner will probably measure the value in terms of the amount of money Professor X spent for meals, drinks, and accommodation.

The meaning of value is sometimes tied to that of 'benefit'. For example, many decisions about whether to initiate public projects are based on the results of a cost–benefit analysis. The benefits of the project are quantitative estimates of the economic rewards or returns that can be attributed to the completion and operation of the public project. In other circumstances, however, 'value' and 'benefit' have different connotations. In our example, the traveller and the employer may think of the value of the trip in terms of subjective, intangible benefits whereas the hotelier will focus on the quantitative economic impact of the trip. This distinction is sometimes expressed in terms of 'use value' versus 'exchange value'.

The use value of some resource is a measure of the personal benefits an individual derives from use or possession of a resource, whereas exchange value is a measure of the price that resource can command in the market-place. A common example used to illustrate the difference is diamonds and water. The use value of diamonds as ornamentation is relatively small compared to the use value of water for drinking, and yet diamonds are expensive while water is cheap. The explanation, of course, is that diamonds are scarce (and that their availability on the market is controlled by an international diamond cartel) whereas water is abundant in many localities and sometimes can be obtained free by collecting rain-water or by digging a well. The exchange value of either water or diamonds reflects not only the demand for the resource but also the availability of alternative supplies. And because exchange value is intended to represent how much someone would be willing to pay for a resource, it is a quantitative indicator of value, whereas use value is more often a qualitative assessment of benefits. As a result, the exchange value of a resource is a more useful and comprehensive indicator of the benefits associated with the resource, and thus a more useful tool for planning and resource allocation.

Exchange value, as a tool for allocating resources, is used in the following way. A basic principle of economics is that resources should be allocated so that the overall benefit to the owner of those resources is maximized. To put this principle of economic efficiency more precisely: resources should be allocated among competing uses in such a manner that the marginal utility of that resource is equal among all uses. If you owned a plot of land and you were trying to decide whether to put that land into housing, tourism, or agriculture, you would want to know the marginal utility of that land in each use – how much money you could make from each hectare of land in each use.

You would rationally decide to put the land to whichever use provided you with the greatest benefit – the greatest economic return. If all land were optimally allocated among society's needs, the return to you would be the same regardless of which use you selected. If the returns were not the same – let us assume that the return would be greatest through tourism development – you would conclude that there was a shortage of land for tourism development and that this shortage had driven up the potential benefits to be derived from land used for that purpose.

As a private landowner, you could rely on the market-place to help you take your decision. Although the intricacies of governmental regulations, zoning, financing, strategic plans, and other issues might make your decisions more difficult, the market-place would give you a reasonably good indication of the value of your land in alternative uses and thus direct you towards the best decision.

When resources are publicly owned, the same principle applies. The public agency controlling the resources should allocate those resources to maximize public benefit derived from those resources. A basic problem, of course, is that governmental resources are rarely allocated through the market-place, so traditional economic measures of their value in competing uses are not available. A public planner should not ignore the principle of economic efficiency, so he must turn to non-market mechanisms to obtain estimates of the benefits of public resources. Many of these mechanisms are based on the concept of 'willingness to pay'. Even though there is no actual transfer of funds, one attempts to obtain an estimate of what typical users would be willing to pay for specified resources in specified applications. These willingness-to-pay measures are sometimes called 'shadow prices'. Two basic approaches are used to derive shadow prices for public goods: (1) the direct method (also known as the contingent value method), which involves some form of survey or direct questioning of users about the value of some resource; and (2) the indirect method, which requires inferring willingness to pay for a resource by observing the expenditures of money on activities associated with the public use of public resources.

We examine several versions of these two basic approaches in this chapter. Before looking at them, though, we must first review some basic concepts.

Basic concepts

The phrase, 'willingness to pay', is self-descriptive, although the methods used to estimate consumers' 'willingness to pay' for a public resource that is not sold through the traditional market-place are not so obvious. Willingness to pay, as a concept, includes both any actual price paid as well as the extra the consumer would have been willing to pay in order to acquire that particular commodity. For example, the admission to a state park for a day's recreation might be $3.00, but a visitor may have been willing to pay an additional $2.00 if required – for a total willingness to pay of $5.00. The extra amount a consumer would be willing to pay is an important measure of the total benefits he anticipated receiving from the resource. Measures of this type are most appropriately applied when evaluating the real or potential benefits derived from improvements or additions to some tourism development, compared to the next best alternative (which might be no change in the existing development). If, in contrast, we are interested in the loss of benefits that might occur if some tourism resource is proposed for elimination, we might wish to estimate the consumer's willingness to sell.

The willingness-to-sell concept is a measure of how much a consumer would need to be compensated for the loss of the opportunity to enjoy a tourism facility through a reallocation of that facility to other uses incompatible with tourism. This measure can also be interpreted as the amount a consumer would have to be 'bribed' to forgo consumption of some resource. Whether or not consumers have any legal entitlement to such compensation or whether they would actually receive compensation are not at issue here. As with willingness to pay, we are concerned with an abstract measurement of value and not with actual financial transactions.

Generally, the monetary value of the willingness to sell will be larger than the value of the same resource assessed through willingness to pay. If there are ample substitutions of similar quality for the resource that is to be reallocated from tourism, the difference will be relatively small. If there are few substitutes, the difference will be relatively great, reflecting the greater reluctance to give up rights to a scarce resource.

Hammack and Brown (1974) and Dwyer, Kelly, and Bowes (1977) have noted that the empirical differences between estimates of willingness to pay and willingness to sell are often greater than one would expect. The exact reasons for this phenomenon are unknown, but these authors have several suggestions. For instance, tastes may change as a result of long-standing access to a resource, with the result that the subjective attributes of the resource to be given up are not the same as those of the same resource when it was first acquired. Consumers thus might expect greater compensation for emotional

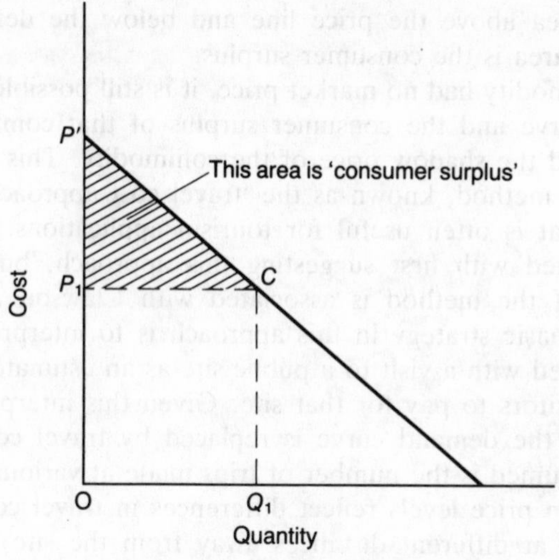

Fig. 9.1 Consumer surplus

reasons – reasons that economists are often ignorant of. There may also be a substantial income elasticity effect (the measure of the change in demand as the individual's wealth or income changes) such that the demand for some commodity increases dramatically as the supply of the resource becomes smaller. An increase in demand would be reflected in a greater value as measured through willingness to sell.

Regardless of the actual reasons for the differences, we can make two observations: (1) willingness to sell is a theoretically valid concept; but (2) it appears to be difficult to measure empirically, especially through direct valuation methods. As a result, we will not pursue methods for estimating willingness to sell and will concentrate on willingness-to-pay methods.

Direct valuation measures require great attention to survey methodology and questionnaire design. Indirect methods are often less sensitive to data-collection difficulties and thus are often more reliable. These latter methods are based on the concept of consumer surplus. It may help in understanding consumer surplus to begin by referring to Fig. 9.1. This figure is a traditional demand curve. Given a cost of P_1, we would predict that consumers would purchase Q_1 units of commodity. Their total expenditure will be the area OP_1CQ_1. From the demand curve we can observe that consumers would actually be willing to pay more than P_1, although the total quantity consumed would decrease. The total additional amount they would be willing to pay is the area above the price line and below the demand curve: $P_1P'C$. This area is the consumer surplus.

If the commodity had no market price, it is still possible to estimate a demand curve and the consumer surplus of that commodity. The trick is to find the shadow price of the commodity. This can be difficult, but one method, known as the 'travel cost approach', has been developed that is often useful for tourism applications. Hotelling is usually credited with first suggesting this approach, but the fullest explication of the method is associated with Clawson and Knetsch (1966). The basic strategy in this approach is to interpret the travel costs associated with a visit to a public site as an estimate of the willingness of visitors to pay for that site. Given this interpretation, the price axis of the demand curve is replaced by travel costs, and the quantity consumed is the number of trips made at various price levels (differences in price levels reflect differences in travel costs faced by people living at different distances away from the site). The actual details of how to estimate consumer surplus of a site using the travel cost approach are described below.

Incidentally, in the following sections, where we describe both the direct and indirect methods of valuation, we will use terms such as 'facility', 'site', 'resource', and 'commodity'. Valuation methods can be applied to any of these as well as to the opportunity to participate in an activity. Remember, therefore, that if we use one term such as 'resource', the method will normally apply to other types of tourism commodities and facilities.

One final comment is necessary before we turn to the details of the valuation or benefit measurement procedures. One of the most important tools developed by resource managers for taking decisions about the feasibility of proposed development projects is cost – benefits analysis (or benefit – cost analysis, depending on which side of the Atlantic the manager or analyst is working). Cost – benefit analysis is essentially a paper-and-pencil experiment designed to estimate whether society would be better or worse off if a proposed resource project is implemented. The decision is based on a comparison of the incremental benefits that would be produced by a project and the incremental costs imposed by the same project. The particular decision may be a choice between approving the project and rejecting it, a choice between several alternative projects, or the optimal timing and scale of a proposed project. The procedures we examine in this chapter are among those used by analysts in estimating the economic benefits of tourism projects. The methods and conventions used in conducting a cost – benefit analysis are beyond the scope of this book, but you can easily find many excellent texts in most research libraries. Some notable books and articles include Grant and Ireson (1970), Hammond (1966), Mishan (1982), Pearce (1978), and Prest and Turvey (1965).

Survey method

Description

The survey method is a process in which individuals are asked directly about their willingness to pay for some improvement in a resource or for additional use of a resource. Practical use of the results of this method depends on the ability of the analyst to estimate the total size of the group or users and his ability to generalize from the survey results to the total user group.

The survey method (also called the contingent valuation method and the direct valuation method) can be more useful than alternative approaches in certain situations. These include:

1. Development of value estimates for facilities that are frequently visited as part of a multiple-destination trip. In such a case the travel cost approach (the primary alternative to the survey method) is very difficult to apply because of the problem of allocating trip costs to the various destinations.
2. Estimating the increase in value resulting from management efforts to reduce congestion, perhaps by opening substitutable sites or overflow facilities. A reduction in the total number of visitors at a given facility would probably increase the value of that facility (if it had been crowded), but the travel cost approach would result in the interpretation of any reduction in use as indicative of declining value.
3. Evaluating management plans to improve user satisfaction in a number of sites, or to evaluate planned improvements for activities not associated with any particular site. A common example of this latter situation are game-management programmes to increase the number of migratory birds and fish.

Dwyer, Kelly, and Bowes (1977) note that the survey method has two key assumptions: (1) consumers can assign accurate values to the resource; and (2) this value can be obtained by direct questioning of the users. With respect to the first assumption, there is some doubt as to whether consumers are able to provide realistic estimates of the maximum they would be willing to pay for a resource that normally does not carry a price. To put this point somewhat cynically: ask someone a hypothetical question about hypothetical prices and you may get only hypothetical answers.

Even if we are able to accept the first assumption, the individual's willingness to pay is greatly influenced by the availability of alternative resources. We are actually interested in how much a consumer is willing to pay for a given resource in comparison to what he is willing to pay for the next best alternative. As a result, we should make sure our respondents understand what, if any, are the alternative resources. Without making this information explicit, we cannot be certain whether the respondent's estimate of his willingness to pay for a given resource is based on an implicit assumption that there are ample alternative resources (which will lower his estimate) or that there are no alternatives (which will raise his estimate).

The second assumption depends greatly on question design. A good question in a survey method will: (1) clearly explain what is being asked; and (2) minimize the chances the respondent will employ a gaming strategy in answering the questions. The issue of clarity implies that you have been able to make explicit the identity and scale of the resource or site being evaluated. As we have already noted, you should also make clear what, if any are the alternative resources.

The issue of a gaming strategy refers to the tendency of some respondents to distort their real opinions in order to influence the researcher in hopes of gaining some personal advantage. A gaming strategy may produce spuriously large values or spuriously low values, depending on the respondent's perception of the purpose of your questions. If the respondent suspects you are going to implement a user fee on the basis of the responses to your survey, he will likely give you a very low estimate of his willingness to pay in order to keep the anticipated fee as small as possible. If he believes his response will be used only to help justify the continued provision of a resource,with no real implications of setting fees, he will likely exaggerate his willingness to pay.

Careful structuring of the questions can minimize such biases. A study on the demand for pay television (Bohm 1971) illustrated one method for discouraging 'game-playing' by the respondents. Bohm told his respondents that some type of payment scheme would be implemented for a desired television service if the aggregate willingness to pay was sufficient to justify the programme, and that the fee would be based on average responses towards acceptable fees. If too few people were willing to pay for the service, the service would not be offered. Such a question discourages respondents from exaggerating their willingness to pay by 'warning' them they might be charged a high fee. On the other hand, they are discouraged from giving an estimate that is unrealistically low because this might lead to the decision not to offer the desired programming service at all.

Procedures

1. Determine as precisely as possible the context of the problem you wish to study. Do you want to estimate the value of a specific site, activity, or management plan? The definition of the problem also requires identification of the group from which you intend to draw your sample and to which you intend to generalize your findings.

2. Develop carefully worded questions aimed at eliciting answers about the willingness to pay. The available experience with question design for direct estimates of the willingness to pay is still sparse. One approach that has been used with some success (Davis 1963) is the use of bidding questions. The researcher asks the respondent whether he would be willing to pay some given price for a certain level of additional consumption. The price is then systematically increased until the respondent indicates he would no longer be willing to pay. This approach yields an 'all or nothing' estimate of the demand. There is no measure of the decline in the amount purchased until the consumer refuses to pay at all. The largest price the respondent is willing to pay is taken as that individual's estimate of the value of the resource.

Another approach has been developed by Cocheba and Langford (1981). They designed a single question with an open-ended response for the amount the respondent was willing to pay. The critical feature of their approach was the elaborate wording of their question. They advised the respondent that the question would be complex, and that it was important to obtain an answer. They anticipated several possible sources of bias such as concern about whether future fee increases would result from their survey, and offered explicit assurances that none of these problems would actually occur to the respondents. They also worded the question in such a way as to make the task as realistic as possible. We will examine their specific question format below in the example for this method.

3. If your study population is easily definable and measurable, such as boat owners or licensed hunters, you can draw a sample directly and administer the survey. The total willingness to pay of the user population can then be estimated from the survey results.

If, on the other hand, your study group is the general population or some large, amorphous group, you may find it necessary to use a two-stage survey. The first stage includes not only the willingness-to-pay question, but also questions about the individual characteristics of respondents that are believed to influence willingness to pay. These characteristics typically include socio-economic variables as well as recreation equipment ownership and travel patterns. A multiple regression equation is then calibrated relating these individual characteristics to the expressed willingness to pay.

The second stage of the survey involves a larger sample of your study population in order to identify the number of people with the characteristics identified in the first stage of the survey. This information is then used in the multiple regression equation to estimate the willingness of individuals in the general population to pay.

Example

Cocheba and Langford's (1981) article provides a useful illustration of how questions might be constructed to elicit reliable information on resource values. The authors were interested in determining the value of wildlife to the population of the Canadian province of Saskatchewan. The authors (Cocheba and Langford 1981) constructed the following elaborate question to impart an air of reality to their survey:

Next, we would like to ask you a question involving something that has not actually happened. Asking you this type of question is the only way of getting the needed information. To fully understand the question you may need to read it more than once, but we would appreciate your best answer.

What we would like to know is how much you would be willing to donate to an organization for the purpose of increasing the goose population by five percent. Suppose the organization would operate in the following way:

a. The organization would spend the money it receives in the most efficient way to keep the goose population five percent above what it would be without the organization's efforts.
b. Both hunters and nonhunters would benefit. For hunters, even though there would be NO change in the length of the hunting season or the daily bag limit, there would be five percent more geese during the hunting season. Nonhunters would benefit because at all times there would be five percent more geese to enjoy.
c. Everyone would pay for all the enjoyment they get from there being more geese. (Don't worry about how this would be done. Just suppose it will be done.) However, everyone's money would be returned if enough money to finance the five percent increase is not collected.

Under these circumstances, what is the maximum amount you would give the organization during this year?

$______

This question is not a model of brevity or simplicity, but Cocheba and Langford found that most respondents were willing to answer and to give plausible answers. The responses to their question were compared to a similar question designed for a 10 per cent increase in the goose population. Responses from both hunters and non-hunters were compared. The authors found that hunters were willing to pay $15.58 for a 5 per cent increase and $23.58 for a 10 per cent increase. Non-hunters were willing to pay only $6.01 and $6.74 respectively.

In another study, Davis (1964) used the survey method to estimate the value of the recreation and tourism use in the Maine woods. He developed a sampling framework for the general population in Maine. A sample of 185 interviews provided information on the amount individual households would be willing to pay for an additional visit to the area they normally used. Information was also obtained on household characteristics: years of acquaintance with Maine, income, and the average length of a trip to the woods. Multiple regression produced the following equation:

$$W = -48.57 + 2.85(A) + 2.88(I) + 4.76(L) \qquad [9.1]$$

where: W = willingness to pay for an additional visit;
A = years of acquaintance with Maine;
I = household income in thousands of dollars;
L = average length of trip in days.

Use of this model to estimate the value of an area in the Maine woods for tourism and recreation required Davis to collect information from a second survey on the general population to collect more comprehensive information on the independent variables identified in equation [9.1]. Data from this survey were then incorporated into the multiple regression equation and a value of W estimated for the sample, which was then weighted to represent the general population of the state.

Travel cost method

Description

The travel cost method is an indirect method for determining the value of a tourism site. This technique is based on the development of a model for predicting site use from observed consumer behaviour. The method may be used to derive values for the same site that provided the original data or for sites similar to the original study site.

The method typically involves some form of regression model relating levels of use to travel costs. Additional variables can be incorporated to reflect the effects of site attractivity and of competition. The use of a wide variety of users facing different travel costs allows the analyst to infer values of a site by observing the relationship between travel costs and levels of use. This is done by estimating a demand curve for which travel costs are a substitute for market prices.

Before we discuss the procedures of the travel cost method, we should consider how travel costs are to be defined. Analysts who use this method generally agree that actual fuel costs such as gasoline for a private automobile should be included. Agreement about the inclusion of other costs as part of total trip costs is less unanimous. Possible costs include: (1) the value of travel time; (2) cost of food and accommodation during the trip; and (3) equipment costs (either rentals for the specific outing or a pro-rated cost of equipment ownership).

Arguments about inclusion of these costs involve debates as to the accuracy of estimation procedures as well as whether they represent costs associated with a specific trip, as opposed to more general 'lifestyle costs' that should not be allocated to actual, specific trips. For example, consumers will eat and will require some form of accommodation whether or not they are travelling. An individual travelling during a paid vacation receives a salary for the time away, so the travel time is perhaps not really a cost (or, more precisely, is a compensated cost). A full review of these arguments is beyond the scope of this book. The interested reader can find an overview of these issues in Walsh (1977). Current practice seems to be to include estimates of time, especially for long trips; food and lodging costs in excess of what the respondent would have spent at home; costs of consumable supplies such as film; and the price of admissions.

This method is based on three assumptions. First, it is assumed that the response of average individuals to a user fee of a given magnitude is the same as their response to a travel cost of the same size. Available evidence suggests that this assumption has some basis in fact. The typical traveller tends to value a dollar largely the same regardless of which item it is spent on as long as the items are fairly priced and contributing to the overall satisfaction of the trip.

It is further assumed that the relationship between travel costs and the number of trips taken is linear. This particular form of the travel cost model presented here is based on the situation where there is no competition from other sites. A modification of this model to accommodate for competing sites is presented in the next section.

Finally, it is assumed that visitation rates are not affected by capacity constraints. If the capacity of a site begins to affect total use levels, the observed level of use does not necessarily reflect the true value of the site. Observed levels reflect, instead, the effects of congestion. The result is a downward bias in the estimate of the value because fewer people are visiting the site than one would expect if capacity did not constrain total usage.

Procedures

1. Define the specific site for which you are developing the valuation estimate. Define, too, the origins of visitors, usually cities or countries.
2. Conduct an on-site survey to determine how many users come from each origin. This usually requires knowledge of the total number of visits at the site for an entire year, as well as some estimate of the proportions of visitors from each origin.
3. Determine the total population of each origin.
4. Estimate the average travel costs for visitors from each origin. This estimate will be a function of distance between origin and destination as well as the specific components of total trip costs.
5. Determine visits per capita for each origin by dividing the total number of trips made by residents from each origin by the population of that origin.
6. Plot visits per capita against cost. Fit, by visual inspection or with least-squares estimation, a line through the points plotted to develop a function for predicting average visitation rates for any particular level of travel cost.
7. Develop an aggregate site demand curve. This curve is based on the assumption that individuals respond to user fees and travel costs in the same way. For example, a person who faces $3.00 in travel costs and is then assessed a $3.00 admission fee will participate at the same rate as someone facing $6.00 in travel costs and no admission fee.

We begin developing the aggregate site demand curve by assuming a zero user fee. If there is a fee, add the fee to total travel costs and continue to work with the assumption of a zero user fee. Recall that in step 6 we developed a function to predict visitation rates for various levels of travel costs. We add, systematically, larger user fees to that function and predict, for each new level of fee, the expected rate of use. The process is continued until all users are priced out of the site. The estimated use levels are plotted against the user fees to generate

Table 9.1 Hypothetical data for deriving trip demand curve for an isolated site

Origin	Population	Number of visits	Visits per capita	Trip costs ($)
A	100 000	50 000	0.50	11.50
B	200 000	200 000	1.00	5.00
C	300 000	75 000	0.25	15.00

the demand curve. The area under that curve is the consumer surplus for the site – and hence its value.

Example

The following data illustrate this procedure. Table 9.1 includes the necessary information for estimating the distance decay curve (the travel demand curve): population of various origins, number of visits from each origin, per capita visits, and travel costs. A regression analysis of trip costs and per capita visits produced the function:

$$V_{ij} = 1.373 - 0.0752(C_{ij}) \qquad [9.2]$$

where: V_{ij} = visits per capita from origin i to destination j;
C_{ij} = trip costs.

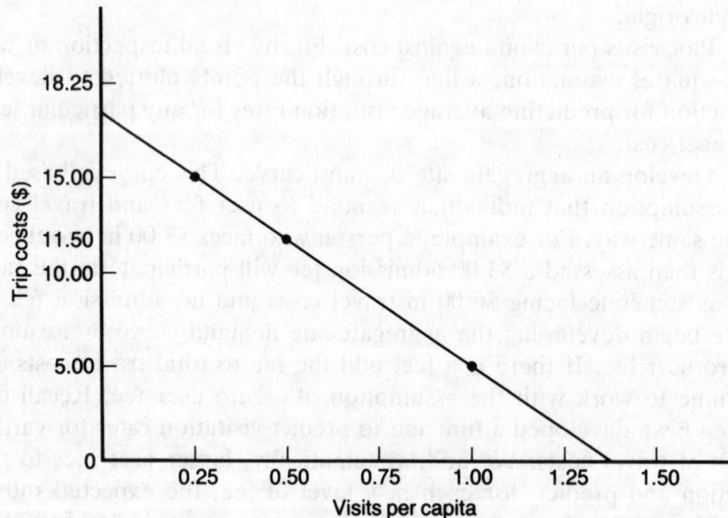

Fig. 9.2 Trip demand curve for an isolated site

Table 9.2 Calculation of the aggregate site demand curve for an isolated site

	A			B			C			
User fees ($)	Total costs ($)	Visits per capita	Visits	Total costs ($)	Visits per capita	Visits	Total costs ($)	Visits per capita	Visits	Total visits
0	11.50	0.50	50 000	5.00	1.00	200 000	15.00	0.25	75 000	325 000
1	12.50	0.43	43 000	6.00	0.92	184 000	16.00	0.16	48 000	275 000
2	13.50	0.35	35 000	7.00	0.85	170 000	17.00	0.09	27 000	232 000
3	14.50	0.28	28 000	8.00	0.77	154 000	18.00	0.02	6 000	188 000
3.25	14.75	0.26	26 000	8.25	0.75	150 000	18.25	0	0	176 000
4	15.50	0.20	20 000	9.00	0.70	140 000				160 000
5	16.50	0.13	13 000	10.00	0.62	124 000				137 000
6	17.50	0.06	6 000	11.00	0.55	110 000				116 000
6.75	18.25	0	0	11.75	0.49	98 000				98 000
7				12.00	0.47	94 000				94 000
8				13.00	0.40	80 000				80 000
9				14.00	0.32	64 000				64 000
10				15.00	0.25	50 000				50 000
11				16.00	0.16	32 000				32 000
12				17.00	0.09	18 000				18 000
13				18.00	0.02	4 000				4 000
13.25				18.25	0	0				0

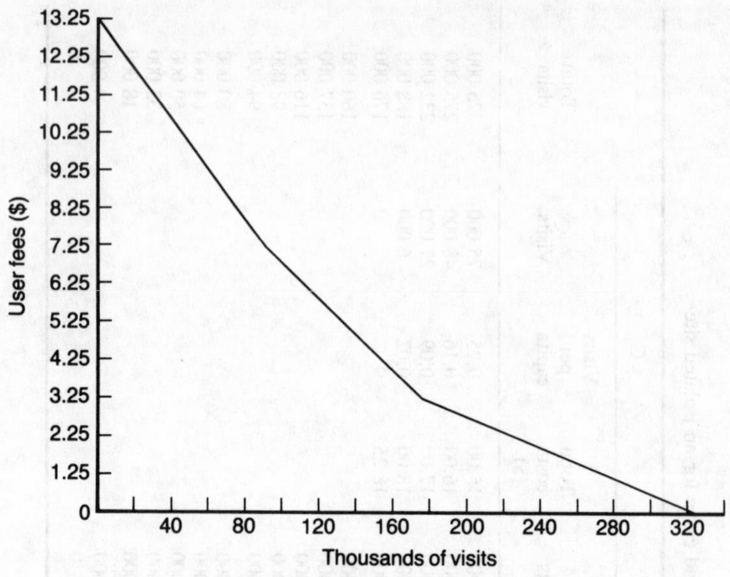

Fig. 9.3 Aggregate site demand curve for an isolated site

This function has been plotted as Fig. 9.2, the 'Trip demand curve for an isolated site'. Note that when travel costs equal $18.25, visits are reduced to zero. Equation [9.2] is then used to calculate the number of trips expected for each origin for a range of user fees in excess of initial travel costs. These calculations are summarized in Table 9.2. The first row of data is the expected user rates under the condition of zero user fee. This, of course, is the same as the per capita visitation rates in Table 9.1. User fees are increased $1 at a time, until a maximum of $18.25 is reached (the last increment needed for each origin to reach exactly $18.25 is not necessarily $1). Per capita trip rates, visits per origin, and total visits are calculated. The total visits are plotted against the incremental user fees to generate the aggregate site demand curve (Fig. 9.3). The area under the curve is the consumer surplus. This may be obtained graphically or by summing the areas under the demand curve for each individual and summing them. The total consumer surplus in this example is approximately $1.8 million.

Travel cost method allowing for site substitution

Description

This version of the travel cost method is a generalization of the basic travel cost method to allow for the effects of one or more substitutable sites in the same market area as the study site. The procedure allows us to estimate the consumer surplus attributable to both sites, although the method can lead to an underestimation of the real value of both sites because of lowered use rates. The process involves the calculation of a trip demand function and derivation of an aggregate site demand model. In this case, we estimate a trip demand function for an existing site and then apply the same function to the substitutable site.

One assumption of this method is that tourists always go to the destination with the lowest overall costs. In fact, of course, this is not always a valid assumption. Tourists do not always act to minimize travel costs. Whether they are exploring new territory, seeking variety, or simply working under a condition of imperfect information, tourists can often be observed going to more distant destinations than to closer ones. Further, destinations are rarely perfectly substitutable. One often finds significant variations in quality or service between destinations.

What all this means is that you might attempt to develop some estimate of the relative market share of each destination in each origin market to obtain an indication of what percentage of tourists from a given origin are likely to be diverted by the creation of a new site (as opposed to the unrealistic assumption of 100 per cent diversion).

The creation of a new destination usually reduces the consumer surplus associated with an existing site. This apparent loss of value at the existing site is exactly that – only apparent. It should not be interpreted as reflecting some lowering of the overall quality or value of the site. The reason for the lowered value is the creation of one or more alternatives. In practice, the creation of an alternative could actually raise the value of an existing site by lowering congestion. The value of a site estimated through consumer surplus is a function of some socially defined worth of the site as well as the price, availability, and quality of alternatives. Values derived with consumer surplus will, assuming accurate data and travel cost estimates, tend to err on the conservative side. As we will see in a subsequent example, the value of any site given the presence of a competing site will be markedly reduced from what we would estimate if there were no competition or substitution.

The creation of an alternative site not only tends to lower the value of an existing site as measured through consumer surplus while conversely raising its value by reducing congestion, alternative sites can also result in direct savings to tourists by reducing the total cost of travel necessary to reach the facilities offered at existing sites. We will examine later a method for estimating the travel savings associated with the creation of substitutable sites.

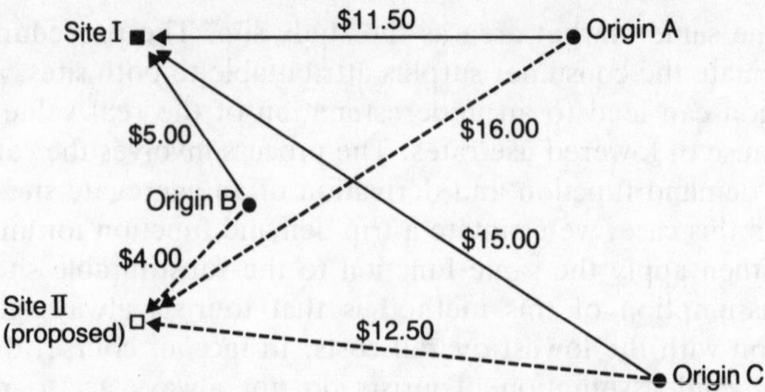

Fig. 9.4 A two-site, three-origin travel system

Procedures

1. Follow the steps outlined in the procedures for the basic travel cost method through step 6.
2. Using the travel demand curve derived in step 6, develop aggregate site demand curves for both sites. This may be done by using the procedures described in step 7 mentioned earlier, but assume that travellers will go only to the site with the lowest travel costs. The area under each curve is a measure of the value of each site.

Example

The following example illustrates the use of this method. Assume another site has been constructed near the site used in our first example. This second site is identical to the first. Its location is such that it is slightly closer to origins B and C but slightly further away from A than the first site. See Fig. 9.4 for the basic data.

Using the demand function calibrated for the first site, we can predict the number of visits to site II under a variety of user fees. Note that there is no user fee level that will permit users from origin A to visit site II. Even at zero user fees, travel costs still exceed the travel costs to site I. Fees of $1.00 and $2.50 are the maxima that users from origins B and C respectively, will pay before switching to site I. These calculations are detailed in Table 9.3.

The aggregate site demand curve for site II is calculated using data from Table 9.3 and it is shown in Fig. 9.5. The area under the curve is approximately $592 000. Note that the consumer surplus for site II is much smaller than for site I without the existence of site II. The

Table 9.3 Calculation of aggregate site demand curve for competing site II

	A			B			C			
User fees ($)	Total costs ($)	Visits per capita	Visits	Total costs ($)	Visits per capita	Visits	Total costs ($)	Visits per capita	Visits	Total visits
0	16.00		—[†]	4.00	1.04	208 000	12.50	0.43	129 000	337 000
1				5.00	1.00	200 000	13.50	0.36	108 000	308 000
2				6.00		—[‡]	14.50	0.28	84 000	84 000
2.50							15.00	0.25	75 000	75 000
3							15.50	—	—[§]	—

† Travel costs from origin A to site II exceed travel costs to site I. No trips will be made to site II.
‡ Once travel costs exceed $5.00, residents of origin B will stop going to site II and switch to site I.
§ Once travel costs exceed $15.00, residents of origin C will stop going to site II and switch to site I.

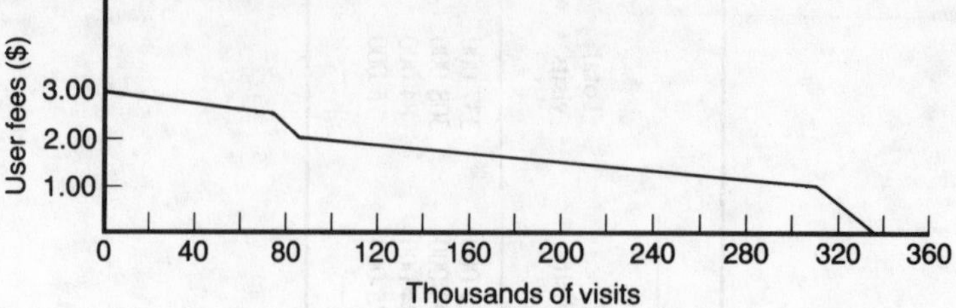

Fig. 9.5 Aggregate site demand curve for competitive site II

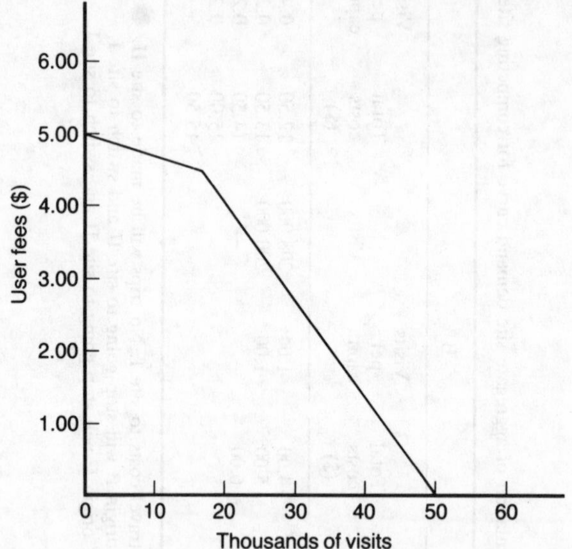

Fig. 9.6 Aggregate site demand curve for competitive site I

reason for the difference is the fact that the consumer surplus for site I without competition reflects the greater value one normally assigns to a resource for which there are no substitutes. The value of site II is lower not because it is in any way an inferior site, but because consumers do not have two sites to choose from, so they value either site less than they would if either were the sole site.

We can also calculate a new value for site I to see what effect the existence of a substitutable site has had on its value. These calculations are shown in Table 9.4. Here site I draws only from origin A when the user fee is less than $4.50. The new site demand curve for site I is plotted as Fig. 9.6. Consumer surplus for site I is reduced to only $140 000.

Table 9.4 Calculation of aggregate site demand curve for competing site I

	A			B			C			
User fees ($)	Total costs ($)	Visits per capita	Visits	Total costs ($)	Visits per capita	Visits	Total costs ($)	Visits per capita	Visits	Total visits
0	11.50	0.50	50 000	5.00	—	—†	15.00	—	—†	50 000
1	12.50	0.43	43 000							43 000
2	13.50	0.35	35 000							35 000
3	14.50	0.28	28 000							28 000
4	15.50	0.20	20 000							20 000
4.50	16.00	0.17	17 000							17 000
5	16.50	—	—‡							0

† Residents of origins B and C do not visit site I because site II is closer.
‡ Residents of origin A switch to site II once travel costs to site I exceed $16.00.

Travel savings estimation

Description

The estimation of travel savings is a procedure for determining the value of a proposed site in terms of reduced travel costs for travellers. This estimate of value is thus independent of any measure of consumer surplus or willingness to pay. As you will recall, consumer surplus is a measure of the hypothetical willingness of a traveller to pay for some non-market tourism commodity. It is, therefore, an abstract value. The value estimated with the travel savings approach, in contrast, represents the savings of real money.

This relatively simple procedure does not indicate anything about the inherent values of either site. Rather, it simply measures the net travel savings attributable to the creation of a new destination. This measure applies only to the savings that accrue to current travellers. It does not represent the value of a site attributable to the creation of new travel.

Procedures

1. Determine the existing number of trips from all origins to some destination and the round-trip costs for each origin.
2. Locate the alternative site and estimate new travel costs to this alternative site from each origin. If the new travel costs are less than the current costs for travel from any origin to the existing destination, subtract the new costs from existing costs to estimate net savings per trip from the origin.
3. Estimate the total number of existing trips that are likely to be diverted to the new facility. This may be done either by assuming that travellers will always go to the site with the lowest overall costs or by conducting a survey to estimate the percentage of travellers that will be diverted by the new site.
4. Multiply the per trip savings by the total number of trips diverted from each origin. Sum these to determine total savings.

Example

Using data from the previous example, we can compare travel costs associated with trips from each of the three origins to either site (Table 9.5). Assuming 100 per cent diversion to the nearest facility, we observe that all travellers from origins B and C will switch to site II.

Table 9.5 Calculation of travel savings attributable to creation of site II

Site	Origin A		Origin B		Origin C		
I	$11.50		$5.00		$15.00		
II	$16.00		$4.00		$12.50		
Savings attributable to creation of II (per trip)	$0		$1.00		$2.50		
Number of trips diverted	50 000		200 000		75 000		
Total savings	$0	+	$200 000	+	$187 500	=	$387 500

We multiply the number of observed trips currently made by residents at each of these origins by the net savings (travel costs to site II minus the travel costs to site I) to determine the total savings travellers will enjoy.

In this example, 75 000 travellers saved an average of $2.50 at origin C while another 200 000 travellers saved an average of $1.00 each at origin B, for a total savings of $387 500. The proximity of site II to origins B and C also stimulates an additional 3440 trips from origin B and 54 000 trips from origin C. No travel savings are attributed to this increase of 57 440 trips.

Differential cost method

Description

The differential cost method is a procedure designed to estimate willingness to pay on the basis of observed differential levels of actual costs borne by participants in some tourism activity. The method is based on the traditional concept of consumer surplus, but it differs from the travel cost approach in that aggregated demand curves are not required. The basic procedure was developed by Pearse (1968). His method involves comparing the actual levels of trip expenditures of consumers to an empirically estimated maximum expenditure. Separate consumer surpluses are defined for different income categories. These are then aggregated to provide total consumer surplus.

An important assumption of this method is that the travellers who come to the site under study have made their trip for the sole purpose of visiting that particular site. If their trip involves other sites, the resulting estimate of the value of the trip will be too high.

One of the more unusual features of this method is the use of income categories for determining consumer surplus. Such a research design implies that all respondents with similar incomes have a similar willingness to pay. Although this is not necessarily true, it is more realistic than the usual assumption – that willingness to pay is the same over all income categories. This latter assumption is usually made implicitly by researchers who use the traditional travel cost approach.

It is interesting to note that if we were to define income categories so narrowly that every respondent were his own category, we would not have any surplus at all. The reason for this is that consumer surplus is defined here as the difference between observed costs in an income category and the maximum cost associated with that category. There could be no difference in single-member groups. In contrast, if all respondents were grouped into one comprehensive income category, the consumer surplus would be determined by comparing everyone's costs to those of a single individual. The result would very likely be an overestimation of the actual surplus. Both designs are unrealistic. Clearly, the researcher needs to find a reasonable compromise. The groups should be small enough so that their behaviour and expenditure patterns are reasonably homogeneous, but large enough so that not all respondents are at the marginal willingness to pay.

Procedures

1. Select a sample of users from a known population of resource users. You must also know the total size of the user population so that you can make inferences from the sample to the total population.
2. Survey the sample of users to collect information on income, participation rates, and expenditures. Expenditures should include actual travel costs, costs of consumable supplies associated with participation, and some pro-rated allowance for equipment and licence fees. An estimate of the value of time associated with travel might also be calculated.
3. Stratify the respondents by income group. Some level of judgement is needed to determine the range of the income categories: categories \$5000 to \$10 000 wide are often useful.
4. Interpret the maximum costs borne by an individual in each income group as the maximum willingness to pay for all individuals in that group. In the event some users made more than one trip per year to the site being studied, calculate total costs for the year. The unit of analysis is user costs per year, not costs per trip.

Table 9.6 Calculation of consumer surplus from big-game hunters in the East Kootenay, 1964: The differential cost method

Income group ($)	Number of observations	Highest cost ($)	Average consumer surplus ($)
Less than 2 000	25	66	47
2 000–4 000	67	183	149
4 000–6 000	219	287	224
6 000–8 000	109	320	221
8 000–10 000	32	267	152
Over 10 000	33	355	196
Total sample	485		(weighted) $197

Source: Pearse 1968.
Total consumer surplus, all hunters = total number of resident hunters × average consumer surplus = 14 346 × $197 = $2 826 162.

5. Subtract the costs borne by every other user in an income category from the maximum for that category. Calculate the average of these differences. This is the estimate of the willingness to pay for individuals in that group.
6. Sum the average consumer surplus over all groups and calculate a weighted consumer surplus for the sample. Multiply the average consumer surplus by the total population of the user group to obtain the total consumer surplus.

Example

Pearse's data (1968) from his survey of big-game hunters in East Kootenay, British Columbia (Canada), illustrate this procedure. Interviews were conducted with 485 hunters of the estimated 14 000 who hunt the East Kootenay each year. He then divided his respondents into the income categories shown in Table 9.6. This table also contains the number of respondents in each income category and the highest costs paid by a member of each category. Finally, the average surplus for the sample was multiplied by the number of hunters to provide an estimate of the annual value of big-game hunting – approximately $2.8 million.

Summary

Methods of valuation are based on expressions of the willingness of travellers to pay for some commodity or resource. Estimates of this willingness may be obtained by asking users directly or by inferring, indirectly, from travel costs. The direct method is more useful when you are making estimates for activities not associated with specific sites, when managers of sites are working to reduce congestion, and when trips associated with the use of a site or resource have several other purposes.

A major problem with the direct method is the potential for respondents intentionally to mislead the researcher. Indirect methods have been developed to avoid this problem.

The most important indirect method is the travel cost approach. This approach produces an aggregate site demand curve from actual travel costs and trips made. The area under the demand curve is a measure of the consumer surplus (economic value) of the resource. Consumer surplus reflects not only the intrinsic worth of a resource but also the number, quality, and costs of alternatives.

Two other methods of estimating values were discussed. The differential cost method is also based on the concept of willingness to pay. In this approach the estimated willingness is the difference between the average payment by users in an income category and the maximum paid by an individual in that category. This method avoids the unrealistic assumption of equal willingness to pay across all income categories. It still requires, however, the sole purpose assumption.

The final method defines value in terms of actual travel savings attributable to the creation of a new site closer to an origin. This method is relevant when the analyst wishes to consider the potential benefits to be derived from opening a new site that will divert users from an existing and perhaps overcrowded site. The approach is a useful supplement to the travel cost approach in that this approach interprets any reduction in use as a lowering of value. The use of both the travel cost and travel savings approaches would yield more valid estimates than either method used alone.

Further reading

Bishop R C and **Heberlein T A** 1979 Measuring values of extramarket goods: are indirect measures biased? *American Journal of Agricultural Economics* **16**: 926–30.

Bowes M D and **Loomis J B** 1980 A note on the use of travel cost models with unequal zonal populations. *Land Economics* **56**: 465–70.

Brookshie D S, Randall A and **Stoll J R** 1980 Valuing increments and decrements in natural resource service flows. *American Journal of Agricultural Economics* **62**: 478–88.

Brookshie D S, Tahyer M A, Schulze W D and **d'Arge R C** 1982 Valuing public goods: a comparison of survey and hedonic methods. *American Economic Review* **72**: 165–77.

Smith V K and **Kopp R** 1980 The spatial limits of the travel cost recreation demand model. *Land Economics* **56**: 64–72.

Strong E 1983 A note on the functional form of travel cost models with unequal populations. *Land Economics* **59**: 342–9.

Walsh, R G 1986 *Recreation economic decisions*. Venture Publishing, State College, Pa.

Wennergren E B 1967 Surrogate pricing of outdoor recreation. *Land Economics* **43**: 112–16.

Wilman E 1980 The value of time in recreation benefit estimation. *Journal of Environmental Economics and Management* **7**: 272–86.

Ziemer R F, Musser W N and **Hill R C** 1980 Recreation demand equations: functional form and consumer surplus. *American Journal of Agricultural Economics* **62**: 136–41.

CHAPTER 10

Estimating the local economic magnitude of tourism

Introduction

One of the major benefits local communities expect from tourism is a significant contribution to their economy: increased local income as well as new jobs. Local business operators, of course, profit directly from tourists' spending. As they pay their employees and as the operators and employees spend their increased wealth locally in other businesses, the entire community eventually benefits. The revenues gained from tourism are considered by economists as 'basic income' (Tiebout 1962) in the sense that they result from export earnings. Money spent by tourists is new money in the local economy, not just a recycling of wealth that already existed there. As a result, the basic income from tourism helps to pay for goods and services imported from other regions and contributes to governmental revenues through taxes.

Such observations are familiar to anyone working in tourism, but they have not always been part of the conventional understanding of local planners, policy-makers, and developers. Tourism was long viewed (with some justification as noted in Ch. 1) as an unorganized unimportant collection of small businesses. The eventual realization that this unorganized collection of small businesses comprises one of the three largest industries in many areas of the world, is the chief earner of foreign income for many countries, and is the world's largest industry prompted many local leaders and planners to look more seriously at tourism.

Unfortunately, as local leaders looked for information about tourism and how it could be developed and managed in their community, they found very little scientific, objective research or case studies. They had to rely on anecdotal information, personal impressions, and enthusiasms of tourism promoters. Not surprisingly, some extravagant claims were made. These fuelled unrealistic hopes for economic growth even in regions totally innocent of tourism attractions and resources. More regrettably, the extravagant claims were occasionally 'supported' by pseudo-economic analyses based on the concept of economic multipliers. While the concept of an economic multiplier is quite legitimate and useful, it can be easily mishandled – either deliberately or accidentally – because of the technical complexities associated with calculating multipliers and the need for large amounts of precise data. One example is a 1983 economic impact assessment of the Recreation Division expenditures of the Ontario Ministry of Tourism and Recreaction. A consortium of three consulting firms prepared a six-volume report, *Recreation: a changing society's economic giant* (Earl Berger Ltd *et al*, 1983) which concluded with the observation that every dollar spent by the Ministry on recreation programmes and activities generated $9.07 in the provincial economy. This extraordinarily high impact ratio was based on a number of methodological and substantive assumptions. Among the more questionable assumptions included the contention that all private spending on recreation associated with activities and clubs that received provincial grants was stimulated exclusively by those grants, and the valuation of volunteer time in recreation leagues and associations could be set equal to the average wage of about $10.00/hour. Further, no distinction was made between actual economic impact created by the expenditure of real money and the value of donated services, such as free space or volunteer time. Archer (1976) has documented some other careless research practices occasionally found in economic impact studies in his paper, 'The uses and abuses of economic multipliers'.

The inevitable result of the misuse of economic impact methodology has been the growth of a backlash against the idea that tourism has any role to play in local economic development. Although this cynicism is rarely published in industry journals, it is expressed frequently in private conversations and sometimes even public addresses by officials. This backlash is understandable, but it is no more accurate or justifiable than the extravagant claims made by tourism boosters.

Not every community can benefit from tourism development. Those that can must carefully plan for and manage development, and they must recognize their unique strengths and weaknesses as tourism destinations. Some communities can take advantage of the large and lucrative convention trade, others would be wise to avoid that highly competitive field. Certain communities can promote cultural attractions and events, while still others may rely on seasonal attractions and resources such as beaches or ethnic festivals. The identification of how a community can plan to benefit from tourism as a community industry is a complex topic beyond the scope of this text. Murphy (1983), in *Tourism: a community approach*, describes several strategies that communities can adopt. Mathieson and Wall (1982), in *Tourism: economic, physical and social impacts*, provide additional information on the various economic and social benefits and costs communities must plan for if they are to take full advantage of tourism development and to manage the potential problems.

A fundamental need for planners and managers of tourism development projects is the measurement of the local economic magnitude of the industry. The magnitude of the industry, in this sense, implies something more conservative than the estimation of economic multipliers. It refers specifically to an assessment of the economic benefits attributable to actual tourist spending in a local community. We have already examined two methods that can be used to give crude or indirect estimates of the local importance of tourism: Defert's *Tf* and the Lorenz curves. We will look next at two methods that provide more direct estimates of economic benefits. Both of these use data sources and analytic procedures that are accessible to most tourism analysts and planners. These measures provide a baseline estimate of gross tourism revenues under current conditions which can then be used to assess the effects of longer-term tourism development and promotion on the local economy.

Local impact model

Description

There are at least three fundamentally different procedures for estimating the effects of tourism on local economies. The first involves input–output modelling. Input–output modelling requires the measurement of financial flows generated by tourists' spending through all sectors of an economy. The end result is the estimation of the tourism multiplier, which we have referred to previously. The data and methodological requirements of input–output research are such that few local planners and tourism agencies should consider this a realistic option. The second procedure is the estimation of tourists' expenditures through analysis of secondary data sources. There are some distinct advantages to this procedure, and we consider an example of this approach in the next section. The local impact model, described here, is an illustration of the third approach – the use of direct estimation methods from primary data sources, particularly tourism businesses and surveys of the tourists themselves.

This particular procedure will help you estimate tourist expenditures in a local region, the number of jobs supported by tourism locally, and the size of the payroll associated with tourism. Although this procedure has been described as being based on primary data sources, it does involve some secondary data sources as well. The basic data, however, does come from business and visitor surveys.

The local impact model is based loosely on procedures developed by Wassenaar (1981) for the California Office of Tourism. His model, in turn, is an adaptation and extension of earlier work done by Frechtling (1974). The basis of the local impact model is the accommodation sector and associated tourism spending on accommodation. Wassenaar notes that there are two reasons for this: (1) tourists who use commercial accommodation are responsible for the greatest portion of tourist expenditures; and (2) the use of commercial accommodation is one of the least ambiguous and most practical working definitions of a tourist as someone distinct from a local resident. There are a couple of problems with the emphasis on commercial accommodation, however. Focusing on overnight accommodation means you will miss the potentially important benefits derived from day visitors in tourism destination regions. The number of day visitors can be roughly estimated through the use of a general population survey of residents who live within 100 to 150 km (60 to 90 miles) of the destination region. This survey can identify the travel and spending patterns of people within this 'fringe' area around the destination.

Another problem with the use of commercial accommodation is the omission of travellers who stay with friends or relatives in private homes. This can be an important segment of all visitors in many regions. Canadian statistics suggest that about one in three travellers stay in private homes and that these travellers are responsible for about half of all visitor-nights generated nationally. Even though their level of spending will typically be less than that of travellers staying in commercial accommodation, you will miss a significant source of tourist expenditures by ignoring travellers in private residences. Again, it might be possible to correct for this omission by conducting a survey to document the extent of this phenomenon and the pattern of tourists' expenditures of those visitors who stay with local residents in the destination region.

When using this method you should be sensitive to variation in definitions of 'tourist', or 'visitor' in any secondary data sources used to obtain state or provincial averages. Some of the different types of definitions were described in Chapter 2. Mixing data from two jurisdictions that used significantly different definitions for collecting and reporting data on tourists would result in meaningless estimates.

Finally, it should be made explicit that this method estimates tourists' expenditures only in the destination region. Spending on airlines, automobile travel, or other *en route* expenditures will not be assessed by this method. This is not necessarily a weakness because the model is designed to apply only to destination regions. It is useful, though, to remember that the total value of a traveller's expenditures is often greater than just the sum of expenditures recorded at the destination.

Procedures

1. Define the geographical limits of the region to be studied. This will usually be a county or a census metropolitan region. Conduct an accommodation inventory of all commercial establishments in the region. This inventory should include the entire range of accommodation firms: hotels, motels, motor inns, bed and breakfasts, and cottages. The total number of rooms or beds in each establishment and in each category should be noted.

2. Conduct a survey of the accommodation establishments in the region. The survey can cover all establishments if the number is small, or it can be based on a sample if the number is large. Collect the following information on either an annual or a seasonal basis, as appropriate for the local pattern of tourism:

(a) average room rate;
(b) average number of customers per room;
(c) average occupancy rate;
(d) average length of stay.

You may also wish to collect other statistics to provide a more complete picture of the tourism industry. These statistics, however, are not essential for this particular procedure:

(e) clientele mix (business, convention, pleasure, personal business);
(f) origins of visitors by county, province or state, and country.

3. Prepare a regional summary of the survey results, either by totalling all responses if you conducted a comprehensive survey or by generalizing to the population of firms if you used a representative sample.

4. Perform the following series of calculations:

(a) Multiply the total room capacity in each accommodation category by the average occupancy rate. Multiply that product by 365 nights per year to obtain the total number of rooms let annually. If you obtained seasonal or quarterly information, calculate totals separately for each season, rather than the entire year.

(b) Multiply the average annual number of rooms let by the average room rate to obtain annual receipts from customers. If you used seasonal data, perform this step for each season and then add to obtain the annual total. Next, obtain the total expenditures for all accommodation categories combined.

(c) Multiply the total number of rooms let annually by the average number of persons per room to obtain an estimate of the total visitor-nights generated.

(d) Divide the number of visitor-nights by the average length of stay to obtain an estimate of the number of visitors per year who use commercial accommodation in each class. Sum these estimates to obtain total visitors for all accommodation categories.

5. Divide the total number of visitors by the percentage of all visitors who stay in all types of commercial accommodation (obtained from national or regional government surveys) to obtain an estimate of the total visitors in both commercial and private accommodation. At this point you now have obtained several basic items of information that are important in summarizing the extent of tourism activity in a region: (1) the total number of visitors who stay in various types of commercial accommodation; (2) the total number of visitors who stayed overnight in the region regardless of type of accommodation; and (3) total expenditures on accommodation. The accommodations survey will also have provided you with information on occupancy rates, which are an indicator of the health of the tourism industry locally as well as a barometer for the potential for expansion in the accommodation sector. You may have also obtained estimates of employment in the accommodation sector if you asked information from each firm about number of employees. This estimate can be used to verify an independent estimate of accommodation employment we calculate later.

The next series of calculations allows you to obtain an idea of the tourism spending in other sectors of the economy and of the total number of jobs supported by tourism in the region.

6. With the support of representatives from the accommodation sector, conduct a survey of their customers. Obtain estimates of their expenditures locally on:

(a) accommodation;
(b) food and drink;

(c) attractions, recreation, and entertainment;
(d) retail purchases, such as souvenirs;
(e) gasoline and auto services;
(f) local transportation, taxis, and rental cars.

Using the totals for each category of expenditure, determine the ratio between each category's total and the expenditure for accommodation. In other words, you want to obtain an estimate of the amount spent by the average visitor on each category for every dollar (or other currency unit) spent on accommodation.

7. Using the expenditure ratios just calculated, multiply the ratio for each category by the total expenditures on accommodation obtained in step 4(b). This provides you with an estimate of the total tourist spending on a variety of major expenditure categories. You may add the individual sums to arrive at a grand total of tourist spending locally.

8. Using national census information, obtain payroll/sales receipts ratios for each expenditure category. Obtain also the average annual wage-rate for employees in each expenditure category. Use local or county-level information if available; otherwise use state or provincial averages.

9. Multiply the total spending in each category by the payroll/sales receipts ratio to calculate approximate tourism-based payrolls.

10. Divide the payroll estimate by the average wage-rate in each category to estimate the number of jobs supported by tourism.

Example

This rather lengthy procedure can be made clearer by the following example. The data are hypothetical, but are typical of many North American counties. In this case, we begin by conducting an accommodation inventory and survey. A county-level summary of the results of this survey is presented in Table 10.1. The number of rooms in each accommodation class was then multiplied by the annual occupancy rate and 365 days per year to determine the total number of rooms let per year. This figure was then used in the series of calculations described in step 4. The results of these calculations are displayed in Table 10.2. The total of visitors in all categories of accommodation was obtained (Table 10.2) and this figure was divided by the estimated percentage (based on the national average in Canada) of travellers who stay in commercial accommodation. This produced an estimate of 243 673 total visitors in the study county, 163 261 of whom stayed in commercial accommodation.

Table 10.1 Local accommodation inventory (hypothetical data)

Accommodation class	Number of rooms	% of total rooms	Average annual occupancy (%)	Average rate per night	Average persons per room	Average length of stay (nights)
Hotels	600	60	65	$40	2	3
Motels	350	35	65	$30	3	4
Bed and breakfast	50	5	50	$15	2	3
Total	1000					
						Weighted mean = 3.25

Table 10.2 Calculation of total visitors and visitor-nights

Hotels

600 rooms × 65% × 365 nights = 142 350 room-nights let per year
142 350 × $40 = $5 694 000 annual receipts
142 350 × 2 persons/room/night = 284 700 visitor-nights
284 700 ÷ 3 nights = 94 900 visitors

Motels

350 rooms × 65% × 365 nights = 83 037.5 room nights
83 037.5 × $30 = $2 491 125 annual receipts
83 037.5 × 3 persons/room/night = 249 112.5 visitor-nights
249 112.5 ÷ 4 nights = 62 278 visitors

Bed and breakfast

50 rooms × 50% × 365 nights = 9125 room-nights
9125 × $15 = $136 875 annual receipts
9125 × 2 persons/room/night = 18 250 room-nights
18 250 ÷ 3 nights = 6083 visitors

94 900 + 62 278 + 6083 = 163 261 visitors in all classes of commercial accommodations
163 261 ÷ 67% (% of all visitors who stay in commercial accommodation) = 243 673 visitors

Table 10.3 Visitor-party expenditure survey (hypothetical data)

	Hotels ($)	Motels ($)	Bed and breakfast ($)
Spending on:			
Accommodation	120	120	45
Food and drink	200	150	100
Recreation and entertainment	60	50	50
Retail purchases	150	120	50
Gasoline and auto service	20	30	30
Local transportation	30	0	0
Accommodation/spending sector ratio			
Accommodation	1.00	1.00	1.00
Food and drink	1.67	1.25	2.22
Recreation and entertainment	0.50	0.42	0.50
Retail purchases	1.25	1.00	1.11
Gasoline and auto service	0.17	0.25	0.67
Local transportation	0.25	0.00	0.00

Results of a visitor survey to determine expenditure patterns is shown in Table 10.3. This table also contains the sector accommodation expenditure ratio described in step 6. The data from this table

Table 10.4 Estimation of tourist spending by sector (hypothetical data)

Sector	Hotels ($)	Motels ($)	Bed and breakfast ($)	Total ($)
Accommodation	5 694 000	2 491 125	136 875	8 322 000
Food and drink	9 508 980	3 113 906	303 863	12 926 749
Recreation and entertainment	2 847 000	1 046 273	68 438	3 961 711
Retail purchases	7 117 500	2 491 125	151 931	9 760 556
Gasoline and auto service	967 980	622 781	91 706	1 682 467
Local transportation	1 423 500	—	—	1 423 500
				38 076 983

Table 10.5 Tourism payroll estimation (hypothetical data)

Sector	Payroll/sales ratio	Estimated annual payroll ($)	Average annual wages ($)	Number of jobs
Accommodation	0.35	2 912 700	8 996	324
Food and drink	0.37	4 782 897	7 332	652
Recreation and entertainment	0.29	1 148 896	11 180	102
Retail purchases	0.25	2 440 139	10 556	231
Gas and auto services	0.22	370 142	9 568	38
Local transportation	0.30	427 050	13 884	31
	Total:	11 059 354	Total:	1378

were then combined with total accommodation expenditures to estimate tourist spending in each of the six sectors of tourist spending identified (Table 10.4). Note that the expenditures in the first row of Table 10.4, 'Accommodation', are identical to the estimated receipts in the various accommodation categories listed in Table 10.2. Total expenditures were estimated to be $38 076 983.

Payroll/sales receipts ratios were calculated from census sources for each expenditure sector and are summarized in Table 10.5. When these ratios are multiplied by the expenditures in each sector, from Table 10.4, the product is the estimated annual payroll in each sector attributable to tourism. Finally, dividing these annual payroll estimates by the annual wages per worker in each sector gives an estimate of the total number of jobs, by sector, supported by tourism (Table 10.5).

Kreutzwiser estimation

Description

The local impact model required the use of questionnaires and fieldwork for estimating local impacts of tourists' spending. The costs of such an approach can become high, especially for a large urban region. Cooperation of the accommodation sector is also mandatory for that model. Both of these conditions can sometimes make use of the local impact model impractical. The method described in this section provides easily obtainable estimates of tourists' spending at a county level through exclusive use of secondary data sources. The cost you must pay for this simpler procedure is that you must settle for only aggregate spending patterns. The Kreutzwiser method tells you nothing about the numbers of jobs or relative levels of spending among various sectors of the economy.

The basic procedure has been developed from a model formulated by Kreutzwiser (1973) for the province of Ontario. One begins by recognizing that the expenditures due to local consumption are usually less than total local receipts. The difference is attributed to visitors from outside the local area. The method considers any resident of a county to be 'local' within the context of that county; it is possible, however, to aggregate data to multi-county regions to account for the mobility of consumers across adjacent county borders. This aggregation, however, must either include all of a county or none of it. It is not possible to divide a county into smaller subunits for analysis.

The Kreutzwiser methodology adjusts for the fact that expenditure on retail commodities is dependent on income levels. Retail expenditures in general tend to increase at a slower rate than disposable income increases (recall Engle's law, discussed in Ch. 5). The model also accounts for county-by-county variations in income levels as well as the more obvious variations due to different population sizes.

As noted, this procedure provides only estimates of tourism receipts. Very often there are no reliable figures from independent sources that can be used to verify the accuracy of these estimates. To be sure, estimates of tourists' spending are available from other sources and procedures in principle – but even when these are available, they are often only estimates, too. Consistency between an estimate derived from the Kreutzwiser method and another source would suggest that the estimate is probably valid. Discrepancy, however, merely indicates that one or both methods are wrong. It could be difficult to decide which method has the greater credibility.

The difficulty of verifying the results of the Kreutzwiser method should serve as a warning not to place blind trust in the results. It is foolish to impute greater accuracy to any procedure than is appropriate. One should not overlook, though, the fact that there is some logic behind the Kreutzwiser method and that the derivation of tourists' spending is based on data from normally reliable sources.

In terms of the internal calculations, Kreutzwiser notes that errors in retail sales estimates and income estimates will cause greater error in the final results than will errors associated with making estimates of regional expenditures. This is fortunate because the procedures used to derive regional expenditure estimates require the most assumptions. Further, error likely to arise from incorrect estimations of the patterns of regional expenditures and consumer mobility can be minimized by aggregating counties into multi-county tourism regions.

This procedure monitors only the total level of tourists' spending. It reveals nothing about the distribution of spending among various sectors nor does it tell us anything about the tourists themselves. In fact, this method defines a tourist to be any traveller outside his home county. Business travellers, people travelling on personal matters, and pleasure travellers are all included. In return for these assumptions and limitations, the Kreutzwiser method provides tourism analysts with a useful, relatively efficient, and practical method for indirectly estimating the economic magnitude of tourism in individual counties.

Procedures

1. The procedure uses census reports and, if desired, newspaper circulation audit figures. This last set of data is used to estimate the magnitude of regional spending. It is possible to exclude regional spending, but the result will typically be an upward bias in the estimate of tourists' spending, which would contribute to the problem of the lack of credibility the tourism industry has in the eyes of many planners and policy-makers. The bias is due to the fact that the failure to adjust for regional spending combines regional spending and tourism spending into a single figure. The seriousness of this error depends on the actual magnitude of regional spending. This can range from negligible to substantial.

The procedure is rather involved, so the steps described below may become clear only after working through the accompanying example. The first step is the collection of data for a number of variables. Most of the required data can be obtained from government census documents. Information on newspaper circulation (used to determine the extent and magnitude of regional spending) can be obtained from audit bureaux that verify and maintain circulation records for newspapers and magazines. The Audit Bureau of Circulations, with offices in Chicago, Illinois, and Toronto, Ontario, serves the USA and Canada.

The data must be obtained for each county you are examining as well as for the major metropolitan areas or county seat in each county. You must also estimate from newspaper circulation figures (or perhaps from informed opinion) the geographical extent of regional retail trade around your study counties. This regional retail trade area is comprised of those counties whose residents make significant levels of retail purchases in your study county. The regional boundaries must, therefore, follow county boundaries.

2. Collect data for the following variables:

Variable description	*Acronym*
Mean family income in each county. Use disposable (after-tax) income if available	*FI*
Mean percentage of family income spent on retail goods and services by county	*%FI*
Total county retail receipts	*CRR*
Total county family income	*CFI*
Total family income in the metropolitan centre	*MFI*
Total metropolitan retail receipts	*MRR*
Total newspaper circulation of all daily newspapers published in the metropolitan centre of the county	*DNC*
Newspaper circulation solely within the metropolitan centre	*MNC*
Newspaper circulation outside the metropolitan centre (extra-metropolitan newspaper circulation)	*EMNC*
Regional newspaper circulation – the circulation of newspapers within the retail region defined above	*RNC*
Total regional newspaper circulation for all counties (total of all *RNC*s)	*TRNC*

3. Multiply *%FI* by *CFI* to obtain an estimate of the county's total buying power, *CBP*.

4. Calculate total retail receipts attributable to people living outside the county by subtracting *CBP* from *CRR*. Call the extra-county receipts *ECRR*. This figure represents the value of purchases made by both tourists and regional residents in the study county. If the level of regional purchases is small, you can end with this step by attributing all *ECRR* to tourists. If, as is more likely, regional purchases account for a significant portion of county receipts, continue with the following steps.

The basic strategy in the following steps is the development of an estimate of average retail sales to regional residents per regional newspaper subscription. Marketing geographers have observed that newspaper circulation volumes and patterns provide a good measure of the extent and magnitude of the retail trade. If we are able to determine a reliable relationship between regional retail sales and regional newspaper circulation, we can use the circulation figures to estimate regional sales. The difference between all extra-county sales and regional sales is assumed to be due to tourists' expenditures. The balance of this procedure describes how we can make an estimate of regional sales that are deducted from *ECRR* to estimate tourist receipts.

5. Calculate the metropolitan area's buying power, *MBP*, by multiplying *%FI* by *MFI*.

6. Calculate the extra-metropolitan retail receipts, *EMRR*, by subtracting *MBP* from *MRR*.

7. Calculate the average extra-metropolitan retail receipts per average extra-metropolitan newspaper by dividing *EMRR* by *EMNC*. Designate this variable as *EMR/N*.

8. Divide *MNC* by *DNC* to determine the percentage of total daily newspaper circulation that occurs within the metropolitan centre: *%MNC*.

9. We have assumed thus far that newspaper circulation figures provide an accurate indication of retail receipts. To some extent, we continue to make this assumption, but we need to correct for two sources of bias in the newspaper circulation figures we have calculated so far (especially *EMR/N*). The value of *EMR/N* is artificially high for two reasons. First, it is only an average figure based on spending patterns and newspaper circulation over all income groups. Second, the value of extra-metropolitan sales includes not only county and regional receipts, but all tourism receipts. To adjust the value of extra-metropolitan sales downward we can do the following calculation.

The value of *%MNC* is proportional to the actual metropolitan centre retail receipts, *MRR*. If the *%MNC* is extrapolated to 100 per cent and *MRR* is extrapolated proportionately to provide a measure of the potential or expected metropolitan centre buying power, *EMBP*, the ratio between *MBP* and *EMBP* can be interpreted to be a reflection of the upward bias in *MBP*.

We need, therefore, to calculate *EMBP* by dividing *MRR* by *%MNC*. Next, divide *MBP* by *EMBP*. The ratio is the adjusting factor, *AF*. We will use *AF* in step 12, below, to calculate the regional retail sales per regional newspaper.

10. We may now calculate a preliminary estimate of regional retail receipts, *ERR*, by multiplying the extra-city sales per extra-city newspaper, *EMR/N*, by regional newspaper circulation, *RNC*. As noted previously, this figure is expected to be biased upwards because it includes both regional and tourist receipts.

11. We begin to correct our preliminary estimate of *ERR* by summing *ERR* for all counties to obtain total regional retail expenditures, *TERR*.

12. Dividing *TERR* by *TRNC* yields an estimate of the average regional retail receipts per regional newspaper for all counties,

Table 10.6 Hypothetical county data for the Kreutzwiser method of estimating county-level tourist expenditures

County	Mean family income *FI*	Mean % *FI* spent on retail goods *%FI*	County retail receipts *CRR*	Total county income *CFI*	Total metropolitan centre income *MFI*	Metropolitan retail receipts *MRR*
A	10 000	64.5	150 000 000	200 000 000	150 000 000	115 000 000
B	12 000	64.0	300 000 000	400 000 000	320 000 000	224 000 000
C	15 000	63.0	500 000 000	550 000 000	342 000 000	222 000 000
D	9 000	65.0	90 000 000	130 000 000	95 000 000	75 000 000
E	10 000	64.5	110 000 000	150 000 000	110 000 000	80 000 000

County	Total daily newspaper circulation *DNC*	Metropolitan newspaper circulation *MNC*	Extra-metropolitan newspaper circulation *EMNC*	Regional newspaper circulation *RNC*
A	14 168	10 573	3595	3 417
B	31 730	24 038	7692	7 290
C	5 658	3 943	1715	1 605
D	6 063	4 355	1708	1 642
E	8 856	6 560	2296	2 010
			Total: *TRNC* =	15 964

Table 10.7 Calculation of total extra-county retail receipts

County	County buying power (*CBP* = *%FI* × *CFI*)	Total extra-county retail receipts (*ECRR* = *CRR* − *CBP*
A	129 000 000	21 000 000
B	256 000 000	44 000 000
C	346 500 000	153 500
D	84 500 000	5 500 000
E	96 750 000	13 250 000

RR/*RN*. The value of *RR*/*RN*, like *EMR*/*N*, is biased high because it includes tourist receipts as well as regional receipts. It may be lowered by assuming that the degree of bias is approximately the same as that calculated for all extra-metropolitan sales (which includes regional sales).

13. To correct for the bias in *RR*/*RN*, we multiply *RR*/*RN* by the appropriate *AF* for each county. This gives us an adjusted regional receipts per regional newspaper ratio for each county, *ARR*/*RN*.

14. Multiply *ARR*/*RN* by *RNC* to obtain a final estimate of the actual regional retail expenditures, *ARE*.

15. The difference between *ECRR* and *ARE* is an estimate of the total tourists' expenditures in the study county, *ETE*.

Example

A careful review of the tables in the following example will clarify this lengthy and complex estimation procedure. The example consists of data taken from five counties, identified here as A, B, C, D, and E. Each county has one newspaper and enjoys some level of retail trade with adjacent counties. The values of the ten basic variables required for the Kreutzwiser estimation are listed in Table 10.6. The next table (Table 10.7) summarizes the calculation of county buying power and total extra-county retail receipts. Finally, Table 10.8 illustrates the determination of metropolitan buying power, extra-metropolitan retail receipts, and all the other intermediate steps, leading eventually to county-specific estimates of tourists' spending.

Summary

We have examined in detail two methods for assessing the economic magnitude of tourism in a local community. The first method provides

Table 10.8 Calculation of regional retail receipts and tourist expenditures

County	Metropolitan buying power (*MBP* = *%FI* × *MFI*	Extra-metropolitan retail receipts (*EMRR* = *MRR* − *MBP*)	Extra-metropolitan receipts per extra-metropolitan newspaper (*EMR/N* = *EMRR* ÷ *EMNC*)	Metropolitan circulation as % of total circulation (*%MNC* = *MNC* ÷ *DNC*)
A	96 750 000	18 250 000	5076	74.6
B	204 800 000	19 200 000	2496	75.8
C	215 460 000	6 540 000	3813	69.7
D	61 750 000	13 250 000	7758	71.8
E	70 950 000	9 050 000	3942	74.1

County	Expected metropolitan buying power (*EMBP* = *MRR* ÷ *%MNC*)	Adjusting factor (*AF* = *MBP* ÷ *EMBP*)	Preliminary estimate of regional receipts (*ERR* = *RNC* × *EMR/N*)	Adjusted regional receipts per regional newspaper (*ARR/RN* = [*RR/RN*] *AF*)
A	154 155 500	0.63	17 344 692	2460
B	295 514 510	0.69	18 195 840	2694
C	318 507 890	0.68	6 119 865	2655
D	104 456 820	0.59	12 738 636	2303
E	107 962 210	0.66	7 923 420	2557
		Total: *TERR* =	62 322 453	
		RR/RN = *TERR* ÷ *TRNC* =	3 904	

County	Adjusted regional retail expenditures (*ARE* = *RNC* × *ARR/RN*)	Estimated tourist expenditures (*ETE* = *ECRR* − *ARE*)
A	8 405 820	12 594 180
B	19 639 260	24 360 740
C	4 261 275	149 238 730
D	3 781 526	1 718 474
E	5 179 770	8 070 230

an estimate of the income and jobs created by tourism in several different sectors of the economy of the host region. This level of detail is possible because you collect specific information on many aspects of the accommodation sector and on the spending habits of visitors. If the cost or effort associated with this local impact model are too high, the second method may be used. The Kreutzwiser method uses secondary data sources to estimate aggregate county-level spending. The cost of the simpler data requirements is a loss of precision and specificity in the spending estimates. The second method tells us nothing about the number of jobs or the distribution of tourists' spending through the various sectors of the tourism industry.

At the beginning of this chapter we referred in passing to both the benefits and the costs of tourism development. You have probably noticed that we have not explicitly considered any method for evaluating the costs of tourism. The omission of cost assessment from this chapter should not be taken to suggest that any analyst evaluating tourism development can afford to ignore costs completely. The decision to emphasize the two methods presented was made for practical reasons. Limitations of space always force decisions about what to include. Beyond this is the fact that the methods for assessing the economic costs of development are reasonably well established and documented in other industrial development texts. The large body of literature on benefit–cost analysis is a major example of this technology. Estimation methods for benefits, however, are somewhat less refined and less clear or documented. Many of the costs of a public project may be estimated directly from the budget proposed for the project (with the important exceptions of opportunity costs and negative externalities). The benefits, however, are rarely entered on any ledger sheet. They must be estimated from available evidence and with specifically developed procedures such as those presented in this chapter.

Finally, we should acknowledge that many of the costs of tourism may be exacted in the form of environmental and social change. The wisdom or fairness of the exchange of these costs for the benefits of tourism is ultimately a social or political judgement. This debate takes you far into issues outside the limited scope of this modest text. With the procedures described in this chapter and throughout the book, you will be able to contribute more effectively and objectively to the making of those judgements.

Further reading

Archer B H 1978 Domestic tourism as a development factor. *Annals of Tourism Research*, **5**: 126–41.

Bryden J M 1973 *Tourism and development*. Cambridge University Press, Cambridge.

DeKadt E 1979 *Tourism – Passport to development*? Oxford University Press, London.

Ghali M A 1976 Tourism and economic growth. *Economic Development and Cultural Change* **24**: 527–38.

Gray H P 1974 Towards an economic analysis of tourism policy. *Social and Economic Studies* **23**: 386–97.

Scottish Tourist Board 1975 *The economic impact of tourism: a case study in Greater Tayside*. Tourism and Recreation Research Unit, University of Edinburgh, Edinburgh, Scotland.

Safavi F 1981 A cost–benefit model for convention centres. *Annals of Regional Science* **5**: 17–37.

Stansfield C A 1978 Atlantic City and the resort cycle: background to the legalization of gambling. *Annals of Tourism Research* **5**:238–51.

Tourism and Recreation Research Unit 1981 *The economy of rural communities in the National Parks of England and Wales*, Report 47. University of Edinburgh, Edinburgh, Scotland.

Wall G and **Knapper C** 1981 *Tutankhamun in Toronto*, Report 17. Department of Geography, University of Waterloo, Waterloo, Ontario.

Willis F R 1977 Tourism as an instrument of regional economic growth. *Growth and Change* **8**(2): 43–7.

Appendices

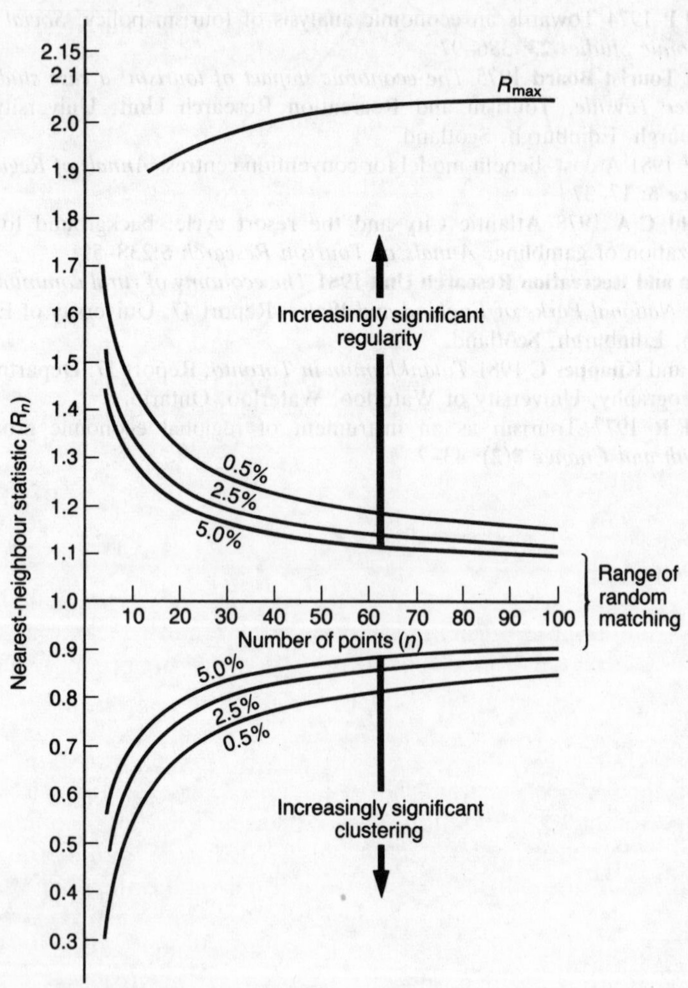

Fig. A.1 Significance graph for testing R_n values (Pinder & Witherick 1975)

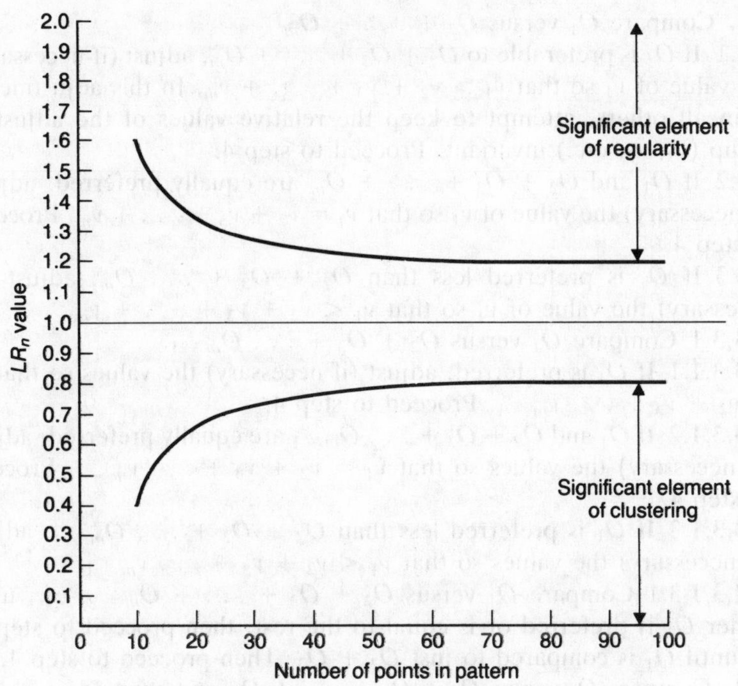

Fig. A.2 Significance graph for testing LR_n values

The Churchman–Ackoff–Arnoff method for weighting objectives*

This method involves the systematic comparison of various 'outcomes' (O_m) (in the context of assessing regional tourism attractiveness, the 'outcomes' are the various regional characteristics) in order to assign weights proportional to the importance or desirability of each outcome. The general symbolic formulation of the method of estimating weights (v_j) associated with the various outcomes or regional characteristics is quite formidable in appearance but not in practice.

1. Rank the outcomes in their order of value. Let O_1 represent the most valued, O_2 the next most valued, . . ., and O_m the least valued.

2. Assign the value 1.00 to O_1 (i.e., $v_1 = 1.00$) and assign values that appear suitable to each of the other outcomes.

* The following material is reprinted from Churchman, Ackoff, and Arnoff (1957) with permission from John Wiley and Sons, Publishers.

† The + sign here designates the logical connective 'and'.

3. Compare O_1 versus $O_2 + \ldots + O_m$[†]

3.1 If O_1 is preferable to $O_2 + O_3 + \ldots + O_m$, adjust (if necessary) the value of v_1 so that $v_1 > v_2 + v_3 + \ldots + v_m$. In this adjustment, as in all others, attempt to keep the relative values of the adjusted group (v_2, v_3, etc.) invariant. Proceed to step 4.

3.2 If O_1 and $O_2 + O_3 + \ldots + O_m$ are equally preferred, adjust (if necessary) the value of v_1 so that $v_1 = v_2 + v_3 + \ldots + v_m$. Proceed to step 4.

3.3 If O_1 is preferred less than $O_2 + O_3 + \ldots O_m$, adjust (if necessary) the value of v_1 so that $v_1 < v_2 + v_3 + \ldots + v_m$.

3.3.1 Compare O_1 versus $O_2 + O_3 + \ldots O_{m-1}$.

3.3.1.1 If O_1 is preferred, adjust (if necessary) the values so that $v_1 > v_2 + v_3 + \ldots v_{m-1}$. Proceed to step 4.

3.3.1.2 If O_1 and $O_2 + O_3 + \ldots O_{m-1}$ are equally preferred, adjust (if necessary) the values so that $v_1 = v_2 + v_3 + \ldots v_{m-1}$. Proceed to step 4.

3.3.1.3 If O_1 is preferred less than $O_2 + O_3 + \ldots O_{m-1}$, adjust (if necessary) the values so that $v_1 < v_2 + v_3 + \ldots v_{m-1}$.

3.3.1.3.1 Compare O_1 versus $O_2 + O_3 + \ldots + O_{m-2}$, etc. until either O_1 is preferred or is equal to the rest, then proceed to step 4, or until O_1 is compared to just $O_2 + O_3$. Then proceed to step 4.

4. Compare O_2 versus $O_3 + O_4 + \ldots + O_m$ and proceed as in step 3.

5. Continue until the comparison of O_{m-2} versus $O_{m-1} + O_m$ is completed.

6. Convert each v_j into a normalized v'_j, dividing v_j by Σv_j. Then $\Sigma v'_j$ will be equal to 1.00.

It should be noted that the resulting estimated values are relative; that is, deletion or addition of an outcome (or regional characteristic) will affect the values obtained for all other outcomes. Furthermore, the estimated values obtained for a set of outcomes may change over time if the true values change.

Significance test for R*

The test is based on the calculation of the standard error of the R^* estimate and on the calculation of a Z variate from the standard error.

$$Z = \frac{|d_o - d_r|}{SE_R{}^*}$$

where:

$$SE_R{}^* = \left\{ \left[\frac{m_1(n_1/a) + m_2(n_2/a)}{(n_1/a)\,(n_2/a)\,\pi} - \left(\frac{m_1\sqrt{(n_1/a)} + m_2\sqrt{(n_2/a)}}{2\sqrt{[(n_1/a)\,(n_2/a)]}} \right)^2 \right] \Big/ N \right\}$$

and all other variables are as defined in the text.
The probabilities for various values of Z are given in the following table (Table A.1).

Table A.1 Probabilities for Z-tests

Probabilities are given for values as extreme as the values observed for Z in the normal distribution.

Z		0.00	0.01	0.02	0.03	0.04	0.05	0.06	0.07	0.08	0.09
0.0	0.	50000	49601	49202	48803	48405	48006	47608	47210	46812	46414
0.1		46017	45620	45224	44828	44433	44038	43644	43251	42858	42465
0.2		42074	41683	41294	40905	40517	40129	39743	39358	38974	38591
0.3		38209	37828	37448	37070	36693	36317	35942	35569	35197	34827
0.4		34458	34090	33724	33360	32997	32636	32276	31918	31561	31207
0.5		30854	30503	30153	29806	29460	29116	28774	28434	28096	27760
0.6		27425	27093	26763	26435	26109	25785	25463	25143	24825	24510
0.7		24196	23885	23576	23270	22965	22663	22363	22065	21770	21476
0.8		21186	20897	20611	20327	20045	19766	19489	19215	18943	18673
0.9		18406	18141	17879	17619	17361	17106	16853	16602	16354	16109
1.0		15866	15625	15386	15151	14917	14686	14457	14231	14007	13786
1.1		13567	13350	13136	12924	12714	12507	12302	12100	11900	11702
1.2		11507	11314	11123	10935	10749	10565	10383	10204	10027	98525
1.3	0.0	96800	95098	93418	91759	90123	88508	86915	85343	83793	82264
1.4		80757	79270	77804	76359	74934	73529	72145	70781	69437	68112
1.5		66807	65522	64255	63008	61780	60571	59380	58208	57053	55917
1.6		54799	53699	52616	51551	50503	49471	48457	47460	46479	45514
1.7		44565	43633	42716	41815	40930	40059	39204	38364	37538	36727
1.8		35930	35148	34380	33625	32884	32157	31443	30742	30054	29379
1.9		28717	28067	27429	26803	26190	25588	24998	24419	23852	23295
2.0		22750	22216	21692	21178	20675	20182	19699	19226	18763	18309
2.1		17864	17429	17003	16586	16177	15778	15386	15003	14629	14262
2.2		13903	13553	13209	12874	12545	12224	11911	11604	11304	11011
2.3		10724	10444	10170	99031	96419	93867	91375	88940	86563	84242
2.4	0.0^2	81975	79763	77603	75494	73436	71428	69469	67557	65691	63872
2.5		62097	60366	58677	57031	55426	53861	52336	50849	49400	47988
2.6		46612	45271	43965	42692	41453	40246	39070	37926	36811	35726
2.7		34670	33642	32641	31667	30720	29798	28901	28028	27179	26354
2.8		25551	24771	24012	23274	22557	21860	21182	20524	19884	19262
2.9		18658	18071	17502	16948	16411	15889	15382	14890	14412	13949

Table A.1 (continued)

Probabilities are given for values as extreme as the values observed for Z in the normal distribution.

Z		0.00	0.01	0.02	0.03	0.04	0.05	0.06	0.07	0.08	00.09
3.0		13499	13062	12639	12228	11829	11442	11067	10703	10350	10008
3.1	0.0^3	96760	93544	90426	87403	84474	81635	78885	76219	73638	71136
3.2		68714	66367	64095	61895	59765	57703	55706	53774	51904	50094
3.3		48342	46648	45009	43423	41889	40406	38971	37584	36243	34946
3.4		33693	32481	31311	30179	29086	28029	27009	26023	25071	24151
3.5		23263	22405	21577	20778	20006	19262	18543	17849	17180	16534
3.6		15911	15310	14730	14171	13632	13112	12611	12128	11662	11213
3.7		10780	10363	99611	95740	92010	88417	84957	81624	78414	75324
3.8	0.0^4	72348	69483	66726	64072	61517	59059	56694	54418	52228	50122
3.9		48096	46148	44274	42473	40741	39076	37475	35936	34458	33037
4.0		31671	30359	29099	27888	26726	25609	24536	23507	22518	21569
4.1		20658	19783	18944	18138	17365	16624	15912	15230	14575	13948
4.2		13346	12769	12215	11685	11176	10689	10221	97736	93447	89337
4.3	0.0^5	85399	81627	78015	74555	71241	68069	65031	62123	59340	56675
4.4		54125	51685	49350	47117	44979	42935	40980	39110	37322	35612
4.5		33977	32414	30920	29492	28127	26823	25577	24386	23249	22162
4.6		21125	20133	19187	18283	17420	16597	15810	15060	14344	13660
4.7		13008	12386	11792	11226	10686	10171	96796	92113	87648	83391
4.8	0.0^6	79333	75465	71779	68267	64920	61731	58693	55799	53043	50418
4.9		47918	45538	43272	41115	39061	37107	35247	33476	31792	30190

(From Fisher and Yates 1948)

References

Addelman S 1962 Orthogonal main-effect plans for asymmetrical factorial experiments. *Technometrics* **4**(i): 21–46.

Advertising Age 1980 Ad beat, 27 Oct: 119.

American Express 1985 *World tourism overview, 1985*. American Express Publishing, New York.

Archer B H 1976 The uses and abuses of multipliers. In Gearing C E, Swart W W and Var T (eds) *Planning for tourism development*. Praeger, New York, pp. 115–32.

Baligh H H and **Richartz L E** 1967 Variable-sum game models of marketing problems. *Journal of Marketing Research* **4** (May): 173–85.

Balmer, Crapo and Associates (no date) *The regional approach to tourism promotion and development in Saskatchewan*. Regina, Saskatchewan.

Barcun S D and **Jeming P** 1973 Airline seat share: a study in false optimization. *Management Science* **20** (Oct.): 146–53.

Bass F M 1977 Analytical approaches in the study of purchase behavior and brand choice. In Ferber R (ed.) *Selected aspects of consumer behavior*. National Science Foundation, Washington, DC, pp. 491–514.

BC Ministry of Tourism and Small Business Development 1980 *Tourism highlights*. British Columbia Ministry of Tourism and Small Business Development, Victoria.

Becker R H 1979 Travel compatibility on the Upper Mississippi River. *Journal of Travel Research* **17**(1): 33–6.

Berry B J L 1966 Interdependency of flows and spatial structure. In *Essays on commodity flows and the spatial structure of the Indian economy*. Department of Geography Research Paper III. University of Chicago, Chicago.

Blank U and **Gunn C A** 1966 *Guidelines for tourism – recreation in Michigan's Upper Peninsula*. Johnson, Johnson, and Roy, Ann Arbor, Mich.

Bohm P 1971 An approach to the problem of estimating the demand for public goods. *Swedish Journal of Economics* **73**: 55–6.

Bose R C and **Bush K A** 1952 Orthogonal arrays of strength two and three. *The Annals of Mathematical Statistics* **23**: 508–24.

British Tourist Authority 1980 *British home tourism survey 1978*. English Tourist Board, London.

Brockhoff K 1975 The performance of forecasting groups in computer dialogue and face-to-face discussion. In Limestone H A and Turoff M *The Delphi method: techniques and applications*. Addison-Wesley, Reading, Mass., pp. 291–321.

Bureau of the Census 1978 *National travel survey*. US Government Printing Office, Washington DC.

Calantone R J and **Sawyer A** 1978 The stability of benefit segments. *Journal of Marketing Research* **15** (Aug): 395–404.

Caprio R J 1970 Centrography and geostatistics. *Professional Geographer* **22**: 15–19.

Chapman G P 1970 The application of information theory to the analysis of population distributions in space. *Economic Geography* **46**: 317–31.

Chilton R J 1969 A review and comparison of simple statistical tests for scalogram analysis. *American Sociological Review* **34**: 238–45.

Christaller W 1933 *Die zentralen orte in Suddentdeutschland*. Gustav Fischer, Jena.

Christaller W 1964 Some considerations of tourism locations in Europe: The peripheral regions – underdeveloped countries – recreation areas. *Papers of the Regional Science Association* **12**: 95–105.

Churchman C W, Ackoff R L and **Arnoff E L** 1957 Weighing objectives. In *Introduction to operations research*. John Wiley, New York, Ch. 6.

Clark P J and **Evans F C** 1955 On some aspects of spatial patterns in biological populations. *Science* **121**: 397–8.

Clawson M C and **Knetsch J L** 1966 *Economics of outdoor recreation*. Johns Hopkins Press, Baltimore.

Cocheba D J and **Langford W A** 1981 Direct willingness-to-pay questions: an analysis of their use for quantitatively valuing wildlife. *Journal of Leisure Research* **13**: 311–22.

Cochran W C and **Cox G M** 1957 *Experimental designs*, 2nd edn. John Wiley, New York.

Coffey W J 1981 *Geography: towards a general spatial systems approach*. Methuen and Company, London.

Cohen K 1968 Multiple regression as a general data-analytic system. *Psychological Bulletin* **70**(6): 426–43.

Cole J P and **King C A M K** 1968 *Quantitative geography*. Oxford University Press, London.

Cooke K 1982 Guidelines for socially appropriate tourism development in British Columbia. *Journal of Travel Research* **21**(1): 22–8.

Coombs D B and **Thie J** 1979 The Canadian land inventory system. In *Planning the uses and management of land*. ASA/CSSA/SSSA, Madison, Wis., pp. 909–33.

Crampon L J 1966 A new technique to analyze tourist markets. *Journal of Marketing* **30** (Apri1): 27–31.

Crompton J L 1979 An assessment of the image of Mexico as a vacation destination and the influence of geographical location upon that image.

Journal of Travel Research **17**(4): 18–23.

Dalkey N and **Helmer O** 1963 An experimental application of the Delphi method of the use of experts. *Management Sciences* **9**(3): 458–67.

Dandurand L 1982 Incorporating casino game preference market segmentation data into marketing plan. *Journal of Travel Research* **20**(4): 15–19.

Davis R K 1963 Recreation planning as an economic problem. *Natural Resources Journal* **3**: 239–49.

Davis R K 1964 The value of big game hunting in a private forest. *Transactions of the 29th North American wildlife and natural resources conference*. Wildlife Management Institute, Washington DC, pp. 54–63.

Defert P 1967 Le taux de fonction touristique: mise au point et critique. *Les cahiers du tourisme.* Centre des Hautes Etudes Touristiques, Aix-en-Provence, C–13.

Dorney R S 1976 Biophysical and cultural–historic land classification and mapping for Canadian urban and urbanizing land, *Proceedings of the workshop on ecological land classification*. Commission on Ecological Land Classification, Toronto, pp. 57–71.

Draper N and **Smith H** 1966 *Applied regression analysis*. John Wiley, New York.

Dwyer J F, Kelly J R and **Bowes M D** 1977 *Improved procedures for valuation of the contribution of recreation to national economic development*. Water Resources Center, University of Illinois, Champaign, Ill.

Earl Berger Ltd, G M Stamm, Economic Research Associates, Mathieu Williams Lethern Associates 1983 *Recreation: a changing society's economic giant.* Ministry of Tourism and Recreation, Toronto.

Ebdon D 1977 *Statistics in geography*. Basil Blackwell, Oxford.

Edwards A 1957 *Techniques of attitude scale construction.* Appleton-Century Crofts, New York.

Edwards S L and **Dennis S J** 1976 Long distance day-tripping in Great Britain. *Journal of Transport Economics and Policy* **10**: 237–56.

Ehemann J 1977 What kind of place is Ireland: An image perceived through the American media. *Journal of Travel Research* **15**(2): 28–31.

Ellerbrock M J and **Hite J C** 1980 Factors affecting regional employment in tourism in the United States. *Journal of Travel Research* **18**(3): 26–32.

Engel J F, Blackwell R D and **Kollat D T** 1978 *Consumer behavior*, 3rd edn. Dryden Press, Hinsdale, Ill.

Engel J F, Fiorillo H F and **Cayley M A** 1972 *Market segmentation: concepts and application.* Holt, Rinehart, and Winston, New York.

English Tourist Board 1983 *Leisure day trips in Great Britain: Summer 1981 and 1982*. English Tourist Board, London.

Etzel M J and **Woodside A G** 1982 Segmenting vacation markets: the case of the distant and near-home travelers. *Journal of Travel Research* **20**(4): 10–14.

Ezekial R S 1970 Authoritarianism, acquiescence, and field behavior. *Journal of Personality* **38**(1): 31–42.

Fechner G T 1889 *Elemente der psychophysik*. Breitkopf und Hertel, Leipzig.

Ferrario F F 1979a The evaluation of tourist resources: an applied methodology, part I. *Journal of Travel Research* **17**(3): 18–22.

Ferrario F F 1979b The evaluation of tourist resources: an applied methodology, part II. *Journal of Travel Research* **17**(4): 24–32.

Fishbein M 1963 An investigation of the relationship between the beliefs about an object and the attitude toward that object. *Human Relationships* **16**(2): 232–40.

Fishbein M 1966 The relationship between beliefs, attitudes and behavior. In Feldman S (ed.) *Cognitive consistency*. Academic Press, New York, pp. 199–223.

Fishbein M 1967 Attitude and the prediction of behavior. In Fishbein M (ed.) *Readings in attitude theory and measurement*. John Wiley, New York, pp. 477–92.

Fishbein M 1972 The search for attitudinal–behavior consistency. In Cohen J B (ed.) *Behavioral science foundations of consumer behavior*. The Free Press, New York, pp. 245–52.

Fisher R A and **Yates F** 1948 *Statistical Tables for Biological, Agricultural and Medical Research*, published by Longman Group Ltd. London (1974) 6th edition. (previously published by Oliver & Boyd Ltd. Edinburgh)

Frank R 1972 Predicting new product segments. *Journal of Advertising Research* **12** (June): 9–13.

Frechtling D C 1974 A model for estimating travel expenditures. *Journal of Travel Research* **12**(4): 9–12.

Fridgen J D, Udd E and **Deale C** 1983 Cognitive maps of tourism regions in Michigan. In *Proceedings of the Applied Geography Conference, 1983*. Ryerson Polytechnic Institute, Toronto, pp 262–72.

Gearing C E, Swart W W and **Var T** 1974 Establishing a measure of touristic attractiveness. *Journal of Travel Research* **12**(3): 1–8.

Gee C Y, Choy D J L and **Makens J C** 1984 *The travel industry*. AVI Publishing Com., Westport, Conn.

Goddard J E 1970 Functional regions within the city centre. *Transactions of the Institute of British Geographers* **49**: 161–81.

Goodrich J N 1978 The relationship between preferences for and the perceptions of vacation destinations: application of a choice model. *Journal of Travel Research* **17**(2): 8–13.

Grant E L and **Ireson W G** 1970 The comparison of alternatives. In Mansfield E (ed.) *Managerial economics and operations research*. W W Norton, New York.

Green P E and **Devita M T** 1973 A complementarity model of consumer utility for item collections. *Journal of Consumer Research* **1** (Dec): 56–67.

Green P E and **Rao V R** 1971 Conjoint measurement for quantifying judgmental data. *Journal of Marketing Research* **8** (Aug):355–63.

Green P E and **Srinivasan V** 1978 Conjoint measurement in consumer research: Issues and outlook. *Journal of Consumer Research* **5**: 103–23.

Green P E and **Tull D S** 1975 *Research for marketing decisions*, 3rd edn. Prentice-Hall, Englewood Cliffs, NJ.

Green P E and **Wind Y** 1975 New way to measure consumers' judgments. *Harvard Business Review* **53** (July–Aug): 107–17.

Greenhut M L 1956 *Plant location in theory and practice*. University of North Carolina Press, Chapel Hill, NC.

Grether E T 1983 Regional–spatial analysis in marketing. *Journal of Marketing* **47** (Fall): 36–43.

Grieg-Smith P 1952 The use of random and contiguous quadrats in the study of the structure of plant communities. *Annals of Biology*, NS **16**: 292–316.

Grigg D 1965 The logic of regional systems. *Annals of the Association of American Geographers* **55**: 465–91.

Guilford J P 1954 *Psychometric methods*. McGraw-Hill, New York.

Gunn C A 1965 *A concept for the design of a tourism–recreation region*. The BJ Press, Mason, Mich.

Gunn C A 1979 *Tourism planning*. Crane-Russak, New York.

Gunn C A 1982 Destination zone fallacies and half-truths. *Tourism Management* **3**(4): 263–69.

Gunn C A and **Worms A J** 1973 *Evaluating and developing tourism*. Texas Agricultural Experiment Station, Texas A&M University, College Station, Tex.

Hammack, J and **Brown G M** 1974 *Waterfowl and wetland: toward bioeconomic analysis*. Johns Hopkins University Press, Baltimore, Md.

Hammond R J 1966 Convention and limitation in benefit–cost analysis. *Natural Resources Journal* **6**: 195–219.

Hawes D K 1978 Empirically profiling four recreational .vehicle market segments. *Journal of Travel Research* **26**(4): 13–20.

Heeley J 1980 The definition of tourism in Great Britain: Does terminological confusion have to rule? *Tourism Review* **2**: 11–14.

Hoover E M 1948 *The location of economic activity*. McGraw-Hill, New York.

House of Commons Debates 1984 *Hansard* (22 Mar): 2349. Department of Supply and Services, Ottawa.

Hunt J D 1975 Image as a factor in tourism development. *Journal of Travel Research* **13**(3): 1–7.

Husbands W 1983 Tourist space and touristic attraction: an analysis of the destination choices of European travellers. *Leisure Sciences* **5**(4): 289–308.

Isard W 1956 *Location and space economy*. MIT Press, Cambridge, Mass.

Johnson R 1972 Pairwise nonmetric multidimensional scaling. *Psychometrika* **38**: 313–22.

Johnson R 1973 *Trade-off analysis: a method for quantifying consumer values*. Market Facts, Toronto.

Johnson R 1974 Trade-off analysis of consumer values. *Journal of Marketing Research* **11**: 251–63.

Jud G D and **Krause W** 1976 Evaluating tourism in developing areas. *Journal of Travel Research* **14**(2): 1–9.

June L P and **Smith S L J** 1987 Service attributes and situational effects on customer preferences for restaurant dining. *Journal of Travel Research* **26**(2): 20–7.

Kakkar P and **Lutz R J** 1975 Toward a taxonomy of consumption situations. In Maze E M (ed.) *Combined Proceedings*, Series 37. American Marketing Association, Chicago, pp. 206–10.

Kellerman A 1981 *Centrographic measures in geography*. Concepts and techniques in modern geography no. 32. GeoAbstracts, East Anglia, Norwich.

Keogh D 1982 On measuring spatial variations in tourist activity. Unpublished manuscript.

King L J 1969 *Statistical analysis in geography*. Prentice-Hall, Englewood Cliffs, NJ.

Kreutzwiser R D 1973 A methodology for estimating tourist spending in Ontario counties. Unpublished M A thesis, Department of Geography, University of Waterloo, Waterloo, Ontario.

Kruskal J B 1964 Multidimensional scaling by optimizing goodness of fit to a nonmetric hypothesis. *Psychometrika* **29**(10): 1–27.

Kruskal J B 1965 Analysis of factorial experiments by estimating monotone transformations of the data. *Journal of the Royal Statistical Society*, Series B **27**: 251–63.

LaPage W F and **Cormier P L** 1977 Images of camping – barriers to participation? *Journal of Travel Research* **15**(4): 21–5.

Lee Y 1979 A nearest neighbor spatial association measure for the analysis of firm interdependence. *Environment and Planning A* **11**: 169–76.

Lefever D W 1926 Measuring geographical concentration by means of the standard deviational ellipse. *American Journal of Sociology* **32**: 88–94.

Leiper N 1979 The framework of tourism: towards a definition of tourism and the tourist industry. *Annals of Tourism Research* **6**(4): 380–407.

Leisure Industry Digest 1985 Leisure travel. *Leisure and Industry Digest* **V**(23): 3.

Likert R 1932 *A technique for the measure of attitudes*, Archives of Psychology, No. 140. Columbia University Press, New York.

Lopez E M 1980 The effect of leadership style on satisfactions of tour quality. *Journal of Travel Research* **18**(4): 20–3.

Lösch A 1944 *Die raumliche ordnung der wirtschaft*. Gustav Fischer, Jena.

Luce R D 1959 *Individual choice behavior*. John Wiley, New York.

Luce R D and **Tukey J W** 1964 Simultaneous conjoint measurement: a new type of fundamental measurement. *Journal of Mathematical Psychology* **1**(1): 1–27.

Lundberg D E 1980 *The tourist business*. CBI Publishing Co., Boston, Mass.

Martin B, Memmott F and **Bone A** 1961 *Principles and techniques of predicting future demand for urban area travel*. MIT Press, Cambridge, Mass.

Massy W F, Frank R E and **Lodahl T** 1968 *Purchasing behavior and personal attributes*. University of Pennsylvania Press, Philadelphia.

Mathieson A and **Wall G** 1982 *Tourism: economic, physical, and social impacts*. Longman, London.

Mings R C 1978 Tourist industry development: at the crossroads. *Tourist Review* **33**(3): 2–9.

Miossec J M 1977 Un modèle de l'espace touristique. *L'Espace Géographique* **6**: 41–8.

Mishan, E J 1982 *Cost–benefit analysis*, 3rd edn. George Allen and Unwin, London.

Moser C and **Kalton G** 1974 *Survey methods in social investigation*, 2nd edn. Basic Books, New York.

Murphy P E 1983 *Tourism: a community approach*. Methuen, New York.

National Task Force on Tourism Data 1985a *Final joint report of the working groups on user needs and current data issues*. Statistics Canada, Ottawa

National Task Force on Tourism Data 1985b Progress Report, unpublished mimeograph. Statistics Canada, Ottawa.

National Tourism Resources Review Commission 1973 *Destination USA: domestic tourism*, National Tourism Resources Review Commission. Washington, DC.

Neft D S 1966 Statistical analysis for spatial distributions, mimeograph no. 2. Regional Science Institute, Philadelphia.

Niedercorn J H and **Bechdoldt B V** 1966 An economic derivation of the 'gravity law' of spatial interaction. *Journal of Regional Science* **9**: 273–82.

Nunnally J 1967 *Psychometric theory*. McGraw-Hill, New York.

OECD Tourism Committee 1973 *Tourism policy and international tourism in OECD member countries*. Organization for Economic Cooperation and Development, Paris.

Ohlin B 1935 *Interregional and international trade*. Harvard University Press, Cambridge, Mass.

Ontario Travel Survey 1983 *Summary report on the Ontario travel survey*. Ontario Ministry of Tourism and Recreation, Toronto.

Osgood C E, Suci G J and **Tannenbaum P H** 1957 *The measurement of meaning*. University of Illinois Press, Urbana, Ill.

Papson S 1979 Tourism: World's biggest industry in the twenty-first century. *The Futurist* Aug: 249–60.

Pearce D W 1978 *Cost–benefit analysis*. Macmillan Press, London.

Pearse P H 1968 A new approach to the evaluation of non-priced recreational resources. *Land Economics* **44**: 87–99.

Philbrick A K 1957 Principles of areal functional organization in regional human geography. *Economic Geography* **33**: 299–336.

Pinder D A and **Witherick M E** 1975 A modification of nearest-neighbour analysis for use in linear situations. *Geography* **60**: 16–23.

Pinder D A 1978 Correcting underestimation in nearest-neighbour analysis. *Area* **10**(5): 379–85.

Pizam A 1978 Tourism impacts: the social costs to the destination community as perceived by its residents. *Journal of Travel Research* **16**(4): 8–12.

Plackett R L and **Burman J P** 1946 The design of optimum multifunctional experiments. *Biometrika* **33**(4): 305–25.

Powell J 1978 *Report of the tourism section consultative task force*. Department of Industry, Trade, and Commerce, Ottawa.

Prest A R and **Turvey R** 1965 Cost–benefit analysis: a survey. *Economic Journal* **75**: 683–735.

Rao R C 1981 *Advertising decisions in oligopology: an industry equilibrium analysis*. Krannert Graduate School of Management, Series 752. Purdue University, West Lafayette; Ind.

Rogers D S and **Green H L** 1978 Analog modelling: A new perspective in store site selection. In *Proceedings of the Applied Geography Conference*, vol. 1. Kent State University, Kent, Ohio

Rosenberg M 1956 Cognitive structure and attitudinal effect. *Journal of Abnormal and Social Psychology* **53**: 367–72.

Ryan M J and **Bonfield E H** 1975 The Fishbein extended model and consumer behavior. *Journal of Consumer Research* **2**: 118–36.

Schuler H J and **Prosperi D C** 1977 A conjoint measurement model of consumer spatial behavior. *Regional Science Perspectives* **7**(2): 122–34.

Seymour D L 1968 The polygon of forces and the Weber problem. *Journal of Regional Science* **8**: 243–6.

Shafer E L, Moeller G H and **Getty R E** 1974 *Future leisure environments*. Forest Research Paper NE-301. USDA Forest Experiment Station, Upper Darby, Pa.

Shepard R N 1957 Stimulus and response generalization: a stochastic model relating generalization to distance in psychological space. *Psychometrika* **22**(4): 325–45.

Shepard R N 1962 The analysis of proximities: multidimensional scaling with an unknown distance function. *Psychometrika* **27**(2): 125–40.

Sheth J N 1972 Reply to comments on the nature and uses of expectancy-value models in consumer attitude research. *Journal of Marketing Research* **9**: 462–65.

Shih D 1986 VALS as a tool of tourism market research: the Pennsylvania experience. *Journal of Travel Research* **24**(4): 2–10.

Simard C and **Hill C** 1986 Measuring the impact of tourism as an industry. Paper presented to the Tourism Industry Association of Canada, Winnipeg, Manitoba.

Smith S L J 1977 Room for rooms: A procedure for the estimation of potential expansion of tourist accommodation. *Journal of Travel Research* **15**(4): 26–9.

Smith S L J 1983 Identification of functional tourism regions in North America. *Journal of Travel Research* **22**(4): 13–21.

Smith S L J 1983 *Recreation geography*. Longman, London.

Smith S L J and **Smale B J A** 1982 The changing demand for culture: estimation of 'cultural elasticities'. *Visions in Leisure and Business* **1**(2): 27–47.

Smith S L J and **Thomas D C** 1983 Assessment of regional potentials of rural recreation businesses. In Lieber S R and Fesenmaier D R (eds) *Recreation planning and management*. Venture Publishers, State College, Pa., and E and F N Spon, London, pp. 66–86.

Smith V K and **Munley V G** 1978 The relative performance of various estimates of recreation participation equations. *Journal of Leisure Research* **10**(3): 165–76.

Smith W R 1956 Product differentiation and market segmentation as alternative marketing strategies. *Journal of Marketing* **21** (July): 3–8.

Sonquist J A and **Dunkelberg W C** 1977 *Survey and opinion research*. Prentice-Hall, Englewood Cliffs, NJ.

Statistics Canada 1978 *Urban family expenditures*, 1978, Cat. 62–549. Department of Supplies and Services, Ottawa.

Stewart J Q 1948 Demographic gravitation: evidence and applications. *Sociometry* **11**: 30–58.

Stutz F P 1973a Distance and network effects on urban social travel fields. *Economic Geography* **49**: 134–44.

Stutz F P 1973b Interactance communities: transportation's role in urban social geography. *Proceedings of the Association of American Geographers* **5**: 257–61.

Stutz F P 1974 Interactance communities versus named communities. *Professional Geographer* **26**: 407–11.

Stynes D J 1978 The peaking problem in outdoor recreation: measurement and analysis. Unpublished paper presented at the Annual Meeting of the National Recreation and Parks Association, Miami, Fl.

Stynes D J 1983 An introduction to recreation forecasting. In Lieber S and Fesenmaier D (eds) *Recreation planning and management*. Venture Publishing, State College, Pa., pp. 87–95.

Stynes D J and **Mahoney E M** 1980 *Michigan downhill ski marketing study: segmenting active skiers*. Research report 391. Michigan State University Agricultural Experiment Station, East Lansing, Mich.

Taylor P J 1977 *Quantitative methods in geography*. Houghton Mifflin Company, Boston, Mass.

Thompson J S 1982 *Site selection*. Lebhar-Freidman, New York.

Thomson C M and **Pearce D G** 1980 Market segmentation of New Zealand package tours. *Journal of Travel Research* **19**(2): 3–6.

Thurstone L L 1927 A law of comparative judgement. *Psychological Review* **34**: 273–86.

Tiebout, C M 1962 *The community economic base study*. Committee for Economic Development, New York.

Tourism Canada 1983 *Directory of courses: tourism, hospitality, and recreation 1983–1985*. Department of Supply and Services, Ottawa.

Tourism Canada 1984 *Tourism tomorrow*. Ministry of Regional Industrial Expansion, Ottawa.

Tourism Research Planning Committee 1975 *Standard definitions and classifications for travel surveys*. Federal–Provincial Conference on Tourism, Ottawa.

United Nations Conference on Trade and Development 1971 A note on the 'tourist sector'. In *Guidelines for tourism statistics: 30*. United Nations, New York.

US Army Corps of Engineers 1974 *Plan formulation and evaluation studies – recreation, vol. ii, appendix a, estimating initial reservoir recreation use-project data*, IWR Report 74-R1. USAE Institute for Water Resources, Fort Belvoir, Va.

US Senate Committee on Commerce, Science, and Transportation 1978 *National Tourism Policy Study: Final Report*. US Government Printing Office, Washington, D.C.

Var T, Beck R A D and **Loftus P** 1977 Determinants of touristic attractiveness of the touristic areas in British Columbia. *Journal of Travel Research* **15**(3): 23–9.

Vickerman R W 1975 The leisure sector in urban areas. In *The economics of leisure and recreation*. Macmillan Press, London. Ch. 8.

Von Thünen J H 1985 *Der isolierte staat in beziehung auf landwirtshaft und nationalokonomie*, 3rd edn. Schumacher-Zarchlin, Berlin.

Wall G and **Knapper C** 1981 *Tutankhamun in Toronto*, Department of Geography Publication Series No. 17. University of Waterloo, Waterloo, Ontario.

Walsh R G 1977 Effects of improved research methods on the value of recreational benefits. In *Outdoor recreation: advances in application of economics*. USDA Forest Service General Technical Report WO-2. Washington DC, pp. 145–53.

Wassenaar D J 1981 *California visitor impact model*. Office of Tourism, Department of Economic and Business Development, Sacramento, Calif.

Weber A 1928 *Alfred Weber's Theory of the Location of Industries* (Friedrich C J, trans.). University of Chicago Press, Chicago, Ill.

Weber A 1911 Die standorslehre und die handespolitik. *Archive für Sozialwissenschaft und Sozialpolitik* **32**: 667–88.

Wennergren E B and **Nielsen D B** 1968 *A probabilistic approach to estimating demand for outdoor recreation*. Bulletin 470. Utah Agricultural Experiment Station, Logan, Utah.

Wells W D 1975 Psychographics: a critical review. *Journal of Marketing Research* **12** (May): 196–213.

Whitehead J I 1965 Road traffic growth and capacity in a holiday district (Dorset). *Proceedings of the Institute of Civil Engineers* **30**: 589–608.

Wilson T P 1971 A critique of ordinal variables. *Social Forces* **49**(3): 432–44.

Wind Y 1978 Issues and advances in segmentation research. *Journal of Marketing Research* **15** (Aug): 317–37.

Winer B J 1971 *Statistical principles in experimental design*. McGraw-Hill, New York.

Wolfe R I 1966 *Parameters of recreational travel in Ontario*, DHO Report R B111. Ontario Department of Highways, Downsview, Ontario.

Wolfe R I 1972 The inertia model. *Journal of Leisure Research* **4**: 73–6

Woodside A G and **Sherrell D** 1977 Traveler evoked, inept, and inert sets of vacation destinations. *Journal of Travel Research* **15**(1): 14–18.

World Tourism Organization 1981 Technical handbook on the collection and presentation of domestic and international tourist statistics. World Tourism Organization, Madrid.

Yokeno N 1974 The general equilibrium system of space-economies for tourism. *Reports for the Japan Academic Society of Tourism* **8**: 38–44.

Young S, Ott L and **Feigin B** 1978 Some practical considerations in market segmentation. *Journal of Marketing Research* **15** (Aug): 405–12.

Young C W and **Smith R W** 1979 Aggregated and disaggregated outdoor recreation participation models. *Leisure Sciences* **2**: 143–54.

Zeller R E, Achabal D D and **Brown L A** 1980 Market penetration and locational conflict in franchise systems. *Decision Sciences* **11**: 58–80.

Zipf G K 1946 The P_1P_2/D hypothesis: an inter-city movement of persons. *American Sociological Review* **11**: 677–86.

Name Index

Subject Index